THE
GODMAKERS

THE GODMAKERS

A Legacy of the Southern Baptist Convention?

Bruce T. Gourley

[signature]

PROVIDENCE HOUSE PUBLISHERS
Franklin, Tennessee

Copyright 1996 by Bruce T. Gourley

All rights reserved. Written permission must be secured from the publisher to use or reproduce any part of this book, except for brief quotations in critical reviews and articles.

Scripture taken from: (1) the King James Version; and (2) the Holy Bible, New International Version. Copyright 1973, 1978, 1984 International Bible Society. Used by permission of Zondervan Bible Publishers.

Printed in the United States of America

00   99   98   97   96   5   4   3   2   1

Library of Congress Card Catalog Number: 95-072407

ISBN: 1-881576-67-1

Published by
PROVIDENCE HOUSE PUBLISHERS
P.O. Box 158 • 238 Seaboard Lane
Franklin, Tennessee 37067
800-321-5692

To my parents,
Thomas and Winifred Gourley,
who taught me to love God and his Word.

Contents

Foreword	9
Introduction	13
1. The Search for Higher Meaning	17
2. Baptists: A Historical Perspective	27
3. The Southern Baptist Convention: A Brief History	41
4. The Southern God	71
5. The God of Exclusiveness	82
6. The God of (Partial) Truth	92
7. The Written God	104
8. The Political God	125
9. The Pharisaic God	142
10. The Organizational God	155
11. The Future: Hope or Despair?	165
Notes	195

Foreword

The making of history books without a point of view has no end. Even when a rare point of view surfaces, it is often blunted, dull, and sanitized, all in the name of historical objectivity. So when a historian comes along such as Isaac Backus, who in the late eighteenth century wrote a history of New England with a honed edge to it, people perk up, pay attention, and read it for years after its publication. When a writer pulls a sword and hacks away at the traditional fare of historians—names, places, and dates, harmlessly strung together and designed to do little more than get a history book published—listen up. Bruce Gourley has a whetted sword in his hand in this his first published book. And we Baptists need to listen up! All other Christians should listen in!

This is another in a growing list of books focused on the fundamentalist-moderate controversy among Southern Baptists. It is a distinctive book, however. Written by an obviously conservative, but not fundamentalist, Southern Baptist, the book cannot be libelously labeled and dismissed as "liberalism." Gourley lays out in unequivocal form his theological position:

> Salvation through Jesus Christ is the basic truth that the Christian community proclaims. Jesus, the Son of God, is the redeemer of humankind. He came in the form of a man, proclaimed to the world the coming of the Kingdom of God, was put to death at the hands of men as a sacrifice for the sins of all humanity, then rose from the dead in triumph over sin and evil, and ascended into heaven to be with God the Father. Salvation is obtained through placing one's faith in Christ and his redemptive work, and thereby entering into a personal relationship with God through Christ. This, in a nutshell, is the foundational truth which the Christian community holds to and proclaims (see page 21).

The major distinctive of this book, however, is not the theological point of view of Bruce Gourley. It is his honed sword, his thesis. By weaving the tragedies of Southern Baptist history with recent Southern Baptist fundamentalist theology, Gourley asserts that the new fundamentalist leaders of the Southern Baptist Convention (SBC) have created a "god" or "gods" out of their own images. They are "The Godmakers." In a word, SBC fundamentalist leaders, says Gourley, have built upon the twisted threads of Southern Baptist history (regionalism, racism, Landmarkism, anti-intellectualism, fundamentalism, etc.) and have created some golden calves. They have worshiped the gods of their own making, and that is their sad, warped legacy to the Baptist future.

I have been carrying a quote around in my files for years, one of those I cannot be sure where it came from, though I think it may have originated with conservative preacher A. W. Tozer. It goes like this: "What comes into our minds when we think about God is the most important thing about us." Surely only a hired hand of the church, a preacher or theologian, would utter such an outlandishly theological bias. But it is true! And Bruce Gourley echoes this sentiment—"What comes into our minds when we think about God is the most important thing about us"—throughout his book.

In the early years of the SBC conflict, I was lecturing at Florida State University, trying to explain the nature of the controversy as I understood it. When I finished, a Lutheran campus minister, one who knew well the recent takeover of the Missouri Synod by fundamentalists, said to me, "You moderates are going to be in trouble if you do not take fundamentalists on regarding the core issue." And then he added, "The core issue is neither politics nor the Bible; the core issue is the nature of God and the fundamentalists' usurpation of God with the Bible, theology, and culture."

Alan Neely, former professor of missions at Southeastern Baptist Theological Seminary in Wake Forest, North Carolina, and present professor at Princeton Theological Seminary, was the first Southern Baptist I ever heard who described the fundamentalist-moderate conflict among Southern Baptists as "fundamentally an argument about God." He whispered that in my ear at a public meeting in Atlanta in May 1991 immediately prior to my reading to the Cooperative Baptist Fellowship "An Address to the Public" regarding the differences between moderate and fundamentalist Southern Baptists. I have never had the opportunity to hear Alan Neely elaborate. I think, however, I know precisely what he had in mind and wish now that the statement I read had been more explicit at this point.

R. Wayne Stacy, former pastor of the First Baptist Church in Raleigh, North Carolina, put part of what Neely had in mind into print in a sermon titled "Risky Business"—*Proclaiming the Baptist Vision: The Bible*, edited by Walter B. Shurden (Macon: Smyth & Helwys, 1994). In describing the major issue in the SBC controversy, Stacy said (page 27), "While most of what you heard and read suggested that the controversy among Southern Baptists focused on what one has described as 'The Battle for the Bible,' the real battle is taking place on a more basic battleground—*what do you believe about God?*"

Now my point: what others have warned, whispered, and whisked away in unread sermons, Bruce Gourley is now saying out loud in a more elaborate, public, and, some will think, shrill form.

But what is Gourley saying? He is saying that a legacy of the SBC, especially as perpetuated by current fundamentalists, is its inferior view of God. And what kind of inferior God has the SBC created? Gourley's chapter titles do not leave you guessing. The SBC has created the "The Southern God" (a god of culture and region), "The God of Exclusiveness" (a god of sectarian denominationalism), "The God of (Partial) Truth" (a god of anti-science and anti-biblical criticism), "The Written God" (a god of biblical inerrancy), "The Political God" (a god of political right-wingism), "The Pharisaic God" (a god of distorted ethics), and "The Organizational God" (a god of ecclesiastical structures).

Moderate and liberal Southern Baptists will doubtless take some consolation in this book. But we should be careful with our exultation. Fundamentalists do not have a monopoly on "humanizing God," as Gourley calls it. Gourley's book has much in common with Luther Copeland's recently released and incisive study entitled *The Southern Baptist Convention and the Judgement of History: The Taint of an Original Sin*. Copeland makes the needed point that Southern Baptist problems did not begin with the rise of fundamentalism in the last two decades of the twentieth century. Those Southern Baptists in control prior to the onslaught of fundamentalism were "godmakers" as well. Will Campbell reminded about four hundred moderates at the Whitsitt Baptist Heritage Society meeting at Fort Worth, Texas, in July 1995 that fundamentalists were not the ones who exiled him from his denominational home; it was those who preceded the fundamentalists.

This is a book for all Southern Baptists, fundamental to liberal, sectarian to ecumenist, Republican to Democrat. Few of us will fail to see our theological and denominational adversaries in these pages. Their "godmaking" will be clear to us, as it always is. Our own homemade idolatries, however—those that blind us to the God of our Lord Jesus Christ—we are unfortunately likely to giggle at and dismiss as moral peccadilloes, mere trifling faults of obviously superior people.

When a book makes one either mad or glad it usually deserves a second, more critical reading. I predict madness on the part of some, gladness on the part of others. I recommend a second reading. And a prayer: "God have mercy on me a...."

—WALTER B. SHURDEN
Callaway Professor of Christianity
Mercer University, Macon, Georgia

Introduction

The Southern Baptist Convention is vitally important to me. I am not a national denominational employee or leader, but rather am an individual who has spent most of his years immersed in Southern Baptist life—first as a child, then as a college and seminary student, and now as a Southern Baptist minister in my "own little corner" of the Southern Baptist world. Throughout the course of my education and ministry, I have experienced the diversity and the richness of faith which characterizes Southern Baptists.

Between the covers of this book is a critical analysis of the first 150 years of the SBC, with particular emphasis upon the current controversy in Southern Baptist life. I am indebted to Baptist historians Walter Shurden, Leon McBeth, Robert Gardner, Robert Baker, and W. W. Barnes. These well-learned men have documented the history of Southern Baptists in an extensive manner, and their works have stamped within me an abiding interest in the history of the denomination in which I grew up and in which I now minister. These authors' writings on Baptist history form the framework upon which I have constructed my critical analysis of the SBC's first 150 years.

These are days of unprecedented theological controversy in Southern Baptist life, so much so that anyone who pens his or her convictions nowadays is, intentionally or not, extending an invitation to be labeled with a term that may or may not be an accurate portrayal of one's beliefs and opinions. Although I do not like this state of affairs, I accept it as inevitable. I also realize that since labels are derived from the standpoint of where the labeler stands, any one person may find himself or herself bestowed with any number of labels.

The current controversy has led me to pen this work. In Southern Baptist life, truth has largely been discarded in favor of power and control. The vision of the national leadership of the SBC has become more self-centered than God-centered. Too many Baptists occupying the pews of Southern Baptists churches have allowed the blind guides in Nashville to directly or

13

indirectly lead them down a new path paved with faulty theology. In the midst of this crisis, too few of the new generation of Southern Baptists have taken a public stand for truth.

Before preceding further, a clarification of terms is in order. Southern Baptist and secular journalists, for the past sixteen years, have wrestled with what labels to employ in describing the opposing parties in the current SBC controversy. To this point, no consensus has emerged. In the essence of such a mandate, I have decided to borrow from Southern Baptist sociologist Nancy Ammerman's work, *Baptist Battles* (Rutgers University Press, 1990), in which she used several surveys to determine how Southern Baptists view themselves theologically in regards to the ongoing controversy.

Ammerman conducted extensive interviews with thousands of Southern Baptists in the mid-to-late 1980s in order to determine how Southern Baptists identify themselves theologically. Her research revealed that eighty-nine percent of Southern Baptists use the words "conservative" and/or "moderate" to describe themselves, while only thirty-three percent use the word "fundamentalist" to describe themselves (there is some overlapping). In accordance with this research, I will identify the two theological camps as "mainline conservatives and moderates" (referring to the group of national leaders who helped to guide the SBC on a national level from its inception until 1979, and who represent the vast majority of Southern Baptists), and "fundamentalists" (referring to the group of national leaders who have controlled the SBC on a national level since 1979, but who represent merely a small fraction of all Southern Baptists).

When I refer to "mainline conservatives and moderates" and "fundamentalists" within this book, I will, by and large, be referring to those camps as represented by their national leaders. The reader should note that prior to 1979, all Southern Baptists were referred to primarily as "conservatives." Self-proclaimed "fundamentalists" formally broke with the conservative SBC leadership in 1979, resulting in the current division in SBC life. It was not until after the fundamentalist insurgence that the word "moderate" became a widely used term to describe non-fundamentalist conservatives.

What do these terms mean? Virtually all Southern Baptists have, historically, held the Bible to be the authoritative Word of God, the written record of the divine revelation of God through his Son Jesus Christ. Mainline "conservatives" and "moderates" are those who hold the Bible to be fully authoritative in regards to matters of Christian faith and practice, and who allow for a latitude of biblical interpretation within the framework of the basics of the Christian faith. "Fundamentalists," on the other hand, are those who subscribe to a Bible which is wholly authoritative and literal in all matters—faith and practice, science, geography, geology, astrology, etc.—while insisting that biblical interpretation be confined to a prescribed, narrow set of creeds and terminology which most conservatives view as extraneous to, and oftentimes distracting from, the basics of the Christian faith. Both parties largely hold the same basically conservative theological tenets, and both champion the authority of Scripture—their differences largely lie in their definitions of "authoritative" (and the manner in which these definitions impact some of the fine points of their otherwise similar theology), and their outward attitudes towards those who express opinions differing from their own (fundamentalists tend to be far more intolerant than conservatives and moderates).

As a student of Baptist history, I feel that the current fragmentation of the SBC is, in many ways, the culmination of the 150 years of SBC history. I believe that the overt racism, southernness, and "organizational arrogance and isolationism" which pervaded the SBC when mainline conservatives and moderates were at the helm, as well as sporadic ultraconservative, fundamentalist (terms which I will use interchangeably in this book) uprisings, paved the way for the current theological crisis within the SBC. However, the present damage done the SBC by the current fundamentalist leadership far outweighs the damage done by their conservative and moderate predecessors. If the former conservative and moderate leadership hindered God from working fully in the SBC, the current fundamentalist leadership has come to the verge of shutting God out of SBC life. Indeed, in the minds of many Southern Baptists, the current leadership is leading the SBC down a path of self-destruction.

History teaches us that the world does not have the power to destroy the church. The first-century church and the underground church of the twentieth-century Soviet Union attest to this fact. Only within the church lies the means to destroy the church, and that means is extremism, which manifests itself in two basic forms: liberalism and ultraconservatism (or fundamentalism). Liberalism has never posed a real threat to Southern Baptist life, but fundamentalism has become a deadly threat to the vitality of the SBC.

My objective in penning this work is to search for truth in the midst of the various controversies, as well as the current full-fledged battle, which have shaped the SBC over its 150 years. It is most unfortunate that even in an overtly Christian environment, truth too often seems to be placed on the back burner. As is the case with the SBC, personal and corporate agendas, crusades, and programs have consistently muddied the line between truth and fiction. The search for truth has not always been a priority in SBC life, and I believe we are reaping what we have sown in years past through the current fragmentation of the SBC.

Finally, although this work seeks to reveal the truth, it is also biased in that I bring to it my own particular slant and understanding of the Southern Baptist picture. True objectivity is virtually impossible for a knowledgeable Southern Baptist to achieve in light of the current heated controversy within the SBC. Although I have been influenced by both major schools of thought in modern Southern Baptist life, the reader will take note that I tend to identify myself with the "mainline conservative and moderate" group as opposed to the "fundamentalist" camp. As Ammerman's surveys have revealed, up to eighty-nine percent of Southern Baptists likewise identify themselves in regards to terminology.

With these precursors and precautions, I encourage the reader to join me on a critical journey through 150 years of Southern Baptist history in a search for truth which will lead us to the current crisis in Southern Baptist life and culminate with the posing of the question, "What will be the legacy of the Southern Baptist Convention?"

CHAPTER ONE

The Search for Higher Meaning

As we stand at the threshold of the twenty-first century, we are bombarded with mixed reviews regarding the state of the world. On the one hand, the world is full of new-found hope. The Berlin Wall has fallen, and communism is almost extinct. Democracy is sweeping around the globe. The Arab states and the nation of Israel are slowly moving towards peace. Thanks to new medicines and cures, people are living longer than ever before. Technology and science are taking us into the far reaches of space and into the inner depths of the human physical makeup. The people of the world are now more educated than ever before. After centuries of wreaking havoc on the earth's ecosystem, nations all over the world are now working together to clean up the world's environment. Modern agriculture allows the farmers of the world to have higher crop yields and healthier food products.

On the flip side of the coin, the world is full of more pain and hurt than ever before. Civil wars and internal strife are tearing many nations apart. Crime plagues the cities of the world. Millions upon millions die each year from starvation and curable sicknesses. AIDS claims the lives of tens of thousands more each year. Accidents and natural disasters kill hundreds of thousands annually. Terrorism poses a threat to the world's most powerful and civilized nations. Prejudice and discrimination are alive and thriving. Injustice and oppression prevail throughout our modern world. Most of the world's wealth rests in the hands of a few. In short, the problems of old have not vanished with progress, but instead have intensified and multiplied.

In the midst of our twenty-first-century world of hope and despair, polls and surveys reveal that even in this modern, technological age, the vast majority of the world's citizens believe in God (some would say a Higher Being, Supreme Being, Creator, etc.). In the United States, for example, a recent Gallup Poll revealed that about ninety-five percent of Americans believe in God. Of those living in southern states, ninety-nine percent expressed a belief in God.[1] Thus, Americans tend to have an extraordinarily uniform belief in God, despite the diversity of religions which exist in the United States. Among other nations of the world, the majority of the world's citizens also believe in God, although the percentages are generally not quite as overwhelming as those found in the United States.[2]

These statistics raise a question: Why do the overwhelming majority of the world's citizens believe in God? This question is particularly intriguing considering the fact that we live in the most advanced technological, scientific, and knowledgeable age the world has ever known. Belief in a supernatural God would seem to be at odds with this modern age.

Perhaps a key to the answer to our question lies in the fact that God is supernatural. God transcends anything the human mind can empirically comprehend—the existence of God is a proposition which can neither be proven nor refuted by empirical means. God lies outside the realm of the scientific or the technological (or at least outside these realms as humankind comprehends them). Perhaps belief in a supernatural God offers something to humankind that scientific and technological knowledge cannot offer.

From the beginning of recorded history, humans have indeed looked beyond their own condition and their own understanding to a higher power of some sort. The earliest humans looked beyond themselves and their world and toward a higher power(s) which oriented and gave meaning to their existence. Each ancient culture had its own peculiar religious belief system centered around a god or gods. These systems served to explain how the world came into existence and how humans came into being, and interpreted the daily life of the believers. Ancient belief systems gave meaning to the natural world (the sun, moon, mountains, animals, disasters, etc.) and to the life cycle (birth, growth, sickness, death, etc.). In the ancient world, religious belief systems gave meaning to life.

At the dawning of the twenty-first century, we understand much more fully the world in which we live. We know that the earth is one of several planets which revolve around the sun. We know how sunlight, the atmosphere, and water combine to sustain life on our planet. We know the reasons behind most sicknesses and diseases. In short, much of what was mysterious and unknown in centuries past has now been identified and explained. However, the world is still plagued by problems such as needless pain, suffering, and death. As such, there remains a very real need for persons to look beyond the self and this world to find meaning to human existence.

For the Christian, there is another explanation of humankind's orientation towards a belief in God. According to Genesis 1:27, God created man and woman in his image. There is much speculation concerning the precise meaning of "in God's image," but one can readily conclude from this passage that in some fashion or another, we as human beings have a "touch" (so to speak) of God within ourselves. From the Christian perspective, this bit of God which is present in each person could be that which pulls us towards our Creator.

FINDING PERSONAL FULFILLMENT THROUGH BELIEF IN GOD

In near-twenty-first-century America, persons are busy searching for fulfillment (or meaning). We can turn on our televisions at any point of the year, for example, and watch men (and women) playing numerous sports. A select few athletes who are very talented make it to the "big leagues," and in the process make "big bucks." In this setting, these athletes seek to find some sort of fulfillment for their lives. Those who perform exceptional feats get their names and accomplishments placed in the record books, and sports fans for decades to come will talk about their skills and statistics. What these athletes (and many other individuals in the entertainment industry, the business world, the political arena, etc.) are often striving for is "fame." Indeed, the American scene in particular is filled with individuals who are out to seek "fame and fortune." By realizing such goals, life will be fulfilled—or so many think.

The capitalistic nature of America fosters a focus on materialism. Personal wealth and possessions are sought by many who truly believe that the more one acquires, the more fulfilled one will be. A well-used saying captures this belief: "He who dies with the most toys wins." Many Americans—and many others throughout the world—are seeking fulfillment in such manner.

Some seek fulfillment in various other ways: sex, alcohol, drugs, etc. Others seek fulfillment in such positive ways as family and friendships. Still others look for ultimate fulfillment through a religious belief system. Christians seek to find meaning through a personal relationship with a loving God who promises a meaningful life in the present and eternal life in the future to those who believe in him.

The fact that humans are creatures who tend to be in a perennial searching mode (the earliest humans were nomadic peoples, constantly traveling in search of better food and shelter) suggests a yearning for something beyond that which is already at hand. This yearning may be attributed partly to human greed (particularly in American culture), but greed does not fully explain the searching dimension of human beings.

Although the search for physical gratification is very real in today's world, it is the spiritual search that commands our attention at this juncture. Human beings, by and large, are creatures who express belief in God. For some, a statement of belief in God is mere lip service. For many others, however, believing necessitates acting in some fashion or another. These latter individuals do more than simply acknowledge the existence of God—they are involved in a spiritual journey towards the God whom they proclaim, and in so journeying they are seeking ultimate meaning and self-fulfillment in their lives. In essence, they seek to do God's will.

Indeed, the world is full of "spiritual pilgrims" who are seeking to draw closer to God through a variety of ways. Christians, Hindus, Moslems, Jews, Buddhists, and adherents of other major religions and an almost untold host of minor religions, cults, and sects are spiritual pilgrims on a journey towards perfection, heaven, nirvana or some other type of higher meaning, self-fulfillment, or self-realization. Although the various religions of the world are often as different as black and white, believers who have embarked on one of these spiritual journeys do generally have a few things in common in addition to believing in a god or supreme being. In essence, the spiritual pilgrim renounces certain "pleasures" or "privileges" and sets about following a "path" which, if traversed properly, will eventually bring meaning and self-fulfillment.

The manner in which spiritual pilgrims seek meaning and self-fulfillment varies greatly. Prayer, meditation, recitations, strict diets, chanting, singing, observances of ceremonies, celibacy, abstinence from this or that—these are but a few methods believers use to work towards spiritual fulfillment. In effect, those who are on such a journey are those whose belief in God (or a god) is lived out through their actions. To the Christian, belief in God is lived out through acceptance of and faith in his Son (John 3:16), with one's faith in Christ being active as opposed to passive (James 1:22). The follower of Christ thus finds self-fulfillment (or meaning) through his/her beliefs put into action.

THE ROAD TO SALVATION

Each religion stresses a distinctive "regimen" or "path" for attaining spiritual self-fulfillment, ultimate meaning, and well-being. Most religious systems focus on the believer or devotee taking specific actions which will ultimately lead the individual to the point where he or she attains spiritual self-fulfillment and ultimate meaning, either in this life or life afterward. In essence, the attainment of self-fulfillment and ultimate meaning is dependent upon the believer or devotee earning "salvation." Therefore, works become vital to salvation.

Christianity, in its truest sense, stands the "salvation-by-works" model on end. Christianity proclaims a sovereign God who created humankind and placed his human creatures in a place of perfection. However, humankind rebelled against God through disobedience, and severed their relationship with him. Christianity teaches that sinful humanity was unable to reach up to a perfect God, and that God, because of his perfect nature, was repulsed and offended by sinful, evil humanity. Only by the grace of God did some obtain "salvation" through faith in God in Old Testament times. However, despite his repugnance with humanity's sinfulness, God deeply loved his errant human creatures, and decided to send his own Son to the earth in the form of a man that he might die a physical death which would serve as a universal sacrifice for humanity's sinfulness. Jesus Christ, the Son of God, thus died on the cross of Calvary, making restitution for the sins of humanity, and becoming the bridge between a perfect God and sinful humanity. Christians believe that by putting one's faith in Christ (that is, in what God has already done on humanity's behalf), one obtains "salvation"—that is, ultimate meaning and self-fulfillment which culminate in a heavenly dwelling.

In essence, the primary difference between these two models of salvation is that the former portrays salvation as coming from human efforts towards God (or a Higher Being, etc.), while the Christian model portrays salvation as coming from God's efforts towards humanity. Human works characterize the first model, while God's grace characterizes the second. The former hinges on adherence to set guidelines or certain activities, while the later hinges on the now-possible relationship between God and the individual. Although the dichotomy between Christianity and most other religions is not always this clear-cut (many Christians, for all practical purposes, espouse a works-oriented view of salvation, for example), it serves to emphasize the basic difference between the Christian belief system and that of other religions.[3]

With these differences in religious belief systems acknowledged, our attention will now turn towards Christianity, then to Baptists, and from there to Southern Baptists, a distinct body within the Baptist community.

DISAGREEMENT BEYOND THE BASICS

Salvation through Jesus Christ is the basic truth that the Christian community proclaims. Jesus, the Son of God, is the redeemer of humankind. He came in the form of a man, proclaimed to the world the coming of the Kingdom of God, was put to death at the hands of men as a sacrifice for the sins of all humanity, then rose from the dead in triumph over sin and evil, and ascended into heaven to be with God the Father. Salvation is obtained through placing one's faith in Christ and his redemptive work, and thereby entering into a personal relationship with God through Christ. This, in a nutshell, is the foundational truth which the Christian community holds to and proclaims.

If this is the basic Christian truth upon which all Christians agree, why, one might reasonably ask, are there so many different groups and denominations within Christendom? The answer lies in the fact that throughout the history of the Christian Church, believers have sought to expound upon these basic tenets in an effort to better understand and be better followers of Christ. A certain group of Christians, focusing on a particular viewpoint in addition to the basic Christian tenets, would soon come to see themselves as distinctive from other Christians who did not agree with them on that particular matter. This pattern has happened many times over since the first century A.D., with the result being that now, on the verge of the twenty-first century, thousands of distinct Christian groups exist throughout the world.

This fragmenting of Christendom can even be seen in the New Testament writings. Christianity at its inception was an offshoot of Judaism. When the message of Christ began to be spread to the Gentile (that is, non-Jewish) world, friction ensued. Circumcised Jewish Christians did not think that Gentiles could become Christians unless they first met the legal requirements of the Jewish law (Acts 11:1-3; 15:1-21). This conflict was a constant source of contention within the early Church, and was only one of many conflicts—Paul's letters in the New Testament are full of discourses about various conflicts (see the epistle to the Galatians, for example).

The disparity and differences in Christendom today are readily apparent. Some Christian denominations and groups are very liturgical in nature, while others shun liturgy and embrace emotionalism. Some groups practice speaking in tongues; others give no credibility to this practice. Some Christians, such as the Amish, avoid contact with anything modern, while others embrace each new revelation that technology and science uncovers, and still others seek middle ground in this regard. Some groups embrace the use of musical instruments in worship services, while others see musical instruments as being of the devil. The Roman Catholic Church practices infant baptism, while certain other Christians believe in believer's baptism (although many Protestant groups practice infant dedications). Some individual Christian churches allow any baptized Christian from another denomination to be accepted into their fellowship without rebaptism, while other churches require that if the candidate for membership has not been baptized in a certain manner or within a certain Christian body, he or she must be rebaptized. Some Christian denominations are creedal, while others historically have avoided creeds. The list goes on and on—differences are numerous and real within Christendom today.

This almost unending list of differences between Christians lends itself to the question of how a religious people with a common belief in Jesus Christ as Redeemer and Son of God could possibly disagree on so many points. The answer to this question can be found in the fact that when we as Christians move beyond the basic truths or tenets of the Christian faith, we make a transition from the realm of absolute truth (within the framework of the Christian belief system) into the realm of perceived truth.

By absolute truth I mean truth that is independent of human mind-set; by perceived truth I am referring to truth which is both dependent upon and a product of the human mind. The existence of the horse, for example, is an absolute truth—the existence of the horse is independent of the existence of human beings. The existence of the horse as a beast of burden or means of transportation, however, is a perceived truth, in our sense of the term. That is, the horse is a beast of burden and a means of transportation only because at some point in human history someone came to view the horse in that light. Horses would exist independently of human beings, but the horse as a beast of burden or means of transportation would not exist without the human race.

In Christendom, the message of John 3:16, the central message of the Bible, is the foundational absolute truth of the Christian faith: "For God so loved the world, that He gave his only begotten Son, that whosoever believeth in him should not perish, but have everlasting life" (KJV). Later on, Jesus, citing Old Testament passages, fleshed out this need for the individual to put his or her faith in the Christ by giving a summary of the commandments of God: "'Love the Lord your God with all your heart and with all your soul and with all your mind and with all your strength. . . . Love your neighbor as yourself.' There is no commandment greater than these" (Mark 12:30-31, NIV). God himself took the initiative to redeem mankind to himself (John 3:16)—it was not humanity's idea, nor could humanity have brought about its own redemption. Only after God's initiative could humankind have a loving relationship with God and neighbor.

However, after God acted on his initiative through Christ's death on the cross and subsequent resurrection, humans began striving to understand the fuller impact of God's redeeming act. Thus, in Acts 11 and 15, where we see some of the early believers arguing over whether Gentiles must fulfill Jewish legal requirements before they could become Christians, we see an example of perceived truth within the Christian community. In this particular example of Acts 11 and 15, the perceived truth on the part of some believers was that Gentiles had to fulfill the requirements of the Jewish law before they became Christians. This was perceived truth, as we are defining the term, because the idea of Gentiles having to fulfill Jewish law was an idea or concept that originated from certain individuals (some early Jewish Christians), and not from God himself.

The believers in Acts 11 and 15 who pronounced that strict obedience to Jewish law was unnecessary for one desiring to follow Christ were also advocating a perceived truth. The view of these particular believers eventually won out over the legalists because the non-legal approach was determined to be more consistent (or compatible) with the teachings, work, focus, and person of Jesus (see Acts 15:11). This debate recorded in Acts was an instance of one perceived truth triumphing over another. This set a precedent for the future of Christianity. Although it may have been the first major dispute within the Christian community, it certainly was not the last.

Over the centuries, Christianity has divided and redivided into numerous distinct groups largely over differences pertaining to perceived truths.

Baptists, for example, came into existence largely over matters such as the proper mode and usage of baptism, and the belief in religious liberty.[4] These were not matters of absolute truth, but rather matters of perceived truth. The earliest Baptists perceived a different truth in these matters than did the Roman Catholic Church or the Church of England. These differences in perceptions of truth led to the founding of the Baptist faith. In turn, over the succeeding centuries, Baptists have had numerous disagreements in regards to perceived truth, resulting in many divisions within the Baptist world.[5]

THE PROBLEM WITH PERCEIVED TRUTH

All Christians harbor many perceived truths within themselves. These truths vary from person to person, church to church, and denomination to denomination. The existence of perceived truths is inevitable and unavoidable for a number of reasons.

To begin with, although the Bible is the written record of God's revelation to and redemption of humankind, it does not spell out everything about God and his workings in the world. Indeed, the Bible, which we as Christians look upon as the written Word of God, is difficult to understand or comprehend in many places. This fact is evident by the massive number of commentaries that have been written about the Bible. For many passages of Scripture, there are literally dozens of possible interpretations that have been put forth by theologians. Thus, Christians oftentimes deal with perceived truth in regards to the interpretation of Scripture or in regards to the silence of Scriptures concerning various issues.

A second reason why perceived truth is unavoidable in the life of the Christian is because each person is a product of his or her environment. The influences of family, culture, and society play an important part in determining the makeup of a person. A young, white boy growing up in the American South of the early 1800s would most likely have been pro-slavery by the time he was a teenager because of the pro-slavery environment in which he would have been reared. If he, in turn, became a Christian, he would tend to incorporate this perceived truth of the rightness of slavery into his "Christian beliefs" (indeed, many thousands did just that). Each person, by the time he or she reaches young adulthood, has absorbed many perceived truths from his or her particular environment. When one becomes a Christian, these environmentally based perceived truths are generally absorbed into one's understanding of Christianity, and subsequently, one's Christian pilgrimage.

Another reason why perceived truth will necessarily be incorporated into the Christian believer's life is that we humans are finite and imperfect creatures. As the writer of Isaiah declares, "'For my thoughts are not your thoughts, neither are your ways my ways,' declares the Lord" (Isa. 55:8,

NIV). According to Scripture, God is *holy* (Josh. 24:19; 1 Sam. 2:2; Ps. 99:3-9; Isa. 5:16, 6:3, 40:25, 43:3; Rev. 4:8), *perfect* (Pss. 18:30, 19:7; Matt. 5:48), *just* (2 Chron. 12:6; Pss. 9:16, 101:1; Isa. 61:8; 2 Thess. 1:6; Rev. 15:3), and *true* (Ps. 119:142-160; Jer. 10:10; John 17:3). In contrast, man is a sinner by nature (Rom. 3:23)—that is, we are not holy, perfect, and just and do not know all truth. Each of us can attest to the imperfection of the human creature by looking at the mistakes and blunders we have made in our own lives. And as imperfect creatures, we are, therefore, neither holy, fully just in our nature, or the knowers of all truth. As such, we each live our lives according to perceived truth, for by our nature, we cannot fully comprehend, nor do we have the capacity to fully understand, the Truth.

We human beings—and Christians—therefore live our lives largely in an atmosphere of perceived truth. We need go no further than our everyday lives to demonstrate this fact. The avid football fan contends that "his" team is the best despite the fact that the team did not win the Super Bowl or make the college Top 20. The college graduate declares that his alma mater is the best institution of higher learning. The patriotic American proudly declares that the United States is the best nation on the face of the earth. The proud father gushes about how his son is the best child in the world. The teenage girl thinks her thirty-seven-year-old mother is "old." The Christian pictures the physical Jesus as the artists from the Middle Ages portrayed him, despite the fact that there are no drawings from the first century depicting the historical Jesus. The car enthusiast adamantly insists that this car or that car is the best automobile ever made. The salesman declares that his products are superior to other's products. Two different soft-drink companies both claim that they have the best tasting cola. In an argument, the husband declares that he is right, while the wife counters that she is right.

The list is virtually endless, but the message is clear: all of us live in our own little worlds of perceived truth, worlds from which we cannot escape. So, what does all this have to do with the follower of Christ? Just about everything.

The perceived truths which we each harbor within ourselves act as filters through which we view the world, our faith, the Bible, and God. Having an "unfiltered" or "untainted" faith is unavoidable—after all, we are mere humans. What is tragic and far too often the case, however, is our tendency to label our personal perceived truths as absolute truths. This oftentimes leads one to project his or her perceived truths onto God. In essence, there is an inherent danger of overlaying our backgrounds, likes and dislikes, prejudices, opinions, etc., into our understanding of the nature of God and his working in the world.

Do you remember when, as a child, you used to enjoy coloring books? I remember as a first grader that my teacher often had us children to color pictures. In a class of thirty first graders who were given the same picture to color, no two would ever turn out exactly the same because no two of us were exactly alike.

==The Bible gives us an outline of who God is: he is perfect, holy, just, and true. The problem is that we humans tend to "color in" that picture of God in accordance with our perception of the world and truth.== By the time we finish coloring in God with our personal prejudices, opinions, and the likes, the result too often is a God who reflects and mirrors ourselves.

The tragic side of this "humanized god" syndrome is that throughout the history of Christianity, influential members of the Christian community have oftentimes held up their personalized, "colored" god as God Almighty. In the Crusades, Christian leaders held up a picture of a warring god who sought converts through threats of death. In the American South of the 1700s and 1800s, Christian leaders displayed a picture of a god who favored the Caucasian race. Today, in the camp of many far right-wing American Christians, the picture is of an American, patriotic, Republican god.

Unfortunately, there tends to be within Christendom a tendency to humanize God as opposed to striving to become godly humans. Baptists, and Southern Baptists in particular, have not been immune to this tendency.

CHAPTER TWO

Baptists: A Historical Perspective

Southern Baptists, unlike Baptists generally, have historically viewed other Christian denominations as suspect, refusing to establish many formal ties with them. However, despite the fact that Southern Baptists have tended to be anti-ecumenical, they emerged in wider religious contexts. The story of Southern Baptists is intertwined both with the history of Protestantism (and the Reformation) and with the history of the Christian Church as a whole. In order to understand Southern Baptists, a foray into the history of Christianity is necessary. Baptists arose out of the background of the Roman Catholic Church, and Southern Baptists, in turn, arose out of the Baptist denomination.

THE FIRST FIFTEEN HUNDRED YEARS OF CHRISTIANITY

When Christ ascended to heaven following the resurrection, he left instructions with his followers: ". . . go and make disciples of all nations, baptizing them in the name of the Father and of the Son and of the Holy Spirit, and teaching them to obey everything I have commanded you. And surely I am with you always, to the very end of the age" (Matt. 28:19-20, NIV). The Gospel of Luke also records Jesus telling his followers to wait for him in Jerusalem until he empowered them with his Spirit (Luke 24:49). Consequently, Jerusalem became the site of the first Christian community, as recorded in Acts 1-7. The members of this first Christian community received the Spirit of Christ (Acts 2:1-12), sought to convert the city masses (2:14-41), sat under the teachings of the apostles (2:42), spent much time in "fellowship" (2:42), ate meals together (2:42, 46), and prayed continuously (2:42). They were, in effect, a Christian commune, with each believer sharing his or her goods and possessions with the others (2:44-27; 4:32-35).

Before long, the spiritual honeymoon ended. The Jewish religious leaders of the city became jealous of the new religious sect (Acts 5:17–42) and took one of the Christian leaders (Stephen) to court (6:8–7:53). Stephen was stoned to death (7:54–8:1), and a "great persecution" began against the Jerusalem Christians. Consequently, the believers scattered throughout the land (8:2-4). As they carried the Good News of Jesus with them, other Christian communities began springing up throughout the Roman Empire.

The early Christian Church spread throughout the first century, with local communities being established in many cities and towns. The persecution continued even as the early Christian leaders wrestled with defining Christianity. The biggest task which faced the first-century Church was the task of coming to an understanding of Jesus, his death, and his resurrection.[1] By the end of the first century, the doctrine of the incarnation (that is, the belief that Jesus was "God in the flesh") was widely accepted among the local Christian communities. However, some Gnostic Christians denied that Jesus had actually been clothed in "flesh and blood." On the other hand, some Jewish Christians maintained that Jesus had been merely human, with no traces of divinity residing within him.[2] Such disagreements within the first-century Church were precursors to thousands of conflicts within Christendom that would arise in the ensuing centuries.

Christianity continued to grow throughout the second and third centuries against the backdrop of continued persecution and numerous internal controversies regarding proper (or orthodox) doctrine and belief. During this time period, a few church communities, such as the congregations at Smyrna, Ephesus, and Rome, gradually became more prominent than others. The prominence given these churches stemmed largely from the fact that each of these communities was able to trace its line of bishops (that is, leaders) to one of the original apostles who either founded or played a direct role in the early development of the church. By the end of the third century, Rome emerged as the singular most prominent church for several reasons: Peter and Paul both had played a part in the early years of the church, and both had died in Rome; Rome was the capital of the Roman Empire and apparently contained the single largest congregation of Christians at that time; and the Roman Christian community was well known for its generosity towards other Christian communities. All of these factors played a part in the Roman congregation's becoming the most prominent Christian church of that day.[3]

The fourth century saw Christianity, a religious sect long persecuted and still struggling to define itself, become the favored religion of the Roman Empire following the conversion of Emperor Constantine. The converted Constantine persisted in promoting Christianity despite the many obstacles that stood in his way, and thus set Christianity on the road to both respect and dominance in the Roman Empire. Internal struggles and controversies, now an inherent part of Christianity, continued to abound during the fourth century. Church leaders, for example, continued their efforts to nail down the nature of Jesus in regards to his divinity and his humanity. Also during this century, contacts between Roman citizens and Germanic peoples of the day eventually led to the spread of Christianity among the Germanic tribes. Some of the Germanic tribes embraced Christianity to some degree, although their acceptance was largely motivated by their desire to be a part of and share in the benefits of the Roman Empire. By the end of the fifth century, in the midst of sporadic hostilities between the Roman Empire and the Germanic tribes, orthodox Christianity had become more accepted among German peoples.[4]

By the end of the fifth century, with Rome being regarded as the preeminent church, the bishop of Rome came to be referred to as the "pope," and the Roman Church claimed to exercise ultimate spiritual authority on earth. The struggle and controversy over the nature of Christ continued to plague Christianity, and led in the sixth century to a division between West and East. Rome remained the center of Christianity in the West, while Constantinople became the center of Christianity in the East. During the ensuing centuries, the East and West grew further and further apart. By the eighth century, church and state in the West were becoming one and the same as the Roman Empire fragmented. Popes and kings often found that their interests were the same, and thus worked together for their mutual benefit. Such was not always the case, however, as the pope and the king were sometimes engaged in political power plays against one another. By the eleventh century, the papacy had fallen on hard times, with the office losing much respect. In the twelfth century, the tug-of-war between church and state reached a compromise, as King Henry V and Pope Calixtus II adopted an agreement which declared that appointed church leaders had to be acceptable to both the civil ruler and the church.[5]

The years 1100-1500 were a period of transition for Christianity. A now-thriving Western Europe cast its eye towards the East with expansion in mind, while the papacy looked to the East with the thoughts of expanding Christianity into Muslim-held territory, particularly the Holy Land, and bringing Constantinople back under Rome's jurisdiction. The state and the church thus united their efforts and launched forays into the East, known as the Crusades, with both parties envisioning favorable results. Although the Crusades did achieve some temporary gains for both the state and the church, long-term gains were nominal. Christianity did expand its borders, but the Muslims eventually took back some lands from Rome. During this time period, an "evangelical awakening" of sorts took place in society at large, spearheaded by a desire of the masses to live like apostles of Christ with the emphasis on renouncing worldly ways (and a worldly church) and living in poverty for Christ. This movement soon turned inward and led to the formation of monasteries and nunneries. Also in Europe, the Cathers and Waldenses, marked by piety and zealousness, arose and challenged the authority of the Roman Church. They evoked a considerable following, and the Roman Church expended much effort to squash these "heretics." Partly out of the church's struggle with the Cathers and Waldenses, orders such as the Dominicans and Franciscans arose within the Roman Catholic Church. These orders embodied medieval piety at its highest, borrowing this characteristic from the "heretical" groups. An increasing emphasis on learning within the church in the form of philosophical study also characterized this time period. The papacy experienced both good and bad times, and the schism between the Western Church and the Eastern Church grew wider. Eventually, in the 1400s, John Wyclif of England and Jan Hus of Bohemia led a major movement against the Roman Catholic Church by protesting ecclesiastical abuses and turning to the Bible (rather than the Roman Catholic Church) as the spiritual authority. They were, in effect, forerunners of the Reformation.[6]

THE REFORMATION

The Roman Catholic Church, had, over the years, become a sacramental institution. To the Catholic Church, certain sacraments (that is, "sacred actions") not only signified the grace of God, but also were the means by which God's grace was conferred to humanity. In 1439 the Council of Florence officially limited the number of sacraments in the Catholic Church to seven (although these same seven had been unofficially acknowledged in the Church for centuries). The seven officially recognized sacraments were: baptism, confirmation, the Eucharist (the Mass or Lord's Supper), penance (the pardoning of sins committed after baptism), extreme unction, ordination, and matrimony.[7]

In 1500 Germany was by and large the most "churchly" of the European nations. Papal authority was greater in Germany than anywhere else except Italy. Piety and devotion characterized laypeople, and the Roman Catholic Church was growing and expanding. There was, however, underlying discontent with the papacy. Rome was in constant financial crisis because of lavish living by the papacy and money spent to maintain its good political standing in Italy. In order to raise more and more money, Rome passed more and more oppressive taxes, fines, and fees, of which the laity eventually bore the burden. Furthermore, loose morals among uneducated Roman Catholic clergy put the Church in a bad light in the face of an increasingly educated and literate laity. All of this led to a deepening desire for church reform from the perspective of the laity.[8]

Martin Luther, an ordained Catholic priest, as well as a "premier scholar and brilliant theologian," stepped into the middle of this simmering unrest.

Through the course of his studies, Luther concluded that true salvation came through a personal relationship with God, rather than through the hierarchical and sacramental structures which characterized the Roman Catholic Church of the Middle Ages. He was particularly appalled with the abuses of the system of indulgences (that is, a method by which a church member who sinned could buy out or otherwise bypass the usual penance required for sin; in recent times, indulgences had been extended to cover purgatory as well, a practice which Luther firmly opposed). The dispute over indulgences (which Luther's famous Ninety-five Theses addressed) initially got Luther into hot water with Rome. However, his emphasis on a personal relationship with God was also a source of contention with the papacy. In his efforts to reform the Church, Luther by and large found a safe haven in his home state of Germany, as the German nobility sided with him and managed to keep him safe despite the fact that the Holy Roman Empire had banned him and his writings. Luther's calls for reforms were well received by his fellow Germans, and by the end of the century, Germany was split between Catholics and Lutherans.[9]

In Switzerland, which was only nominally a part of the Holy Roman Empire, the reform movement was led by one Ulrich Zwingli, a Catholic priest who was a popular leader and a trusted interpreter of Scripture in his homeland. Zwingli went a bit further than Luther in his denouncements against the Catholic Church: he declared, among other things, that salvation is by faith alone, rather than through the Church, the sacraments, or good works, and that purgatory did not exist. The one point that Luther and Zwingli most strongly disagreed on, however, concerned the Lord's Supper (the Eucharist). Luther believed the wine and bread included the actual body and blood of Christ, while Zwingli believed the elements signified Christ's body and blood. However, Zwingli (like Luther) greatly influenced his homeland. By 1525 Zurich had disassociated itself with Rome, and most of Switzerland soon followed suit.[10]

In the midst of Zwingli's reformations, another movement arose in Switzerland and opposed the Roman Catholic Church. The Anabaptists declared that infant baptism was unscriptural, and in its place instituted adult baptism for regenerated believers. In essence, they viewed themselves as a "separate" community of "gathered believers." They found themselves in opposition to both Zwingli and Rome, but flourished nonetheless, eventually becoming known as Mennonites.[11]

On the heels of Luther, Zwingli, and the Anabaptists came John Calvin of France. A well-educated humanist, Calvin had been exposed to Protestant (the name given to the movement which "protested" against the Roman Catholic Church and its practices) thought through his education and a number of friends. However, Calvin displayed no interest in religion until he had a "sudden conversion" that placed God first in his life. Already familiar with the rapidly growing Protestant movement, Calvin threw himself into the movement as a defender of his fellow French Protestants who had been unjustly slandered by the French king. In 1536 Calvin published the first edition of his *Institutes of Christian Religion*, which quickly became a hallmark presentation of doctrine and Christian living during the Reformation. Calvin set forth the theory of "predestination," which, in essence, is the belief that God divinely elects those who will be saved, independent of a person's efforts or decisions. He also believed in only two sacraments—baptism and the Lord's Supper—as opposed to the seven sacraments of the Catholic Church. By the mid-1500s, the city of Geneva had become thoroughly Calvinistic in its political and religious makeup, and Calvin's influence was spreading abroad.[12]

Thus, the Protestant Reformation, as it came to be known, continued its sweep across Europe and what had once been known as the Holy Roman Empire. The Catholic Church underwent a reformation, focused largely on efforts to secure more worthy clergy, during this age of change and upheaval. Near the end of the century, Jacob Arminius, from the Dutch Protestant tradition, brought controversy within the ranks of Protestantism with his rejection of Calvin's predestination and espousal of human choice (in essence, the individual being allowed to accept or reject God's saving grace) as leading to salvation or damnation. Although persecuted by Calvinists, what came to be known as Arminianism also thrived and spread abroad.

In England the Roman Catholic Church was ousted in the face of the growing Protestant movement. In its stead was placed the Church of England, a state-controlled church which was similar to the Catholic Church in many respects (as in regards to many of the old traditions), but incorporated the basic reforms that the Protestant movement demanded. Such a "compromise" did not sit well with all English Protestants, however, and some, who wanted to purge all vestiges of Rome and put forth the Bible as the basic religious authority, sought to "purify" the Church of England from within. This group came to be known as Puritans, and they followed a course which they hoped would eventually bring the Church of England into line with their wishes. Others, however, were not content to sit back and wait for results. These radicals, who wanted to separate completely from the Church of England, became known as Separatists, and advocated a congregational polity (that is, the placing of policies in the hands of the local church).

Baptists, in turn, originated out of the Separatist movement in the early seventeenth century. Puritans and Separatists were persecuted by the Church of England, and it was not until the late seventeenth century that Protestant dissenters, such as Baptists, were granted freedom to worship through the Toleration Act of 1689. Although the dissenters had to continue paying taxes to the Church of England, they were basically free to worship as they pleased.¹³

Thus, the sixteenth century was a time of turmoil and fragmentation for Christianity. The Catholic Church was rapidly losing control of the Holy Roman Empire to those who demanded reform and who came to be known as Protestants. These reformers refused to recognize the supreme authority of Rome, declaring instead that the Bible was able to speak for itself and championing a personal relationship between the individual believer and God. Within the Protestant movement itself were many varied beliefs on finer points of worship and doctrine, which in turn led to a rapid splintering of the Protestant movement. During this period, Christianity was radically altered and forever changed.

BAPTIST BEGINNINGS

The Protestant Reformation continued into the seventeenth century in Europe and England, finally coming to an end when the Peace of Westphalia in 1648 gave limited recognition of Protestantism. Baptists emerged early in the seventeenth century out of these reform movements, shaped by Puritanism, Separatism, and (some historians contend) Anabaptists.

In England Baptists originated out of the Separatist movement. The Separatists were those who, in the sixteenth century, had pulled out of the Church of England, declaring that the Anglican Church (as the Church of England came to be known) had not removed itself far enough from Roman Catholicism. The Separatists sought to live according to the Bible's teachings, insisted that the true church consisted only of the redeemed, and believed in participatory church government, such as congregationalist or presbyterian form (as opposed to the hierarchy in the Catholic Church).¹⁴

John Smyth, an ordained Anglican priest who left the Church of England to join the Separatist movement, is credited with establishing the first identifiable Baptist church. Smyth, following his forsaking of the Anglican Church in 1606, became associated with a group of Separatists in Gainsborough, England. This group came under intense persecution from James I, and eventually fled to Holland. Smyth and Thomas Helwys, a layperson, were the recognized leaders of this group as they settled in Amsterdam in 1607. During the next two years, Smyth's beliefs evolved to the point where, in 1609, he advocated a pure church comprised of believers who had been baptized as a sign of their confession of Christ. Accordingly, the little congregation was reconstituted as a church which practiced believer's baptism and viewed the Bible as the ultimate written authority for their faith.

Shortly thereafter, Smyth had a change of heart regarding the validity of the believer's baptism which the congregation had undergone, and he and a number of church members made an attempt to become a part of the Mennonite flock. Thomas Helwys, however, broke with Smyth in maintaining that the believer's baptism they had received was valid, and accordingly took up the leadership of the remainder of the group. In 1611 Helwys led the group back to England, settling in London, and founding what historians consider the first Baptist church on English soil.

Although the Helwys congregation maintained the practice of believer's baptism, the method they employed was not immersion at this point. The group had departed from the Calvinism which tended to mark Separatists, embracing instead the concept of free will (that is, Arminianism), and eventually becoming known as General Baptists (because of their belief in a "general" salvation—the belief that Christ died for all). The local church was responsible for electing its leaders, including preaching elders and men and women deacons. Helwys himself, in 1612, began attacking the authority of the Church of England and championing religious liberty for all believers. For his outspokenness, he was thrown into prison, where he apparently died in 1616. Others carried on the leadership of the General Baptists, continuing to champion religious liberty, autonomous local-church government, biblical authority, and the right for each individual to stand directly before God (the latter came to be known as the "priesthood of all believers"). By 1650 at least forty-seven General Baptist churches existed. Particular Baptists (so called because of their adherence to the Calvinistic belief that salvation had been extended to only particular individuals) came on the scene in the 1630s, and by 1644 there were at least seven such churches in or near London.[15] Therefore, virtually from the beginning, there were divisions within Baptist ranks.

By the mid-1600s, English Baptists had begun practicing immersion as the biblical mode of baptism. Furthermore, they drew up confessions in order to clarify their faith, inform church members, provide a basis for fellowship, and to deal with controversy. These early Baptists also pronounced their belief in the Trinity, the final authority of Scripture, salvation (General and Particular Baptists disagreed over who could be saved), the autonomy of the local church, the nature of ministry (which they distinguished between preaching the Word and meeting the needs of individuals; preachers and deacons were comprised of both men and women), believer's baptism by immersion, communion as a way of remembering and reflecting upon the death of Christ (as opposed to the Catholic belief that Christ actually existed in the bread and wine), and religious liberty.[16]

In the American colonies, Baptists first appeared in New England in 1639. Roger Williams, a former Anglican priest turned Separatist who had gotten into trouble with the Boston authorities because of his dissenting religious beliefs, founded the first Baptist church on American soil in

Providence, Rhode Island, sometime early in 1639. Although Williams remained a Baptist for only a short while, he made some important contributions to early Baptist thought through his beliefs in religious liberty for all, separation of church and state, and democratic church government.

Other Baptist churches sprang up in the New England colonies during the century, some of which counted among their members both General and Particular Baptists. However, Baptists quickly came under persecution from the militant Puritans who controlled the governments of most of the New England colonies and had established the Congregational Church as the state-sponsored church of most of New England. The persecution of Baptists at the hands of the Puritan-controlled, state-church governments included fines, imprisonments, and public whippings for a number of Baptists. Some Baptists moved to the Middle Colonies to escape persecution, and by 1700, several Baptist churches in that area had been founded. A few Baptists moved to the southern colonies, although some of the migrants initially met with severe persecution from the established Anglican Church in South Carolina and parts of Virginia. The first Baptist presence in the South has been traced to a pastorless "house church" in Charleston, South Carolina, in the 1680s. In 1696 the First Baptist Church of Charleston was officially and visibly organized. Thus began the story of Baptists in the American South.[17]

EARLY BAPTIST GROWTH IN AMERICA

In 1700 there were only twenty-four Baptist churches with 839 members in America.[18] Baptists at that time were not a denomination, had no organized associations, sponsored no organized missionary or evangelistic efforts, and only had limited awareness of one another.[19] However, the widespread revival which came to be known as the First Great Awakening led to sudden and explosive growth among Baptists. By the end of the eighteenth century, Baptists had become the largest denomination in America.[20] By 1790 there were 979 Baptist churches and 67,500 Baptist church members in America. They were organized into at least 42 associations and were discussing plans to form a national organization.[21]

Although Baptists had little to do with initiating the First Great Awakening, they benefited immensely from the revival fires which swept the land. The new interest in religion among the colonies led to tremendous growth in Baptists' ranks, as well as a division of the ranks. Out of the revival atmosphere emerged two basic strains of Baptists in America: Regular Baptists, who were suspicious of the emotionalism which characterized the revival movement, and Separate Baptists, who saw the hand of God in the revivals and embraced the emotionalism which accompanied the First

Great Awakening. In New England, despite these differing views which emerged, Regular and Separate Baptists eventually merged ranks. Regular Baptists preceeded Separates in the South, but Separates migrated southward and eventually constituted a different and distinct group from their Regular brethren.[22]

The most significant Baptist growth of the century occurred after 1740. Between 1740 and 1790, a fifty-year span, the number of Baptist churches increased from sixty to nearly one thousand. The New England colonies experienced a good deal of growth despite opposition and persecution from the state-supported, Puritan-founded Congregational Church. Baptists of the Middle Colonies, not having to strive against a state-supported church, experienced the most growth during the century. In the South, where the Anglican Church was the official state church, Baptists experienced slow growth throughout the century. The sparse population of the area played a part in restricting Baptist growth. The bulk of the expansion that did occur was from Baptists migrating to the South from the Northern and Middle Colonies.[23]

In the second half of the eighteenth century, Separate Baptists were transplanted into the South. The first Separate Baptist church was the Sandy Creek Church of North Carolina, established in 1755. The Separate Baptists were caught up in the emotional, evangelistic zeal which characterized the revivals. Worship services were marked by emotional preaching and worship. Advocating a modified Calvinism, the Separates believed that Christ offered salvation for all, and that the decision of life or death was left up to the individual. As other Separate Baptist churches followed the Sandy Creek Church, a trend developed toward uneducated, anti-intellectual preachers. Most Separatists opposed ministerial salaries as well. Generally speaking, Separate churches held to nine "rites": baptism, Lord's Supper, love feast, laying on of hands, foot washing, anointing the sick, the right hand of fellowship, the kiss of charity, and the dedicating of children. The Separate Baptist churches of the South also helped popularize the "evangelical invitation" and allowed women to serve as deaconesses and, in some cases, preachers.

In 1758 nine Separate Baptist churches in the South joined forces to form the Sandy Creek Baptist Association. Soon, however, Separate and Regular Baptists (who were characterized by their orderly and liturgical worship services and educated ministers; the First Baptist Church of Charleston was a model for Regular Baptist congregations) of the South began gravitating towards one another, partially over their shared strong emphasis on religious freedom. In 1787 the Separate and Regular Baptists of Virginia merged, followed by North Carolina in 1788. The Baptists of South Carolina, Georgia, and Kentucky gradually merged within their respective states. The mergers turned out to be permanent unions, but the Separate and Regular

Baptist emphases still remain, as does the tension that results from the differences which characterize the traditions.

The Southern Baptist Convention, in many ways, traces its roots back to both the Separate and Regular Baptist traditions: evangelistic preaching, a heavy emphasis on an emotional conversion, emotional worship services, a modified Calvinism that makes room for a personal decision, and the gospel song tradition are characteristics that are found in many Southern Baptist churches today. On the other hand, many SBC churches have orderly worship services and seminary-trained ministers, which are characteristic of the Regular Baptist tradition. The SBC of today is a mixture of both traditions.[24]

Generally speaking, Baptists of the eighteenth century were suspicious of education. On the other hand, Baptists in the South did begin to see the need for local churches to join together in common efforts. Late in the century, and largely after the American Revolution, Baptist churches began forming associations in earnest. Churches grouped themselves into associations for several reasons: to clarify and monitor doctrine, give advice on Baptist practices, help connect available pastors to needy churches, promote benevolent works (particularly in regards to Christian education, the struggle for religious liberty, and home missions), provide model preaching (preaching was a major feature of early Baptist associational meetings), and provide a means of fellowship for Baptists who were oftentimes isolated and sometimes persecuted.

Within the local churches of the eighteenth century, some Baptist congregations incorporated hymn singing as a part of the worship service, while others avoided singing. Baptism and the Lord's Supper became the two major rites of local Baptist churches. Sunday Schools did not exist, and holidays such as Christmas and Easter were not observed because they were considered to be worldly and popish (if not downright pagan).[25]

The late 1700s and early 1800s saw Baptists unite in their efforts to secure religious liberty for all persons. Severe persecution of Baptists by state-controlled churches in both the Northern and Southern Colonies continued immediately after the American Revolution, partially in the form of the continuing taxation of Baptists to support the state churches. From their beginnings in America under the leadership of Roger Williams, Baptists had always fought for religious liberty, not only for themselves, but for others as well. Just prior to the Revolution, some Baptists had championed religious liberty through civil disobedience by refusing to pay taxes to support the state church. One Baptist association sent a delegate to the Constitutional Congress in Philadelphia in 1774 to lobby for religious liberty. This civil disobedience brought some relief for Baptists, but the Philadelphia delegation could not fully persuade the Congress to their views.

Following the Revolution, which most Baptists supported, individual states began drafting constitutions. Baptists incessantly petitioned state leaders to keep state governments out of religious matters. In Virginia, for example, Baptists sent written petitions to the state leaders protesting the use of taxes to support the state church and demanding religious liberty for persons of all faiths. Virginia's leaders eventually strove to adopt a compromise between the current establishment and the radical demands of the Baptists by proposing to levy a general tax which would be used to support all religions. A number of Christian denominations were prepared to accept such a compromise, but Baptist leaders would not bend. James Madison eventually lent his support to the Baptist stance, and his eloquent cries for religion to be "wholly exempt" from government made an impression on Thomas Jefferson, who in 1785 introduced a bill establishing religious freedom in Virginia. The bill passed with the support of Baptists.

On the national level, Baptists likewise played a key role in the drafting and ratification of the First Amendment, which guaranteed religious liberty for all and disassociated the federal government from religious matters. The term "separation between church and state" was later coined by Thomas Jefferson in a letter he wrote to a group of Baptists in Danbury, Connecticut, in 1802, in which he used the term to describe his understanding of the First Amendment which he had helped draft.[26]

1800-1840: BAPTISTS IN THE SOUTH

Baptists, by 1800, had become the largest denomination in America. Their support of the American Revolution and their successful battle for religious liberty in the new nation had won them friends in high places, such as James Madison, Thomas Jefferson, and George Washington. As such, Baptists had acquired, for the most part, a good public image. Now, early in the nineteenth century, they sought to pull together and form a national structure to promote the modern missionary movement which was then underway. William Carey, missionary to India, had inspired the formation of the Baptist Missionary Society in 1792, raising the awareness of Baptists in regards to missions. Subsequently, Luther Rice had evoked missions awareness through his tireless efforts to raise money for foreign missions through local Baptist churches. As such, Baptists were, for the first time, being exposed to the idea of sending out foreign missionaries.

In 1814, at the First Baptist Church of Philadelphia, thirty-two delegates met and formed the General Missionary Convention of the Baptist Denomination of the United States for Foreign Missions. This national Baptist organization quickly became known as the General Convention, and then as the Triennial Convention, for it met once every three years.

In the beginning, Northern Baptists had a stronger representation than Baptists from the South in the Triennial Convention. There were differences of opinion between North and South as to how the organization should be structured, and the constitution adopted in 1814 was a compromise between the North's desire for a "society" method (whose base support would come from interested individuals and churches) and the South's preference for a "convention" plan (which would involve across-the-board participation from local churches, and, Baptists of the South believed, would give them fairer representation). The compromise contained elements of both plans, but this initial balance shifted towards the South's convention method over the next decade, only to shift towards the North's society plan by 1826.

The Triennial Convention quickly expanded its base to accommodate more than just foreign missions. In 1817 home missions was added, with the emphasis being placed on the expanding West. However, the Convention disbanded the home missions effort in 1820, deciding instead to focus only on foreign missions. Also in 1817, the Convention voted to sponsor theological education and, to that end, established a seminary, only to sever ties with the institution in 1823 when the seminary came into financial ruin. The Triennial Convention also moved into the publication arena in 1818 with the publication of a Baptist newspaper.

By 1826, however, the overall mood of the Convention had changed. The Convention of that year was held in New York, with the result being that Baptists from the North had more delegates in attendance than did Baptists from the South. The Northern Baptist majority body, expressing the opinion that expansion efforts had hindered the foreign mission work of the Convention, voted to refocus solely on foreign missions. The delegates also voted to change the Convention's organization to the society method, the preference of Baptists in the North.

Baptists from the South did not take lightly the power which their brethren from the North had exercised over the Convention. Nevertheless, the number of foreign missionaries dramatically increased following the 1826 meeting, as the Triennial Convention refocused on foreign missions.[27]

During this time, two additional societies were formed in Baptist life. In 1824 the Baptist General Tract Society was formed with the mission of publishing written materials for Baptists. A decade later, in 1832, the American Baptist Home Mission Society was established. This society picked up where the Triennial Convention had left off in 1820 when it abandoned home missions.[28]

Although the three Baptist societies grew throughout the 1830s, there was simmering dissatisfaction and discord among Baptists in America. In the 1820s, an antimission movement arose from within Baptist ranks. The leaders of this movement ardently held to strict Calvinism, which espoused the belief that God had already chosen those who would be saved (this belief is known as "predestination"). Thus, missionary activity and evangelism were deemed unnecessary. Also, the leaders of the antimissionary movement declared that the Bible made no provisions for missions organizations. This call to strict biblicism (taking the Bible literally and refusing to recognize any institutions or practices which are not specifically mentioned in Scripture), along with the Calvinistic leanings of many Baptists, led many to rally around the antimission effort.[29] Furthermore, the suspicion among uneducated ministers toward educated preachers, as well as the belief among some Baptists that ministers should not be paid (whereas the missionaries were being paid), helped fuel the antimission movement.[30]

Most of the antimission sentiment came from Baptists in the South, where another factor came into play: the headquartering of the mission societies in the North, which was bringing about growing resentment and suspicion among many Baptists in the South. Nevertheless, only a small minority of the entire Baptist population of the 1820s and 1830s actually embraced the antimission movement.[31]

The antimission movement was the first major internal doctrinal controversy which Baptists in America experienced. Baptist historian Leon McBeth summarized the movement as ultraconservatism confronting the "progressive spirit" of mainline Baptists. The leaders of the movement evoked the name of biblical authority in order to undercut biblical teachings and practices (namely, the spreading of the gospel). The legacy of the antimission movement, which was confined largely to the South, still lives on today among Southern Baptists in the form of ultraconservative opposition to denominational programs (which was most evident in the 1960s-1980s), suspicion of education (prevalent among many ultraconservative Southern Baptists to this day), and rigid biblicism (also prevalent among ultraconservative Southern Baptists).[32]

Finally, out of the antimission environment of the 1820s, Alexander Campbell, a former Presbyterian and non-denominationalist, led an ultraconservative "reformation" which countered historic Baptist principles regarding believer's baptism and the right of the individual to stand before God and personally read and interpret Scripture (the "priesthood of all believers"). The Campbellite movement caused division among Baptist churches on the local level. Preaching that baptism was necessary to salvation and that the Bible should be interpreted in a strictly literal fashion, Campbell disrupted Baptist life and caused splits among local churches and associations, particularly in Kentucky and Virginia, resulting in the formation of the Church of Christ denomination.[33]

Although Baptists entered the nineteenth century ready to work together to spread the gospel, by the 1840s, sectionalism and doctrinal conflicts had torn the Baptist family apart. Unfortunately, worse was yet to come.

CHAPTER THREE

The Southern Baptist Convention: A Brief History

The Southern Baptist Convention is only one of many different Baptist groups, albeit the largest. The SBC is an organization of like-minded Baptists (to some degree) within the Baptist denomination. As its name implies, the stronghold of the SBC is the South, commonly referred to as the "Bible Belt." In 1995 the SBC celebrated its 150th anniversary. Those 150 years were marked by diversity, controversy, and, until the 1970s, rapid growth.

THE BIRTH OF THE SOUTHERN BAPTIST CONVENTION

By the 1830s, Baptists in the South were somewhat distraught by the northern dominance of the Triennial Convention. Also by this time, Baptists in the South were accusing the Home Mission Society, based in New York, of neglecting the South in its missionary appointments. This suspicion and distrust of their northern brethren had led some Baptists in the South to call for a separate organization based in the South as early as 1835.

The straw that broke the camel's back, however, was the issue of slavery. To be sure, some Baptists in some southern states, such as Virginia and Kentucky, were on record as opposing slavery prior to 1830. However, the deep-South states—Georgia and the Carolinas—witnessed no organized anti-slavery movement among Baptists. In fact, a number of Baptist leaders in the South were slaveholders, some having numerous slaves.

The South, by this time, was vigorously defending the institution of slavery against the anti-slavery sentiment that was sweeping the northern states. Southerners believed slavery to be necessary if the South's economy, based almost exclusively on agriculture, were to remain stable. Baptists, like other Southerners, defended slavery on these same premises, seeing no contradiction between slavery and Christian principles.

In 1840 the Baptist Anti-Slavery Convention was formed in New York, and the organization immediately proceeded to warn Baptists in the South to renounce their support of slavery. Over the next four years, however, Baptist leaders from the North and South strove to work together despite their intense differences of opinion concerning slavery. Although they succeeded for a short while, in 1844 their efforts at neutrality fell apart. The Home Mission Society (HMS), meeting that year, refused to take action on the appointment of a southern slave owner as a missionary. The HMS also voted to look into the dissolution of the organization, largely because of the conflicts between Baptists over the slavery issue. In a separate incident that year, Alabama Baptists tested the board of the Triennial Convention by asking for the foreign mission appointment of a slaveholder and stating that the Convention should share its missionary appointive powers with the local churches. Alabama Baptists tied these two requests together, and the Convention's reply stated its intentions to make no arrangements which could be construed as supporting slavery.

Baptists in the South read the worst into these actions of the HMS and the Triennial Convention. Some Baptists in the South urged immediate separation from their northern counterparts, while others urged caution. The voices of the separationists won as Virginia Baptists called for a consulting meeting on May 8, 1845, in Augusta, Georgia, to discuss options for Baptists in the South. Nearly three hundred people attended the meeting, all but twenty being from Georgia, South Carolina, and Virginia. Although the group met only to discuss options, sentiment for separation was high, and the meeting led to decisive action. The delegates voted to form the Southern Baptist Convention, adopted a constitution employing the convention method of organization, and established two mission boards (foreign and home).

Admittedly, many Baptist leaders of the day did not attach profound significance to the actions of May 8, 1845. There were already a number of Baptist groups and societies, and the formation of yet another Baptist organization was not significant in and of itself to many observers. However, the splintering of Baptists along North-South lines was to have a tremendous impact on the future of Baptists.[1]

1845-1900: GROWTH AND CONTROVERSY

From the inception of the SBC, foreign missions was viewed as being of primary importance to Baptists in the South. Shortly after the formation of the Convention, the Civil War raged across the United States, and the Foreign Mission Board (FMB) suffered both during and after the conflict. The FMB also faced other obstacles during the last half of the nineteenth century:

continued opposition from the antimission faction, apathy, lack of information in the local churches, and doctrinal controversy. Nevertheless, by 1900 Southern Baptists had ninety-four foreign missionaries who had founded 113 churches with sixty-five hundred members in six nations.[2]

The Board of Domestic Missions (renamed the Home Mission Board in 1874) also faced many problems. In addition to struggling with the same difficulties the FMB faced, the Home Mission Board had difficulty locating capable leaders, winning the support of local churches (many of whom felt home missions should be the work of local churches and associations), and staying financially afloat. By the 1870s, there was serious talk of dissolving the board, but in 1882 the SBC decided to try and revitalize the board by electing new leadership and trustees and moving the board to Atlanta (it had been located in Marion, Alabama). With new leaders and in a larger city, the HMB finally became a solid organization. In 1900 there were 671 home missionaries on the field who started 195 new churches.[3]

In 1891 the SBC added the Sunday School Board. This completed the schism of 1845, for many southern churches, following the formation of the SBC, had continued buying educational materials from the American Baptist Publication Society in Philadelphia. With the establishment of a publishing board in the South, southern churches began buying their church materials from their own publishing agency, cutting off the last ties to Northern Baptists.

In the area of educational institutions, Christian colleges mushroomed in the wake of the religious awakenings which had swept across the nation. Initially suspicious of education by and large, Baptists in the South warmed up to the idea of an educated clergy during the 1800s, once they began realizing that educated men made good pastors who could better defend the faith against such challenges as the antimission and Campbellite movements. The first half of the 1800s witnessed the formation of individual state Baptist conventions in the South, followed by the formation of state-sponsored Baptist colleges. In 1825 the institution which is now known as Furman University was established by South Carolina Baptists, followed by Georgetown (Kentucky, 1829), the University of Richmond (Virginia, 1832), Mercer University (Georgia, 1833), and Wake Forest (North Carolina, 1834). Many others followed, although the Civil War led to the demise of more than a few of the newly founded Baptist colleges. The late 1800s, however, witnessed a resurgence in the founding of Baptist colleges in the South.

The shift towards education also resulted in the founding of the Southern Baptist Theological Seminary (thanks largely to the efforts of Georgia and South Carolina Baptists) in 1859. Originally located in Greenville, South Carolina, it relocated to Louisville, Kentucky, in 1877. Although the Civil War threatened the demise of the seminary, the institution survived and prospered following the move to Louisville.[4]

Following the Civil War, women of most major denominations developed their own national organizations. Southern Baptists were a bit slower in following suit, but when messengers at the 1885 annual SBC meeting rewrote the Convention's constitution to deny messenger status for women, Southern Baptist women were stirred into action. In 1888 the Woman's Missionary Union (WMU) was founded as an auxiliary to the SBC. In its early years, the WMU tended to focus solely on supporting the foreign mission work of the SBC.[5]

Despite growth and expansion, the SBC was plagued by a major internal doctrinal controversy which hung around for most of the remainder of the nineteenth century. The Landmark Controversy, as it came to be called, started in the 1850s as certain popular Southern Baptist leaders begin putting forth the notion that only Baptist churches were true Christian churches.[6] James Robinson Graves, editor of the *Tennessee Baptist*, and an influential Southern Baptist (although not a pastor), espoused a new doctrine (which Graves had picked up from someone else) concerning Baptists which won many Baptists over to his side. In essence, Graves taught that only Baptist churches were true Christian churches, that "church" should refer only to the local church, that "kingdom" and "church" are synonymous terms in the Bible (meaning that the Kingdom of God would be made up of the sum total of all Baptist churches), that non-Baptist ministers could not preach in Baptist pulpits (since they were not ministers of true Christian churches), and that Baptist churches could be traced back through history to John the Baptist. Graves used the latter belief to validate Baptists as being the only true church, since it portrayed Baptist churches as the only churches whose foundations could be traced to the New Testament. However, Graves' revision of Baptist history was pure fantasy, as opposed to fact.

Graves' views were widely circulated in Baptist circles, and won over more than a few Baptists. With his views gaining acceptance among the Baptist public, he began acting vehemently towards those Baptist leaders who openly opposed him. In 1858 his own church convicted him of slandering the pastor (who was opposing Graves), seeking to divide the church, publishing "foul" statements, using the *Tennessee Baptist* to attack other Baptist leaders, and speaking or publishing nine specific lies. He was soon evicted from the church, whereupon he started his own church and, the following year, unsuccessfully sought to have the SBC dismantle the Foreign Mission Board. The mean, exclusive spirit of the movement had begun to show itself by now, and this, along with the Civil War, slowed the movement considerably, but did not put it to death.[7]

By the end of the century, Landmarkism had raised its head several more times in Southern Baptist life. In Texas and Arkansas, Landmark proponents tried to gain control of the state conventions, but both states repelled the attacks and the two Landmark groups eventually left the SBC and formed their own respective associations; both would exert much influence.

The most well-known facet of the Landmark controversy, however, was the Whitsitt controversy. William H. Whitsitt, newly elected president of the Southern Baptist Theological Seminary, had begun publishing articles in the 1880s which affirmed that Baptist beginnings could be traced back to the early 1600s. The Landmarkists did not openly attack Whitsitt until 1896, following his appointment to the presidency of Southern Seminary the previous year. The 1895 publication of an article by Whitsitt regarding Baptist history,[8] and a subsequent monologue in 1896, further outlining his views of Baptist origins, resulted in an all-out Landmarkist war against him.[9] In response to these writings, two prominent Southern Baptist Landmarkists (one of whom was a seminary trustee) challenged Whitsitt, claiming he was teaching heresy. For the next three years, these two individuals spearheaded an attack against him.

Although the Landmarkists did not succeed in turning the seminary trustees against Whitsitt, they did succeed in damaging the reputation of the seminary, and in 1899, a weary Whitsitt decided to resign the presidency of the seminary in order to save the institution. This appeased the Landmarkists by and large. Whitsitt's view of Baptist history, despite his resignation, came to be accepted as truth among most Baptists.[10]

Birthed in the midst of controversy, the SBC closed out the nineteenth century caught up in another controversy. The controversy, however, did not hinder the numerical growth of Southern Baptists.

1900-1930: CONSOLIDATION AMIDST CONTROVERSY

The SBC, at the onset of the twentieth century, consisted of three general boards (Foreign Mission, Home Mission, and Sunday School), one seminary, one auxiliary organization (the Woman's Missionary Union), and no central structure. The arrival of the new century marked new hope and a new direction for the SBC, however. It was an opportunity to put Reconstruction behind and look to the future South with new-found optimism. Into this atmosphere came a search for greater efficiency in Southern Baptist life in order to cope with the expanding Convention. The state Baptist conventions led the way in becoming more efficient, beginning with Texas Baptists' consolidation of their work under a central executive board in 1914. Other states soon followed Texas' example.

On a national level, Southern Baptists finally made the first move towards streamlining the Convention (following several years of discussion) with the creation of the SBC Executive Committee in 1917. For the first time, the boards of the SBC were joined together under a central, unified structure. Soon afterward, the SBC addressed the issue of systematically raising funds to operate the national boards and agencies, which resulted in the formation of the Cooperative Program in 1925. The Cooperative Program was designed to be a means whereby Southern Baptists could collectively fund the various agencies of the SBC. Local churches sent a certain percentage of their offering receipts to their respective state conventions, which, in turn, sent a certain percentage of those gifts to the national Cooperative Program. Cooperative Program money was then divided among the various SBC agencies. The same basic structure is still largely intact in today's SBC.[11]

Several new SBC agencies were established during the early years of the twentieth century, underscoring the need for efficiency and consolidation. In 1918 the SBC voted to establish a Relief and Annuity Board (now known as the Annuity Board) for the purpose of providing financial protection for Southern Baptist pastors in case of injury, illness, or retirement. In 1907 the Laymen's Missionary Movement (later changed to the Brotherhood Commission, recently incorporated into the North American Mission Board) was formed to involve men in the support of missions. The Social Service Commission, the forerunner of the Christian Life Commission (CLC), was founded in 1914 in order to confront the perceived evils of society (alcohol in particular). Today the CLC has a broad-based social and political agenda. In 1938 the Southern Baptist Historical Society was formed in order to gather and preserve "historical records of Southern Baptists." Two SBC seminaries were added in the early 1900s: Southwestern Baptist Theological Seminary (1908) and New Orleans Baptist Theological Seminary (1917).[12]

In the midst of the tremendous surge of growth which the SBC experienced in the early years of the twentieth century, controversy again reared its head. In the latter half of the nineteenth century, Darwin's theory of evolution and the emergence of new schools of biblical criticism had had the effect of putting some Christians on the defensive in regards to traditional views of the Bible. In the face of what some considered an onslaught upon long-held beliefs about the Bible and God, there arose within the ranks of Christians an anti-modernist movement. In essence, this ultraconservative movement (which came to be known as fundamentalism) rejected any trappings of modern science and learning and rallied around long-held interpretations of Scripture and notions of God. Southern Baptists, being conservative (but not ultra-conservative) by nature, had long managed to remain largely unaffected by the ongoing controversy (with the exception of the forced resignation of Crawford H. Toy, professor of the Southern Baptist Theological Seminary, in 1879, because of his open embrace of new methods of biblical criticism in regards to the understanding of the Old Testament).[13] However, the fundamentalist-modernist controversy could not be kept out of Southern Baptist life forever.

The opening years of the twentieth century saw developing tension in the Christian world in regards to the "confrontation" between science and religion. E. Y. Mullins, Southern Baptist theologian, president of the Southern Baptist Theological Seminary, and Southern Baptist leader during the first quarter of the century, rose to lead Southern Baptists through these turbulent times. He opposed the small, but growing, powerful fundamentalist faction within the SBC which appealed to the uneducated and sought to overtake the SBC.[14] Although a self-identified moderate-conservative (that is, a conservative, but not in the strictest sense) who believed that Christianity was compatible with "modern culture,"[15] and who accepted higher criticism (that is, the scientific study) of the Bible,[16] Mullins remained evangelistic.[17] The fundamentalists, however, refused to concede any point to "modernism" and waged war against both Mullins and the mainline conservative SBC.

In 1907 fundamentalist leaders played an instrumental part in founding Southwestern Baptist Theological Seminary. Southwestern was established as a theological training ground for Southern Baptists in the Southwest, and, for fundamentalists, as an alternative to the perceived liberalism of Mullins and Southern Seminary.[18] Fundamentalist Southern Baptists began rallying around certain beliefs as outlined in a series of articles entitled *The Fundamentals* (from which the fundamentalist movement derived its name), which became, in effect, the creeds of the ultraconservative movement. The five "fundamentals" which ultraconservatives rallied around included: 1) an inerrant Bible, 2) the virgin birth of Jesus, 3) the substitutionary atonement of Christ (the sacrificing of his life for our sins), 4) the physical resurrection of Christ, and 5) the second coming of Christ. The fundamentalists believed subscription to these beliefs was mandatory if one was to be a true Christian.[19] The latter four were common Southern Baptist beliefs, but the concept of inerrancy was divisive, as inerrancy per se was virtually unknown in SBC life.

By 1920 the fundamentalists, though only a small minority in SBC life, were growing more vocal. Southern Baptist fundamentalists, echoing lingering adherence to Landmark principles, had long battled Mullins' efforts to lead the SBC into dialogues and partnerships with Northern Baptists.[20] In Texas fundamentalists argued among themselves over the direction of Southwestern Baptist Theological Seminary.[21] When Southern Baptists launched the Seventy-Five Million Campaign (the first attempt to systematically raise money for SBC causes, and the forerunner of the Cooperative Program) in 1919, the fundamentalists quickly voiced opposition.[22]

J. Frank Norris, pastor of First Baptist Church in Fort Worth, Texas,[23] became the visible leader of the Southern Baptist fundamentalist movement. Norris led an attack against the SBC, charging that Southern Baptists held "modernistic" teachings on Scripture (an allusion to the newly developed methods, at that time, of examining Scripture) and were not taking a stand against the ever-growing theory of evolution. Norris was also upset that the

SBC did not hold to his own personal strict views of premillennial eschatology (that is, the belief that the rapture will take place prior to Christ's thousand-year reign on earth, an interpretation of the end times derived from the book of Revelation).[24] By the 1920s, in fact, premillennialism had become synonymous with fundamentalism.[25]

Although fundamentalists continued to attack the SBC leadership on many points, in the 1920s, evolution became the focal point of fundamentalist campaigns. Fundamentalist Southern Baptists fervently opposed the teaching of evolutionary thought in the public schools, and subsequently took their case to state governments in the South, beginning with Kentucky. Mullins (not seeing any danger to Christianity from evolutionary thought) led the mainline Southern Baptist effort to combat this fundamentalist maneuver by helping to defeat ultraconservative efforts to have the Kentucky House of Representatives outlaw the teaching of evolution in that state's public schools.[26]

In the 1923 SBC meeting, fundamentalists sought to lead the SBC to take a strict stand against the teaching of evolution. However, the messengers rallied behind Mullins, who was presiding as president, and accepted a compromise which neither condemned nor openly condoned evolution.[27] The following year at the annual SBC meeting, Norris led the efforts to condemn evolution, but once again Mullins prevailed. The Southern Baptist fundamentalist minority also failed in 1925, but in 1926, after intense politicking and emotional appeals in Southern Baptist churches, they did succeed in leading the messengers of the SBC annual meeting to accept as the "sentiment of the body" the rejection of evolutionary theory.[28] This was a victory for the fundamentalists, although their measure against evolution never became an official SBC stance.[29]

In the midst of the evolution controversy, the SBC, in 1925, adopted its first written statement of doctrine and faith, The Baptist Faith and Message. This first formal SBC confession of faith traced its beginnings to 1919 when, at the annual SBC meeting, a resolution was passed calling for a committee, to be led by E. Y. Mullins, to prepare a statement of formal greeting to "Baptists of the world." The motive behind the resolution was to reestablish communication with Baptists of Europe following the dark years of World War I. The paper which the Mullins-led committee presented to the annual SBC meeting the following year was in the shape of a doctrinal summary, reaffirming Baptist principles and practices, and addressed to Baptists around the world. The treatise was not intended to be a confession of faith, but rather a summary of Southern Baptist beliefs and practices. The paper received positive attention, and certainly helped pave the way for the formal confession which would soon follow.[30]

By 1924 the attacks upon the SBC by J. Frank Norris were a source of consternation for many Southern Baptists. Partly in response to Norris, the

SBC voted that year to issue a more complete doctrinal statement. A committee, chaired by Mullins, was elected, which, in turn, drew up a formal doctrinal statement and presented it to the messengers of the 1925 annual SBC meeting. The Baptist Faith and Message, as it was called, restated the 1833 Baptist New Hampshire Confession of Faith "revised . . . and with some additional articles growing out of present needs." The committee's introductory statement explicitly noted the nature and function of confessions in Baptist life: "They constitute a consensus of opinion of some Baptist body . . . for the general instruction and guidance of our people." Confessions were noted as being incomplete statements of faith with no "finality or infallibility." The introduction reaffirmed Scripture as "the sole authority" for Baptist "faith and practice," while noting that confessions, although "drawn from Scriptures, are not to be used to hamper freedom of thought or investigation in other realms of life."[31]

The confession itself made declarations on such things as the Bible ("divinely inspired"), God, the Fall of Man, Salvation (by grace through Christ), Justification, Baptism and the Lord's Supper, Religious Liberty, Education, Stewardship, and Evangelism and Missions. There were a total of twenty-five articles, none of which dealt with the pressing issue of evolution (although the committee did address the theory of evolution, neither condemning nor condoning it, in a statement following the twenty-five confessional articles).[32] Southern Baptists of the day, by and large, received the confessional statement positively, although Southern Baptist leaders had mixed feelings about adopting confessions of faith. Some felt that there had really been no need for the confession to be made, and others (including Mullins) went further by noting the danger of creedalism which confessions invoke.[33] The current doctrinal crises in Southern Baptist life attest to the wisdom of these Baptist leaders of yesteryear.

Fundamentalists within the SBC were quite furious over the absence of an anti-evolution statement within the confession. The anti-evolution statement which was endorsed by the fundamentalists and passed by the messengers of the SBC annual meeting the following year was never added to The Baptist Faith and Message. Norris, the fundamentalist ringleader within the SBC, became discouraged and frustrated over not getting his way, and eventually left the SBC to start his own independent fundamentalist denomination.[34] By the 1930s, the fundamentalist-modernist controversy had faded in the face of the newly formed Cooperative Program (which completed the SBC trend towards centralization), the Great Depression, and a united SBC effort to oppose the presidential nomination of anti-Prohibitionist Governor Albert Smith.[35]

Thus, although the first three decades of the twentieth century were a time of growth and expansion for Southern Baptists, they were also a time of continuous conflict between mainline conservative-moderate Southern

Baptists and a vocal minority of ultraconservative fundamentalists who wanted to pit the SBC against anything which hinted of the modern world. Although winning a few skirmishes, fundamentalists gained no long-term victories in Southern Baptist life. Their vocal and fervent opposition in SBC life, however, did help lead the SBC to make a formal confessional statement which indirectly refuted fundamentalism, but which also opened the door towards potential creedalism within the SBC.

1930-1960: DEVELOPING A NATIONAL VISION

In 1912 Southern and Northern Baptists had reached an agreement that there should be only one convention (either North or South) represented in each state, with the basic understanding that southern states would be affiliated with the SBC. From this agreement, Oklahoma, which had had dual state conventions for several years, opted for the SBC in 1914. The 1912 agreement was generally expected to put an end to southern aggression in the northern states.[36]

The agreement worked well for several decades. However, in 1942 the SBC broke its end of the bargain in the face of changing demographics.

During the Great Depression, families from Oklahoma, Texas, and Arkansas left their homelands and traveled to California in search of something better. Many of those who migrated to California were Southern Baptists. They soon began forming their own independent churches, followed by associations, and, in 1940, a state convention. The following year, 1941, the state convention applied for affiliation with the SBC. An SBC committee was appointed to study the proposal, and, in 1942, reported back to the annual SBC meeting, clearly leaning towards a stance of refusing admission to the California group. However, a committee member presented a minority report which urged recognition of the California Baptists, and the messengers "overwhelmingly" approved the minority report, sensing a need to provide more structure for Southern Baptists in the far West.

The Northern Baptist Convention (NBC) protested, but to no avail. In 1944 the SBC voted to remove all territorial limits. In the face of this removal of territorial barriers by the SBC, the NBC changed its name to the American Baptist Convention (ABC) in 1950, and extended an invitation to other Baptist groups to affiliate with it. Southern Baptists, quickly moving into northern and western states, held annual SBC meetings in Chicago (1950) and San Francisco (1951). At the 1951 meeting, the SBC, noting the inclusive name change of the Northern Convention, voted to make its boards and agencies free to serve "any community or any people in the United States."[37] Any remaining harmony between the SBC and the ABC was dissolved, and Southern Baptists lurched at the reins of expansion.

In the 1940s and 1950s, Southern Baptist churches sprang up all across the country, spurred on by relocated Southern Baptists who wanted Southern Baptist fellowship in their new home states. Besides California, the states of Ohio, Utah, Oregon, Washington, Kansas, Michigan, Alaska, and Hawaii acquired Southern Baptist works in the 1940s. But the majority of non-southern states were opened up to Southern Baptists in the early and mid-1950s: Wyoming, Idaho, Nevada, and Delaware (1951); Montana (1952); North Dakota, South Dakota, and Wisconsin (1953); Iowa (1954); New York and Nebraska (1955); and Minnesota (1956). Southern Baptists expanded into the New England states in the 1960s. Churches were first formed; then associations and state conventions or fellowships followed. Today there are Southern Baptist churches in all fifty states and Puerto Rico.[38]

The SBC expansion into northern and western states was not initially received well by American (Northern) Baptists. Since 1960, however, relations between the two Baptist conventions have grown better. The expansion has also led to some tension between the old South states and the new convention areas (sometimes called "pioneer areas"). The SBC policy of not recognizing a state convention until there are fifteen thousand resident Southern Baptists is not looked upon with favor by some of the new state conventions, while some old state conventions do not want the new states to receive too much representative power on SBC agencies.

The territorial expansion of Southern Baptists has transformed the SBC. Numerical growth in terms of membership, the founding of new institutions (including seminaries in Mill Valley, California and Kansas City, Missouri), and an enlarged financial base, as well as a national vision, were by-products of Southern Baptists' foray into the entirety of the United States.

The expansion has also led to new theological conflicts. Landmarkism, long dormant, found new expression and new life in some new convention areas. Leon McBeth surmised that the isolation of Southern Baptists in many pioneer areas led to some of the same old insecurities which plagued some Baptists of the early nineteenth century, leading those earlier Baptists to a point of defending their faith as the one true faith, out of which arose Landmarkism. McBeth also suggested that the Landmarkism which flamed up in new convention areas may have been funneled back to the Bible Belt states and fueled the major theological controversies which have plagued the SBC since the 1960s.[39]

1960-1977: THEOLOGICAL POLARIZATION

Although the fundamentalist-modernist controversy had played itself out by the 1930s, the SBC expansionistic policies of the 1940s and 1950s had created tension both externally (between Southern Baptists and Northern

Baptists) and internally (the stirring up of ultraconservative—or fundamentalist—Landmark principles and attitudes). Kansas City was destined to be the powder keg where these tensions were to clash and eventually ignite the most turbulent theological controversy which the SBC has ever experienced.

In the 1950s, the SBC began looking for a midwestern or western site for its sixth seminary. The feeling was that such a location would be beneficial to the newly expanded Convention. In the meantime, the SBC had voted not to support any longer any institution whose trustees it did not elect. This policy led the SBC to reevaluate its relationship with Central Baptist Theological Seminary, an American Baptist seminary which served both the ABC and the SBC. Although some of the trustees of Central Baptist Seminary were Southern Baptists, as were a number of students and teachers, and although many Southern Baptists were quite content with this joint venture between Baptists of the North and South, the aforementioned new policy of the expansionistic-minded Convention seriously hampered relationships between the two Baptist bodies in regards to the seminary. In 1956 the officials of Central Seminary invited the SBC to dialogue with them in hopes of continuing cooperation, but the talks soon fell through and the education board of the ABC recommended that the seminary align itself solely with the ABC. Several Southern Baptist trustees and teachers resigned, and a number of Southern Baptist students left the seminary.[40]

Following the Southern Baptist pullout from Central Seminary, several of the Southern Baptist trustees who had resigned worked toward having the newly proposed SBC seminary placed in Kansas City. As a result, Midwestern Baptist Theological Seminary was established in Kansas City in 1957,[41] and the former Southern Baptist trustees of Central Seminary were placed on the trustee board of Midwestern.[42] Accordingly, Midwestern's relationship with a number of area churches was strained from the beginning, as a number of area Southern Baptists were sympathetic with Central.[43]

Internally, some of the new very conservative Midwestern trustees, who were formerly Central trustees, soon became disenfranchised with some of the administrative decisions at Midwestern. Although Midwestern's first president, Millard Berquist, tried to steer the seminary through the controversy by not selecting faculty or staff persons who had been a part of the conflict with Central, his efforts would prove futile, partly because by avoiding bringing former Central employees on board, he incurred their wrath.[44]

In the midst of this stewing animosity, Berquist hired young Ralph H. Elliott, previously on the faculty of the Southern Baptist Theological Seminary, as Old Testament professor. After having been at Midwestern for only a short time, Elliott published his first major book, *The Message of Genesis*, in 1961.[45] Shortly after the publication of this book by Broadman Press of the Baptist Sunday School Board, ultraconservatives, who were already irate about the Midwestern situation, seized upon what they perceived to be liberal teachings within the book.

Elliott used biblical criticism (nothing new in itself) to examine Genesis, and focused more on determining the meaning of Genesis than on a literal interpretation of the book. Ultraconservatives quickly accused Elliott of advocating "unacceptable" views of biblical inspiration and espousing liberalism. While debates waged in state Baptist papers, the Sunday School Board and Midwestern trustees at first defended Elliott. However, by late 1962, under intense pressure from vocal and well-organized fundamentalists, both the Sunday School Board and the Midwestern trustees backed off of their support of Elliott.[46] A committee of trustees of Midwestern asked Elliott to withdraw *The Message of Genesis* from any future publication. Elliott agreed to comply if the full trustee board and the president also requested withdrawal of the book, but the full trustee board never took such action. Instead, acting on recommendation of the trustee committee, Elliott was dismissed for insubordination. Thus, although Elliott was never convicted of theological wrongdoing, pressure from the ultraconservative faction led to his firing.[47]

A couple of things should be noted about the "Genesis controversy." To begin with, Elliott's book espoused mildly progressive viewpoints on certain passages of Scripture,[48] nothing new in the life of Southern Baptist academia.[49] Elliott reported that ninety percent of the letters he received from Southern Baptist laypeople during the controversy were supportive of him and *The Message of Genesis*, while about ninety percent of the letters from Southern Baptist clergy were extremely critical.[50]

The contents of Elliott's book were certainly not "liberal" in the life of Christianity as a whole. The author's main "sin" in the eyes of his detractors was his de-emphasis of the literal interpretation of portions of Genesis, which was nothing new in the Christian world, or in Southern Baptist academia, at that time. However, Elliott's book did serve to jolt Southern Baptist fundamentalists, a small but vocal minority, into action. This faction quickly rallied around a literal Bible and began dividing Southern Baptists into two categories: orthodox (literalists) or heretics.[51]

The repercussions of the Genesis controversy began almost immediately. As a direct result of the controversy, the messengers to the 1962 SBC meeting, spurred on by the fundamentalists' charges of liberalism in Southern Baptist seminaries, voted to establish a committee to draw up a new Southern Baptist confession of faith. The committee presented its work the following year, and the Convention voted on and passed a revised version of The Baptist Faith and Message. The 1963 confession was a revision of the 1925 Baptist Faith and Message, containing some modifications, such as dropping a few articles and combining others, and further clarifying, but making no radical change to, the article on Scripture.[52] It was certainly an effort to appease the minority, but vocal, fundamentalists whose alarmist cries of liberalism were threatening to fragment the Convention.

Having been spurred to action by the Elliott incident, fundamentalist Southern Baptists continued to decry perceived liberalism in the Convention and its seminaries. Their emotionally charged message of the need to go "back" to the Bible enticed many Southern Baptists. As a result, in 1964 a leading fundamentalist and one of Elliott's foremost opponents (K. Owen White, pastor of First Baptist Church, Houston, Texas) won the SBC presidency. His election was indicative of the growing fundamentalist faction in the SBC, and was, in all likelihood, the first time an SBC president had won the position based on his known theological position.[53] Unfortunately, this development proved to be a harbinger of what was to come.

The fallout from the Genesis controversy also led to a rising feeling of mistrust among Southern Baptists in regards to theological education and publications.[54] This anti-theological education mind-set was also a prelude of what was to come.

The militant fundamentalists, although somewhat appeased by the outcome of the Genesis controversy, had by no means given up their crusade to defend their understanding of the Bible. More theological trouble within the SBC was unavoidable. The next major flare-up began in 1969 over the Sunday School Board's publication of a particular commentary volume.

Baptist leaders had, for quite some time, been aware of the absence of quality commentaries on certain portions of the Bible.[55] As a result, the Baptist Sunday School Board, in 1961, had approved the writing of a twelve-volume commentary which would cover the entire Bible. Volume 1 of *The Broadman Bible Commentary* was published in October 1969. Even before Volume 1 rolled off the press, there was some fear that the material would lead to controversy.[56] Indeed, a few months before the commentary was released, W. A. Criswell, the popular fundamentalist pastor of First Baptist Church, Dallas, Texas, and former opponent of Elliott, had been elected to the presidency of the SBC.[57]

By January 1970, fundamentalists were blasting the writings of an author in the commentary who had questioned the literal reading of Genesis 22 in regards to God telling Abraham to sacrifice his son. Although a number of Southern Baptist leaders defended G. Henton Davies (an English Baptist) and the right to present different understandings of biblical interpretation (which was in line with the historic Baptist principle of the "priesthood of all believers"), militant fundamentalist Southern Baptists once again raised the cry of liberalism. On May 30, fundamentalists met prior to the annual SBC meeting in what was called an "Affirming the Bible Conference." Participants attacked perceived liberalism and affirmed their belief in a literal Bible.

During the 1970 SBC meeeting, held June 1-4 and presided over by fundamentalist W. A. Criswell, one fundamentalist messenger, declaring that some of the interpretations presented in Volume 1 of the *Broadman Commentary* were "out of keeping" with the beliefs of the "vast majority" of Southern Baptists (a statement which probably had some merit), made an emotional plea for the Convention to withdraw Volume 1 and have it rewritten from a more "conservative" (i.e., fundamentalist) viewpoint. The executive secretary of the Sunday School Board and the general editor of the commentary both urged the messengers not to censure the book, noting that there was no official SBC position regarding the interpretation of Genesis and stating that Baptists should have an open mind, under the leadership of the Holy Spirit, in matters of scriptural interpretation. Nevertheless, the emotional cries of the fundamentalist faction won the day as the Convention voted to withdraw the commentary and instructed the Sunday School Board to have it rewritten.

Following the SBC annual meeting, the Sunday School Board voted to rewrite Volume 1 of the commentary, and decided to allow the original authors to do the rewriting. When fundamentalists learned that the Sunday School Board had not acquired new writers, they were incensed. As a result, they led messengers of the 1971 SBC meeting in narrowly passing a motion instructing the board to seek other writers to rewrite it.[58]

In 1972 fundamentalists, by now suspicious of the whole commentary, presented a motion at the annual SBC meeting requesting that since much of the material within the commentaries was at odds with The Baptist Faith and Message (an unfounded and untrue charge), that the entire set of commentaries be suspended. They were unable to rally the messengers to their cause, and the motion was defeated.[59] That same year, fundamentalists organized Mid-America Theological Seminary (now located in Memphis, Tennessee) followed by the Criswell Biblical Studies Center (now Criswell Bible College), in an effort to teach and spread fundamentalist views.[60]

In the meantime, the Sunday School Board had hired Clyde Francisco, a respected Old Testament scholar at the Southern Baptist Theological Seminary, to rewrite the Genesis portion of the commentary. Although Francisco used more cautious language in the revised commentary issued in 1973, fundamentalists grumbled that only minor changes had been made.[61]

During the 1960s and early 1970s, following the Elliott controversy, conservative-moderate Southern Baptists sought to establish several organizations to counter the rising fundamentalist wing within the SBC. These organizations were short-lived, and their impact was minimal.

Fundamentalists had better grassroots organizational success. One organization which gained some influence in Southern Baptist life was the Baptist Faith and Message Fellowship, formed in 1973 by fundamentalists determined to push their agenda despite setbacks during recent SBC annual meetings.

The main objective of the Baptist Faith and Message Fellowship (BFMF) was to battle perceived liberalism within the SBC and its agencies. Fundamentalist members of the BFMF attacked by name those Southern

Baptist leaders whom they felt were liberals. The BFMF also sought to combat the Sunday School Board by providing alternative literature. By the late 1970s, the BFMF had evolved into an organization that catered to the most extremist of fundamentalists, prompting many fundamentalists to severe connections with the group. A split occurred and the organization never recovered.[62]

Perhaps the most important event of the 1970s in regards to the increasing theological polarization of the SBC was an increasing interest in "inerrancy," a fundamentalist concept of scriptural authority which had arisen to some prominence in the early part of the century, but which had gained little attention in Southern Baptist circles. Although the term was not used during the Genesis controversy or during the *Broadman Commentary* controversy, and although Volume 3 of the comprehensive *Encyclopedia of Southern Baptists*, published in 1971, did not mention the term, "inerrancy" was poised to gain a following in the Southern Baptist fundamentalist camp. In the early 1970s, a prominent Southern Baptist fundamentalist sought to introduce resolutions identifying inerrancy as the normative Southern Baptist view. The resolutions were completely unfounded and were soundly defeated.

Although some fundamentalists were already using the term "inerrancy" by the mid-1970s, it attracted virtually no attention in Southern Baptist circles until the publication of fundamentalist Harold Lindsell's book, *The Battle for the Bible*, in 1976. The book included a chapter on the SBC in which Lindsell assumed (wrongly) that inerrancy had always been the standard Southern Baptist position in regards to biblical authority. Lindsell also decried what he perceived as a shift away from inerrancy in SBC life.[63]

Lindsell's book and the 1977 formation of the International Council on Inerrancy (cofounded by none other than W. A. Criswell[64]) greatly impacted fundamentalist Southern Baptists and galvanized them into action around the concept of biblical inerrancy. Rallying around cries of biblical inerrancy, the fundamentalist wing of the SBC gathered momentum for a new assault upon the SBC.[65] This time, the militant, ultraconservative fundamentalist attack upon the mainline conservative-moderate SBC would result in full-fledged victory for the invaders.

Despite the ever-gathering storm on the horizon, the SBC continued to prosper in its home and foreign missions efforts, which continued to serve as a point where the vast majority of Southern Baptists (with the exception of many fundamentalists) could find common ground. Membership in Southern Baptist churches continued to rise, despite a numerical plateauing of many Christian denominations during the sixties and seventies.

1979-1995: THE TAKEOVER OF THE SOUTHERN BAPTIST CONVENTION

During the 1970s, Southern Baptist fundamentalists Paul Pressler (a Southern Baptist layman and judge in Texas) and Paige Patterson, president of the Criswell Center for Biblical Studies, became friends through their mutual desire to see the SBC come under fundamentalist control. They discussed what could be done to capture the SBC, and soon came to the conclusion that the Baptist Faith and Message Fellowship, despite its strong fundamentalist stance and publications, would be unable to take over the SBC.

Thus, in 1978 they became convinced that a new fundamentalist organization was needed if the SBC was to be conquered. That year Pressler and Patterson organized a meeting in Atlanta at which select fundamentalist pastors from each state with a Southern Baptist presence were invited to attend. Pressler and Patterson presented their plan to those present: the key to gaining control of the SBC would be to elect fundamentalist presidents and to use presidential powers thereafter to appoint only fundamentalists to key SBC positions of leadership. The group decided to put their plan into action at the 1979 annual SBC meeting, at which time there would not be an incumbent running for the presidency of the SBC.[66]

The power of the SBC presidency must be noted at this point. The president, who generally serves a two-year term, is empowered to appoint the members of the powerful Committee on Committees, which, in turn, nominates members to the also-powerful Committee on Nominations (formerly Committee on Boards). The latter group, in turn, nominates the trustees and directors of Southern Baptist agencies, as well as members of the Executive Committee and SBC standing committees.[67] As such, the appointive powers of the presidency reach throughout virtually all SBC life.

Prior to the fundamentalist Atlanta meeting of 1978, there had been no organized effort in SBC life to use the presidency as a tool for gaining political power for a particular faction of Southern Baptists. W. A. Criswell, a key fundamentalist leader, noted that he was not aware of the powers of the presidency when he served as SBC president during 1968-70.[68]

Following the 1978 Atlanta meeting, Pressler and Patterson took visible leadership of the new fundamentalist strategy, while the pastors who had attended the meeting went back to their home states and began organizing fundamentalist pastors in their states for a strike at the 1979 annual SBC meeting. Although the pastors who were at that meeting are unknown, some of the more well-known Southern Baptist fundamentalists at that time were W. A. Criswell, Adrian Rogers, Charles Stanley, Jerry Vines, Fred Wolfe, and Robert Tenery, among others.[69]

At the 1979 SBC meeting, held in Houston, Texas, homestate to both Pressler and Patterson, the fundamentalists made their first open move. The

Pastors' Conference, which preceded the Convention and was dominated by fundamentalist pastors, was characterized by continuous attacks upon the six SBC seminaries. Also, the fundamentalists established "inerrancy" as the buzzword of the Convention as they rallied around the narrow, creedal view of scriptural authority which strict inerrancy represented. Since that time, Southern Baptist fundamentalist leaders have continued to rally around inerrancy in the strictest since.[70]

The fundamentalists succeeded in getting their candidate (Adrian Rogers, a popular pastor) elected to the presidency,[71] but the methods they employed were both unethical and illegal. When messengers learned that Pressler, Patterson, and other key fundamentalists had been operating a political "command post" in the "sky boxes" high above the stadium floor, keeping floor contact through an elaborate communications network, they were incensed and quickly made it known that no such political activity would be permitted during the SBC meeting. Adding insult to injury, it was discovered that Pressler had registered as a messenger from a church in which he did not hold membership. Thus, the fundamentalists began their takeover of the SBC in a most underhanded manner.

The following year, flush with initial victory, Pressler in particular became the spokesman for the fundamentalist faction. He described trustees of SBC agencies as "dummies" and "rubber stamps." He openly declared that the fundamentalists were "going for the jugular" of the SBC, indicating the mean spirit of the movement.

True to Pressler's words, the new fundamentalist members on the Committee on Boards sought to replace SBC agency trustees who were not fundamentalists. Trustees in some states were questioned about their belief in inerrancy, with the intention of sorting out those who did not believe in inerrancy. In 1981, at the annual SBC meeting, the Committee on Boards presented a slate of fundamentalist nominees, specifically omitting many non-fundamentalist trustees who were eligible for reelection. The messengers, however, reversed the board's action and reelected all trustees who were up for reelection.[72]

The 1981 trustee incident proved to be only a minor setback for fundamentalist forces, however. Mainline conservatives and moderates, long accustomed to figurehead presidents and trusting those who held power on the national level, were uncertain how to act toward the fundamentalist grab for political power. The established leadership initially believed that the fundamentalist victory in 1979 was a fluke. In the following year, when Pressler began bragging about how the fundamentalists were going to go "for the jugular," some mainline Southern Baptists began to get wind of the plot underfoot. Even so, their opposition to the fundamentalist threat was neither focused nor intense, largely because there continued to be widespread disbelief that a fundamentalist coup could actually succeed.

For example, despite Pressler's open and oft-repeated statements about focusing on presidential elections, the mainline conservatives and moderates did not seem to take the threat seriously. Indeed, they continued believing in the old mind-set, which deemed that the position of president was only an honorary post. And, as in years past, the moderates continued to welcome open multiple nominations for the presidency. What resulted between 1979 and 1985, therefore, was a unified fundamentalist force pitted against the mainline conservative-moderate leadership of old which was more interested in a spiritual agenda than a political agenda. In 1979 five moderate candidates opposed Rogers. In 1980 five more ran against the one fundamentalist candidate, Bailey Smith. In 1982 two moderates opposed fundamentalist James T. Draper, while in 1984 two moderates opposed fundamentalist Charles Stanley.

Not until 1985 did mainline conservatives and moderates as a whole realize that the presidential contests were not what they used to be. The truth finally became unavoidable: the unified fundamentalist faction was winning the presidential elections because they were pitting one candidate against a divided conservative-moderate slate.[73] By this point, it may well have been too late to turn back the momentum of the fundamentalists, as the usurpers had won every presidential election between 1979 and 1985.

To be certain, some denominational leaders did recognize the fundamentalist coup for what it was and sounded the alarm in the early 1980s. Long-time Southern Baptist leaders Cecil E. Sherman and Kenneth L. Chafin soon rose to lead the loosely organized opposition to the fundamentalist machinery.[74] In 1984 Roy L. Honeycutt, president of Southern Seminary, declared war on the "Inerrancy Party," claiming that the inerrantists were in league with "unholy forces" within the Convention.[75] Meanwhile, Russell H. Dilday, Jr., president of Southwestern Seminary, published *The Doctrine of Biblical Authority*, affirming that Southern Baptists had historically accepted the Bible as having absolute authority, but that they had never accepted the strict inerrancy of Scriptures which the fundamentalist wing was trying to impose upon the SBC. Although fundamentalist James T. Draper, president of the SBC from 1982 to 1984, brought a moderating influence by not insisting upon the usage of the term inerrancy, the "toning down" of the fundamentalists was only temporary.[76]

By the time mainline conservative-moderates finally woke up to the reality of the fundamentalist takeover, the fundamentalists, under the emotional banner of inerrancy, had sown seeds of denominational distrust among Southern Baptists. In 1986 sixty-three percent of Southern Baptist respondents to a survey indicated that they believed that some professors in Baptist seminaries and colleges did not "believe what Baptists ought to believe." The leaders of the fundamentalist movement, largely super-church pastors and evangelists, had succeeded in winning crowds to their side by using their winning personalities and their remarkable preaching abilities to evoke emotional responses from their hearers.[77]

The success of the fundamentalists was certainly noteworthy. A survey of Southern Baptists taken in the middle-to-late 1980s revealed that only thirty-three percent of respondents identified themselves as holding fundamentalist beliefs,[78] despite the major inroads the fundamentalists had made in Southern Baptist life at this point. The fundamentalists had, in fact, won many non-fundamentalists to their sides, when it came voting time, through the natural charisma of their leaders and their "back to the Bible" message.[79] In fact, of all the individuals who heard fundamentalists speak, fifty-six percent were non-fundamentalists, while only forty-three percent of all persons who heard conservative-moderate speakers were not conservative-moderates. The fact that fundamentalists made better use of mass media played no small part in their getting their message out more effectively than their conservative-moderate counterparts.[80]

The fundamentalists were not always ethical in their drive to gain control of the SBC. In 1985, which some regard as the turning point for the fundamentalist faction, Charles Stanley, the presiding president, used his parliamentary power to overlook and dismiss discussion and points of order from conservative-moderate messengers in forcing through the fundamentalists' slate of SBC committee members. Furthermore, the fundamentalists used the year-to-year strategy of busing in voters whom they could count on to vote for their agenda. Busloads of messengers would be bused in for the express purpose of being present for the presidential voting.[81]

For all practical purposes, the fundamentalists were more concerned about their political agenda than spiritual matters. Stories of unethical practices by the fundamentalists abounded. Some messengers reported seeing five-year-old children with official messenger badges and ballots (to be a messenger at the annual Convention, one must be baptized and a member of a local Southern Baptist church). Others reported entire ballot boxes from conservative-moderate sections of the auditorium disappearing on their way to the counting room. The 1985 Convention served only to further convince mainline conservatives and moderates that the fundamentalist wing was unscrupulous and was out to win at any cost.[82]

During 1985-1988, conservative-moderate leaders, now sensing the imminent danger to the SBC, went all out to beat back the fundamentalist encroachment. The conservative-moderates presented only one presidential candidate during these years, and each time the conservative-moderate candidate expressed theological beliefs which matched those of many fundamentalists. The fundamentalists opposed the conservative-moderate "inerrantists" because the latter were willing to include non-inerrantists among their appointees and nominees, while the fundamentalists vowed to have nothing to do with mainline conservatives and moderates.[83] The exclusive nature of the fundamentalists was evident.

The conservative-moderate faction, now unified, stood ready to squarely challenge the fundamentalists. The momentum of the fundamentalists would have been hard to overcome, no doubt, but another development may have been the larger culprit in the thwarting of conservative-moderate efforts. A few months prior to the furor of the 1985 Convention (which the conservative-moderates lost to fundamentalist Charles Stanley), a call for the organization of a Peace Committee had been voiced. The committee was thus formed, comprised of fundamentalists, mainline conservative-moderates, and unaligned persons, for the purpose of bringing peace to the divided SBC. However, conservative-moderates on the Peace Committee soon discovered a fundamentalist agenda and realized that cooperation was not possible. Nevertheless, the fundamentalist-controlled Peace Committee did propose that both factions cease to be involved in active political campaigning, only to have the fundamentalist leadership turn around and violate their own recommendations.

The Peace Committee had the effect of hindering the conservative-moderate cause. As revealed in a survey taken following the 1985 Convention, during which the Peace Committee was appointed, over half of the anti-fundamentalists and undecideds left Dallas believing that peace between the two warring parties was at hand. The significance of this statistic was that the anti-fundamentalists who believed peace was at hand were much less likely to organize opposition to the fundamentalist takeover than were those anti-fundamentalists who did not believe peace was on the horizon. In effect, nearly half of the conservative-moderate constituency, wanting to believe the fight was over, did not get involved in organizing for the conservative-moderate cause following the 1985 Convention.[84]

Whereas conservative-moderate leaders tried to honor the Peace Committee's call for the cessation of political activities prior to the 1986 Convention, fundamentalists largely ignored the committee's recommendations. The net result was that mainline conservatives and moderates lost the presidential elections of 1986-1988 by slim margins. Also, with each successive year and loss, conservative-moderate hopes for peace grew dimmer. By 1988 conservative-moderate hopes for peace had largely dissipated. The initial hopes for peace had led to a defeat in the 1986 election, and by 1988, the conservative-moderate camp was feeling routed. The minority fundamentalist faction had emerged victorious largely because mainline conservative-moderates had been unable to channel their energies into a singular, cohesive voting bloc.[85]

Although the fundamentalist political machinery was in high gear by this time, mainline conservatives and moderates ran their own "inerrancy" (but not fundamentalist) candidates in 1989 and 1990. Their efforts were to no avail, as the fundamentalists had the momentum on their side.

The 1990 election marked a watershed. Much like the 1985 annual meeting, anger, hostility, and conniving marked the Convention. Despite the fact that the evangelical, conservative-moderate candidate, Daniel Vestal, received over forty percent of the vote (although many, if not most, conservative-moderates had given up attending the annual SBC meeting at this point), the spirit of the fundamentalist leaders towards the mainline conservatives and moderates was one of meanness and treachery. There were parliamentary maneuvers made against the conservative-moderate faction, as well as unscrupulous moves to silence those conservative-moderates who attempted to address the Convention.

Following the meeting, defeated conservative-moderate candidate Daniel Vestal called some key conservative-moderate leaders to a meeting at Dallas-Fort Worth airport in July 1990. The leaders present decided to call an informal open meeting in August for anyone who felt disenfranchised by the current fundamentalist leadership of the SBC. With a lead time of only a few weeks, the organizers anticipated about two hundred attendees. To their surprise, some thirty-one hundred people attended. Participants decided to take steps towards forming a formal organization for disenfranchised mainline conservatives and moderates.[86]

More than just the loss of the SBC presidency to fundamentalists led to the August 1990 meeting of conservative-moderates. Having won each presidential election since 1979, the fundamentalists had been using their political power to change SBC agencies to fit their ideology. The fundamentalists, long isolated dissenters in SBC life, now wielded great political power, and they did not hesitate to use that power. Annual SBC meetings, at which fundamentalists mustered a majority of messengers because of their well-orchestrated busing strategies, became a key time for fundamentalist power plays.

The "purge" began at the SBC Home Mission Board. In 1984 the fundamentalists led SBC messengers to adopt a resolution excluding women from pastoral positions. The HMB, however, had historically supported mission churches with either male or female pastors. Outraged fundamentalists began an all-out campaign to force the HMB to change its stance on supporting women-led churches, contending that they were trying to bring the HMB in line with "the historic Baptist position" of not supporting women pastors. Despite the fact that the fundamentalist claim of championing historic Baptist principles was totally erroneous, by 1986, with a majority of fundamentalist trustees for the first time, the ultraconservatives forced the HMB to suspend support of women-led churches.

Also in 1986, the fundamentalist trustee majority led the HMB to elect its first fundamentalist president. In 1987 trustees voted not to allow divorcees (except for those who were victims of their spouses' sexual infidelity or desertion) to serve as home missionaries. Although no wholesale purge of office employees took place in the 1980s, key HMB positions were doled out to fundamentalists, and, by the end of the 1980s, all potential key employees were forced to undergo a doctrinal grilling to make certain that their theological beliefs were "correct." As a result, mainline conservatives and moderates were effectively excluded from employment at the HMB.[87] Similar patterns would emerge in other SBC agencies.

At present, fundamentalists continue to exercise an iron fist over the Home Mission Board. Many longtime conservative-moderates have resigned or left, and morale among those that remain is very low. Also, for the first time, the HMB has become a very outspoken proponent of the hardline anti-abortion agenda.[88]

The Foreign Mission Board was next to come under the ax of the fundamentalists. Although the FMB had long had strict theological requirements for foreign mission appointees, and Keith Parks, the FMB president, was an avowed conservative (but not a fundamentalist), fundamentalists wanted the FMB to fully embrace their ultraconservative character. Fundamentalists considered all six SBC seminaries to be liberal, and, therefore, considered all FMB missionaries as suspect liberals. By "liberal," the fundamentalists meant "less conservative" than fundamentalists.

As the ultraconservatives won every SBC presidential election, they were able to begin putting fundamentalist trustees on the FMB's trustee board. By 1988, for the first time in the board's history, the majority of trustees were fundamentalists. That year, the fundamentalist-led trustees overturned the FMB's long-standing policy of requiring missionaries to have taken seminary classes at one of the six Southern Baptist seminaries. The trustees widened the requirements to include other seminaries. This move was aimed primarily at giving graduates of fundamentalist Baptist (but not Southern Baptist) seminaries, such as Mid-America Seminary in Tennessee, the opportunity to serve as FMB missionaries.

A doctrinal purge also began in 1988 at the FMB. Those who did not voice agreement with the ideology of the fundamentalists were less likely to be appointed as missionaries. Trustees granted more power to themselves and took it upon themselves to screen potential candidates (something which trustees of the FMB had not done previously) to ascertain doctrinal correctness. Keith Parks, president of the FMB, came under scrutiny of the trustees for his non-fundamentalist conservative theology.[89]

An event in 1991 led to dramatic upheaval at the FMB. The fundamentalist-controlled board of trustees voted that year to defund the Baptist seminary in Switzerland, due to perceived "liberalism" within the seminary. The FMB had long supported Rushlikon Seminary, the only Baptist seminary in that part of Europe, helping defray operating costs and keeping the seminary in operation. The FMB had a contract with Rushlikon through 1993, but in the midst of this agreement, the trustees decided to defund the seminary, effectively breaking the FMB's promise to European Baptists. European Baptists were appalled and infuriated at the breach of trust brought about by the "witch-hunting" tactics, and the FMB's integrity was irrevocably damaged in Europe.[90]

The fundamentalist agenda which had come to a head in the Rushlikon incident of 1991 soon led Foreign Mission Board president Keith Parks and three other top-ranking FMB administrators to resign from the FMB in 1992. Many FMB missionaries also resigned during the year, and hundreds of other foreign missionaries voiced their desire to leave the FMB.[91] Since that time, the resignation of top-ranking FMB officials and missionaries has continued in reaction to the fundamentalist agenda.

Virtually all other SBC agencies and committees have also been captured by fundamentalists. The powerful Executive Committee is under firm fundamentalist control with a fundamentalist president-treasurer at the helm. At the Baptist Sunday School Board, the non-fundamentalist president was ousted in 1990 by trustees and replaced by a fundamentalist. Also, for the first time in history, the board has stated its commitment to base all its curriculum material on a verbal-plenary (that is, the belief that God verbally dictated the Bible word-for-word to the men who penned the manuscripts), inerrancy platform.

The Christian Life Commission (CLC), the ethics agency of Southern Baptists for many years, has also undergone a radical transformation. Under fundamentalist leadership, the CLC has moved from its primary role as an ethics agency to a political action committee. The fundamentalists have seemingly ignored the historic Baptist principle of separation of church and state and have, for all practical purposes, aligned themselves squarely with the Republican Party. The current CLC president, for example, has close connections with the Republican Party, while the CLC itself cozied up to the Republicans during the Reagan-Bush years. Also, fundamentalist SBC leaders led the SBC to drop its support of the Baptist Joint Committee on Public Affairs, the church-state watchdog group based in Washington, D.C., which traditionally represented the SBC on religious liberty matters during recent decades.

The loathed SBC seminaries have also come under fundamentalist attack. The ultraconservatives, long complaining of the perceived "liberalism" of the SBC seminaries, claimed their first victory in 1988 with the capture of Southeastern Seminary in Wake Forest, North Carolina. When the fundamentalist-led trustees forced president Randall Lolley to resign that year, enrollment at the institution immediately plummeted from about twelve hundred to four huindred, and the accreditation of the institution was threatened because of the unethical manner in which the new trustees re-routed the seminary. Paige Patterson (an early architect of the fundamentalist SBC takeover) was eventually awarded the presidency of Southeastern (following a term of service by President Lewis Drummond, who had come from the faculty of the Southern Baptist Theological Seminary), but the number of enrolled students is less than the enrollment of the pre-fundamentalist Southeastern.[92] The takeover of Southern Seminary followed in 1993, while Southwestern Seminary fell under the ax in 1994,[93] and Midwestern in 1995.[94] Enrollment at these institutions is less than it was in pre-fundamentalist days, and fundamentalist control of all six seminaries is imminent.

No SBC agency is safe from the crusading fundamentalists. The ultraconservative leadership even went to the point of preventing publication of Leon McBeth's (a well-known and well-respected Baptist historian) history of the Baptist Sunday School Board, which was to be published in 1990 by the board, because fundamentalists thought that McBeth's account of the fundamentalist takeover of the agency put them in a bad light.[95] Such an episode is reminiscent of the former communist Soviet Union's banishing of history texts which put communists in a bad light.

In 1993 Woman's Missionary Union (WMU), an auxiliary of the SBC (not a board or agency) since 1888, came under the wrath of the fundamentalist leadership for its stated intention of supporting other Southern Baptist groups, as well as the SBC. Fundamentalist leaders likened WMU to an "adulterer" and vowed to "hardwire" the organization into the SBC (that is, bring it directly under the control of the SBC Executive Committee). Should the WMU continue its ways, fundamentalists declared, another organization would be put together to replace it. Many feel that such action against the WMU would be the worst wound yet to an already faltering SBC, for WMU, through its sponsoring of the annual Lottie Moon and Annie Armstrong offerings for missions, has traditionally raised about half of the money which supports SBC missionaries.[96] The fundamentalist leadership of the SBC, in retaliation for WMU's refusal to bow down to their wishes, stripped WMU of being in charge of promoting the aforementioned home and foreign mission offerings as a part of the 1995 "restructuring proposal" for the SBC.[97]

The "other" Southern Baptist group which the WMU was specifically alluding to in the 1993 incident was the Cooperative Baptist Fellowship, an organization of mainline conservatives and moderates which was conceived at the aforementioned meeting of Southern Baptist mainline conservatives and moderates in Atlanta in August 1990.

The participants at that August 1990 meeting, tired of being shoved aside by the new fundamentalist leadership of the SBC, decided to call yet another meeting in Atlanta in May 1991 in an effort to give the conservative-moderate movement a cohesive voice through a national organization. In the meantime, the conservative-moderate leadership worked on a constitution which would be presented during the second Atlanta meeting.[98]

Also, at the August 1990 meeting, the Baptist Cooperative Missions Program was incorporated for the purpose of giving Southern Baptists the option of sending their tithes and gifts to Southern Baptist agencies and institutions of their choice without having to go through the now fundamentalist-controlled SBC Executive Committee, which recommends to the SBC the annual distribution of Cooperative Program funds on the national level.[99] In a similar manner, the Baptist Fellowship (also known at that time as the United Baptist Fellowship), a conservative-moderate organization devoted to giving mainline conservatives and moderates a voice in SBC life, was birthed out of the summer meetings of 1990.[100] The May 1991 meeting was planned as a time to solidify and determine the direction of these new conservative-moderate organizations.

The conservative-moderate initiatives in the summer of 1990 did not develop overnight. Organized conservative-moderate resistance to the fundamentalist encroachment had begun in the early 1980s under the direction of longtime Southern Baptist leaders Kenneth Chafin and Cecil Sherman. These early efforts met with limited success, for reasons previously mentioned.

These efforts did, however, result in the founding of *SBC Today* in 1983 (renamed *Baptists Today* in 1991), a national Baptist paper targeted at mainline conservatives and moderates. Several years later, in 1986, as Southern Baptist conservatives and moderates debated over whether or not to continue the then-political battle against the fundamentalists, one group of moderate-conservatives, wishing to move beyond politics, formed the Southern Baptist Alliance (renamed Alliance of Baptists in 1992), an organization dedicated to preserving historic Baptist principles. The Alliance, although never large in numbers, played an important role in the crusade against fundamentalism by starting a "free" Baptist seminary in Richmond in 1989 and laying the groundwork for the establishment of the "free" publishing firm Smyth and Helwys (named after the two Baptist founders) in 1990. Also in 1990, Associated Baptist Press, a national news organization, was founded in response to fundamentalist attempts to control and place their "spin" on Baptist Press, the traditional source of news in Southern Baptist life.[101] The Alliance of Baptists now numbers only a handful of Southern Baptists, and has moved to the background of the Southern Baptist controversy. Many Southern Baptists from both sides of the controversy view the Alliance as harboring a moderate-liberal element in its midst.

Accordingly, the May 1991 meeting in Atlanta was a culmination of mainline conservative-moderate "resistance" efforts over the past several years. Over six thousand disenfranchised Southern Baptists attended the meeting for the purpose of officially establishing a national conservative-moderate organization. The net result was the formation of the Cooperative Baptist Fellowship (CBF)—which emerged out of the aforementioned Baptist

Fellowship—an organization dedicated to traditional Baptist ideals and principles and designed to give a voice to conservative-moderate Baptists upon whom the fundamentalist leadership of the SBC looked down. A three-year constitution was adopted and the organization was chartered. Southern Baptist conservative-moderates had chosen to retain their affiliation with the SBC, but had decided to chart their own course rather than continue to fight the politically powerful fundamentalist leadership.[102] Other conservative-moderate organizations quickly rallied around the CBF.

Since the formation of the CBF, the growth of the SBC has stagnated,[103] only to recently move forward again (although current statistics are being manipulated by the fundamentalist leadership), while the CBF has initially experienced phenomenal growth.[104] More and more Southern Baptist churches are joining CBF, and the organization has a rapidly increasing number of missionaries on the field, many of whom are former Foreign Mission Board missionaries who fled from the board in the wake of the fundamentalist takeover. In November 1992 Keith Parks, who had recently resigned as president of the board, accepted the call to take the helm of the CBF missions program.[105] By July 1993, two other former high-ranking board officials had followed Parks in taking positions with CBF.[106]

Thus, as the 150th anniversary of the SBC came and went, Southern Baptists were and are a sharply divided people. The fundamentalist faction, long dissenting outsiders within SBC life, now have almost total control of SBC agencies. Although only a small minority of Southern Baptists are self-identified fundamentalists, fundamentalists appear to have a firm grip upon the SBC for the foreseeable future. A survey by Nancy Ammerman revealed that fundamentalism continues to be a minority mind-set in Southern Baptist life.[107] The current leadership of the SBC is now almost exclusively drawn from the eleven percent of self-identified fundamentalists, and the twenty-two percent who are "fundamentalist conservatives" (who share basically the same theology as "self-identified fundamentalists," but do not uniformly align themselves with that group). "Conservatives," fifty percent of the denomination, share some beliefs with "self-identified fundamentalists," but clearly distance themselves from that group. "Moderate-conservatives" (eight percent) reject most fundamentalist beliefs, while "moderates" (nine percent) are conservatives who actively reject virtually all fundamentalist beliefs (see Nancy Ammerman, *Baptist Battles*).

From these statistics, the exclusiveness of the "self-identified fundamentalist" faction in Southern Baptist life is self-evident. Whereas the current SBC leadership is fully representative of only eleven percent of Southern Baptists (and fully supported by no more than thirty-six percent of Southern Baptists), the conservative-moderate camp represents most of the other eighty-nine percent of Southern Baptists, with the CBF itself drawing more and more support from that majority. The current fundamentalist leadership has consistently labeled as "liberals" a large bloc of the eighty-nine percent with whom they do not fully identify. As Ammerman's survey indicates, however, there are, in truth, only varying degrees of conservatism in the SBC. True liberalism—that is, the denial of the deity of Christ and the atoning work of his death and resurrection—simply does not statistically exist in Southern Baptist life.

Perhaps the greatest tragedy of the fundamentalist takeover is that most of the eighty-nine percent of Southern Baptists who are not in the "self-identified fundamentalist" camp never saw what was hitting them until it was too late. The political power play and questionable ethics of the fundamentalist group served to pull the rug out from under the SBC before the mainline conservatives and moderates were able to formulate a cohesive response to the hostile challengers.

The 150th anniversary of the SBC in 1995 marked a time of uncertainty for Southern Baptists. Despite the fact that the majority of Southern Baptists do not identify themselves with their national leaders, many employees of the denomination have chosen to quietly "sit-out" the siege in the hopes that the pendulum will eventually swing back from the extremities. Such individuals, already having invested their lives fully in the former SBC, have chosen the route of persevering rather than changing careers and risking personal upheaval in midlife.

Southern Baptist laity have also, to this point, largely ignored or chosen to "sit-out" the fundamentalist upheaval on the national level because of traditional ties to the SBC. Indeed, two-thirds of Southern Baptist laity in a recent survey said it was "very true" that they could not imagine themselves as being anything other than Southern Baptists. "The relationships, activities and cultural norms that surrounded and constituted their church membership were far too strong to be dislodged by the winds of this controversy."[108]

There is a strong possibility of a complete schism within Southern Baptist life. Although the CBF has chosen to remain within the SBC at the moment, there is much sentiment among some CBF members for a formal break with the SBC. This sentiment has been fueled by a decision made at the 1994 SBC annual meeting in Orlando that SBC agencies no longer accept money channeled through the CBF. However, strong traditional SBC loyalty among the majority of Southern Baptists who are at odds with the current SBC leadership would, at this point, make it difficult for the CBF to garner the open support of a majority of either the eighty-nine percent who are not self-identified fundamentalists, or the sixty-four percent through eighty-nine percent who do not fully support the fundamentalist leadership.

The future of the SBC is uncertain, and continues to be masked by the seemingly apathetic attitude of the majority bloc. Although the current fundamentalist leadership has boldly pushed aside and slandered longtime conservative Baptist leaders, flagrantly mangled Baptist history, and violently shaken many SBC programs and institutions to the point of extinction, the majority conservative-moderate bloc of Southern Baptists nationwide has largely remained surprisingly passive. The past three years have seen fundamentalist leaders of the SBC take large steps to formally finish their crusade by seeking to force all non-fundamentalists out of meaningful roles in all levels of SBC life. The 1995 SBC Executive Committee-led restructuring plan reflected attention to the global, business world in which we live, but it also did away with several SBC agencies, including the Education Commission and Historical Commission (which have continually voiced warnings about the fundamentalist takeover), and has removed the Woman's Missionary Union from its primary role in the raising of money for SBC missions. The restructuring of the SBC is, thus far, the capstone of the political power play which began in 1979. Yet, the majority bloc of Southern Baptists continues to show limited resistance at best.

In the midst of such dire upheavel, the SBC has continued to move forward to some degree. The mission boards' work and the overall church membership of the SBC continue to increase numerically, although many of the numbers reported to the public have, in recent years, been manipulated by the fundamentalist leadership to paint a better picture than would be otherwise. Enrollment at SBC seminaries has been declining over the past decade, a fact which even doctored statistics cannot hide.

A Southern Baptist commitment to missions and evangelism continues to keep the SBC from completely shattering. SBC foreign missionaries are in more countries now than ever, and on the home front, the Mission Service Corps program has boosted home missions. Many thousands of lost souls continue to be saved through churches which are affiliated with the SBC.

And yet, with each passing year, the credibility and integrity of the SBC come ever more into question—from the secular world, the Christian world, and the Baptist world. The strict, legalistic nature of the fundamentalists who control the Convention has led many unsaved persons to view Southern Baptists as unethical, ungodly, hypocritical, and more politically oriented than spiritually oriented. Many Christians of other denominations now view Southern Baptists as political extremists who will use almost any means, regardless of ethics, to achieve certain political goals. Within Baptist circles, more and more laypersons and ministers are questioning the actual integrity and true intentions of the fundamentalist leadership of the SBC. A number of large state Baptist conventions, under instruction from their Southern Baptist constituency, have changed their definition of Cooperative Program to include the CBF and other non-SBC-owned entities.

The SBC is at the crossroads of history. Will the minority continue to exercise dominance over the majority? Although God is still working through the SBC to some degree, will the current leadership drag the

Convention so low into the quagmire of deception, duplicity, and hypocrisy that the Spirit of God is totally pushed aside? Will more Southern Baptists in the pew stand up for the truth before it is too late?

The answers to these questions are beyond our knowing at this point. Perhaps a more through analysis of the first 150 years of Southern Baptist history can lead to a better understanding of the crucial situation which now faces Southern Baptists, which, in turn, can help each individual make a better decision on where he or she stands in the midst of this current conflict.

CHAPTER FOUR

The Southern God

The Southern Baptist Convention was founded in the southern United States by Baptists who lived in the South some 150 years ago. Today, on the eve of the twenty-first century, despite five decades of seeking to expand outside the South, the SBC remains firmly anchored in the "Bible Belt." The vast majority of southern Baptists live in southern states, and virtually all SBC agencies are located in the South or Southwest (Midwestern and Golden Gate seminaries are the exceptions). The SBC has, and continues to be, shaped and molded to a large degree by southern culture, mentality, and environment. In the same way, individual Southern Baptists have, and continue to be, shaped by southern mores in regards to their understanding of God and the living of the Christian life.

A WHITE GOD

The final straw that led to the schism between Northern and Southern Baptists in 1845 was the issue of slavery. Baptists in the South felt their northern counterparts were placing more and more pressure upon them to denounce and abandon their long-held practice of slavery. This perception led Baptists in the South to sever ties with their Baptist counterparts in the North rather than free their slaves.

The decision to place slavery over continued union with Northern Baptists was some years in the making. The South of the early 1800s was modeled after Athenian democracy—a society of privileged citizens (white aristocrats, in the case of the South) built on an economic base of slavery. This system worked satisfactorily for the agricultural, labor-intensive South for quite some time. By the 1840s, however, the morality of slavery was being questioned in the North, and the South found itself defending a culture and society which continued to be based on the institution of slavery.[1]

Southerners, being of the firm belief that slavery was necessary in order for their agricultural society to maintain economic stability, were averse to the anti-slavery sentiment that was spreading throughout the North. When the North started suggesting that the South abandon its practice of slavery, Southerners perceived that the North, with its factories and large cities, was trying to lord it over the South.[2]

The cultural and social acceptance and dependence upon the institution of slavery in the South had worked its way into southern churches. Christians who lived in the South, long accustomed to the institution of slavery, by and large believed that the enslavement of the black population was in total harmony with the teachings of the Bible. Christians in the South defended slavery in the name of God, declaring the practice to be ordained by God. Slavery had been so incorporated into the belief system of southern Christians that an attack upon the institution of slavery was considered to be questioning the character of southern believers. In the face of such "attacks," Christians throughout the South disfellowshiped themselves from Christians in the North. Methodists in the South first broke away from their northern counterparts, followed by Baptists and Presbyterians.[3]

A letter from Richard Furman, one of the most influential Baptists of that day and the namesake of Furman University, to the governor of South Carolina in 1822 reflected the pro-slavery feelings of most Baptists in the South during the early 1800s. In the letter, Furman declared that "the right of holding slaves is clearly established in the Holy Scriptures, both by precept and example." Furman continued, "In the Old Testament, the Israelites were directed to purchase their bond-men and bond-maids of the Heathen nations." Regarding the New Testament, Furman asserted that slavery was acceptable in that day, and noted that when slaveholders were converted to Christianity, "their relationships, as master and slaves, were not dissolved." Furman thus concluded that "the holding of slaves is justifiable by the doctrine and example contained in Holy Writ . . . consistent with Christian uprightness, both in sentiment and conduct . . . slavery, when tempered with humanity and justice, is a state of tolerable happiness."[4]

While it may be true that most Christian slaveholders, including Baptists, treated their slaves better than most non-believing slave-owners, the gist of the pro-slavery stance which Christians in the South stood upon—the appeal to biblical precedence—seems both perverse and immature to most professing Christians of the late twentieth century. Nevertheless, the SBC was birthed from within the framework of a self-righteous, pro-slavery mind-set.

When Baptist delegates from the South formed the SBC in 1845, a key paragraph from the public statement they released suggested the racial nature of the decision to sever ties with the North. "Our objects, then, are the extension of the Messiah's kingdom, and the glory of God . . . the upholding of . . . God's glory, and Messiah's increasing reign . . . we find no necessity of relinquishing any of our civil rights. . . . We will not compromise what is God's."[5] In this allusion to slavery, the founders of the SBC seem to have upheld slavery as both a civil right and God's created order.

From our late twentieth-century perspective, we now know that the upholding of slavery by our Christian forefathers was an example of cultural conditioning of Christian beliefs. During the early years of the New World, the Caucasian race was considered the superior race, and the black was accordingly subjugated to the white race. Out of this setting emerged, not surprisingly, the belief in a God who favored the white race.

Although the Civil War served to liberate blacks from the bondage of slavery, resentful Southerners—including Southern Baptists—did not waver in their belief in the supremacy of the white race over against the black race. A Georgia Baptist editorial in 1883 regarding race revealed the prevailing attitude of the post-Civil War era. After declaring that whites "love" blacks (as well as the Chinese and Indians), the editorial qualified such "love" by stating that it is not the same love "which we have for the Caucasian race." The editorial continued: "We do not believe that all men are created equal . . . nor that they will ever become equal in this world, and perhaps not in the world to come." Regarding the proper place of blacks in the context of the various races of the world, "we do not know where to place him; perhaps not at the bottom of the list, but certainly not near the top." Also, it "is our opinion that any intermingling of these races . . . is a misfortune and an evil. . . . We prefer to have as little business with them as possible." The editorial proclaimed the treatise was a Southern Baptist "Confession of Faith," and considered the treatment of the subject of race relations as "orthodoxy."[6]

A few years later, in 1891, the SBC Home Mission Board, which was working with the black population, issued its own statement on racial relations. Among other things, this statement declared that "nothing is plainer to anyone who knows this race than its perfect willingness to accept a subordinate place, provided . . . it will receive justice and kindness." The statement noted that subordination is the condition the black "prefers above all others, and this is the condition in which it attains the highest development of every attribute of manhood." As such, whenever the black "shall understandingly and cheerfully accept this condition, the race problem is settled forever." The Home Mission Board declared its belief that "an expenditure of . . . fifty thousand dollars a year for the next ten years will settle this race question forever." The report concluded, "What greater good could come to our country, or what greater triumph to Christianity than so easy and perfect a solution of a question which has been and is now the despair of the statesmanship of the world?"[7]

Southern Baptists of the late 1800s, albeit paternally minded, helped black Baptists form their own churches, under the guise of home missions.

In 1891 the Home Mission Board reported that the majority of blacks in the South were Baptists.[8] In 1895 black Baptists consolidated their efforts and formed the National Baptist Convention (NBC). In 1915 this black Baptist convention was legally corporated.[9] In 1914 the SBC adopted a resolution supporting the funding of a black seminary which the NBC was advocating. The NBC, in turn, expressed thanks to its "white brethren" for their cooperation,[10] and the seminary opened in 1925.[11] The paternalistic attitude of white Southern Baptists seems to have been accepted by black Baptists, at least on the surface.

In the 1940s, a discernible, if not openly recognizable, shift began surfacing in the SBC in regards to relationships with blacks. During 1942, as Hitler and his anti-Semitic crusade held Europe in the grip of fear, one Southern Baptist state editor wrote, "Until we break down racial prejudices within the boundaries of our own land . . . we shall be heard with little serious attention when we speak about removing the larger and far more complicated racial antipathies and antagonism which the would-be dictators of the world are using today for their own advancements."[12] The horrors of Hitler's hate campaign against Jews were waking some Southern Baptists to the ultimate danger of promoting one particular race as being supreme over other races.

Five years later, messengers to the SBC annual meeting adopted a special report regarding race relations. The report declared such things as, "we shall think of the Negro as a person and treat him accordingly," and "we shall continually strive as individuals to conquer all prejudices" as well as "teach our children that prejudice is unChristian." A new current in race relations was slowly ebbing forth, although it was more often than not undetectable in local Southern Baptist churches.[13]

The 1950s would prove to be the beginning of major upheavals in regards to race relations in the United States. With America now conscious of the dangers of racial prejudice, the Supreme Court issued a ruling in 1954 declaring that the public schools of America should be desegregated. The Christian Life Commission of the SBC lauded the Supreme Court's decision, noting that it was "in harmony with the constitutional guarantee of equal freedom to all decisions, and within the Christian principles of equal justice and love for all men."[14] At least in words, Southern Baptist leaders had done an about face from their stance on race relations during the 1800s.

When the desegregation ruling was issued, the SBC had already opened the doors of its seminaries to blacks, although only a few years prior. Wayland Baptist College, in 1951, had become the first Baptist college to enroll a black student. Nevertheless, many Southern Baptists, long accustomed to the separation of the races, resisted the enforcing of mandatory public school desegregation and opposed the growing civil rights movement. These stances illustrated the attitude of white supremacy which was still widespread throughout the South.[15] This defiance of the civil rights movement, spurred on by long-held prejudices, led to the formation of thousands of white-only private "Christian" schools in the 1960s and 1970s, some of which were sponsored by local Southern Baptist churches.[16]

Southern Baptists gradually came to accept the civil rights movement, which gave black citizens equal rights. Although many white Southern Baptists no longer look down upon blacks, many others are, to this day, highly prejudiced against blacks. Some Southern Baptist churches have blacks on their membership rolls, but many do not. This continuing "church segregation" may partially be due to the fact that black Baptist worship styles tend to be different than white Baptists' worship styles, and people generally like to worship within the style in which they feel most comfortable. It is a tragedy, however, that the white God which Southern Baptists of the 1800s worshiped is still alive in the minds of many Southern Baptists, particularly in fundamentalist circles. The current fundamentalist-controlled SBC Christian Life Commission has, at times, displayed openly racist attitudes, and Adrian Rogers, fundamentalist pastor and past SBC president, recently revealed his racist beliefs when asked about slavery: "Well, I believe slavery is a much-maligned institution. If we had slavery today, we would not have this welfare mess."[17]

In recent developments, the 1995 SBC resolution, backed by the Christian Life Commission, expressing repentance for racial sins and acknowledging the wrongfulness of slavery has been heralded by its supporters as the final step towards racial reconciliation. However, many non-Southern Baptist blacks question the real motive behind the fashioning of the resolution.

Indeed, black Baptists across America are suspicious that Southern Baptist leadership issued the resolution in an effort to attract more black congregations into the SBC fold, with the intention of increasing the number of local churches aligned with the SBC. The SBC resolution turned out to be a hot topic during annual meetings of national black Baptist conventions and organizations in the second half of 1995. Despite denials from SBC leaders, numerous national black leaders and local pastors see the resolution as a smoke screen for a larger agenda. More than a few black Baptist leaders have openly condemned the resolution.

"The Baptist resolution may have been meant for good," according to one black Baptist minister who speaks for many of his black brethren. "But many are interpreting it as a means of seducing black congregations and trying to sucker African-Americans into joining the Southern Baptist Convention."[18]

At the very least, the motives of the current SBC leadership are questionable in regards to the racial resolution. Now that they are manning the helm of the SBC, it is important that they maintain the appearance of a growing, vibrant organization. Bringing large numbers of black Baptists into the SBC fold would certainly be a relatively easy way to enforce that appearance.

Although it is much too early to truly assess the results of the racial resolution, early indications are that it may do as much harm as good.

A GENTEEL GOD

The southern colonies were generally settled more slowly than their central and northern counterparts. By the late 1800s, however, migration from the northern and central colonies led to a steady population growth in the "uncivilized" southern region of the new nation.

Into this picture entered what came to be known as the "Second Great Awakening." Hints of revival were in the air during the 1790s, and in 1800, full-fledged revival, in the form of "camp meetings," broke out in Kentucky. Within a few years, these camp meetings had spread all across the South and had encompassed Baptists, Methodists, and Presbyterians. Fervent, emotional preaching, as well as fervent, emotional responses on the part of the masses, characterized the camp meetings. Some Christian leaders of the day, such as George A. Baxter, president of Washington College in Virginia, wholeheartedly believed the revivals brought morality to the uncivilized citizens of the frontier South: "I found Kentucky . . . the most moral place I had ever been. A profane expression was hardly ever heard. A religious awe seemed to pervade . . . It has confounded infidelity, awed vice into silence, and brought numbers beyond calculation under serious impression."[19]

In the frontier, uncivilized South, the message of individual salvation and piety which the revival preachers focused upon made a solid impact on Southerners. In that day, many southern families lived miles from their nearest neighbors, and were thus forced to rely upon their own skills and know-how in order to survive. Necessity oftentimes led families to play the roles of farmer, doctor, blacksmith, potter, and carpenter. Largely because of this prevailing rugged individualism, a gospel of individual salvation and piety, as well as local church autonomy (which Baptist churches tended to advocate), was well received in the South.[20]

The camp meetings, to be sure, did not last long. Dependent upon the frontier atmosphere of the day (particularly in the Ohio Valley region), the camp meetings faded away as the scattered population and isolated life of the region gave way to settled communities which, in turn, grew into established towns.[21] Nevertheless, the "puritanical" revivals of the early 1800s left a lasting impression upon southern religion and morality.

Out of this awakening in the South arose a growing Baptist population and a general sense of piousness throughout the region. Baptists and other denominations of the South, noting the difference the revivals had made in the lives of individuals and witnessing the blossoming of a pious southern society, sought to spread their influence at this opportune time. With evangelism at the heart of southern religion (thanks to the revivals), and piousness at the center of a growing regional consciousness (again, thanks to the revivals), Christians of the South, including Baptists, began touting their cultural religion as the best possible amalgamation of both worlds. Baptists of the South sought to spread their evangelistic zeal and moral purity through the Baptist mission boards and the newly founded Baptist colleges of the South.[22]

By the 1840s, the South, considered "uncivilized" only a few decades previous, had developed its own culture, which was clearly identifiable from that of the North. Southern culture was rural, whereas the North, once boasting a rural culture, had largely abandoned agriculture in the face of the Industrial Revolution. The South, in contrast, saw no need to abandon its rural atmosphere, and instead found stability in the status quo. Indeed, the rural life was elevated to the highest social status in the South, with industry being looked upon in disdain. There was, in fact, a belief among many Southerners that the Industrial Revolution could not have happened and could not be sustained without the cotton which the South provided for textiles.

The religious conservatism (characterized by individualism and moral purity) which the Second Awakening had spread throughout the South was by now firmly entrenched. In fact, Southerners now tended to be conservative in all matters. There was no vision for change on the part of the South; the maintaining of the status quo was considered primary. "Gracious cultural values" and "relaxed social intercourse" marked the white South. Politics, hunting, social gatherings, and leisure pursuits were sources of happiness and contentment for many white Southerners. Individualism was cherished. There was a general belief among Southerners that their rural civilization could be traced to England, and this connection was a source of pride. All in all, there was a sense among many white Southerners that theirs was a "perfect" life. They had, in effect, built in the South a "City of God"—a society where God was honored (so they thought) and life was pleasant.[23]

In the midst of this "perfect" existence, the only thorn in the flesh was the growing political and economic power of the North, which the South viewed as a threat to its way of life. The perceived northern threat led the South to take defensive, preservationist actions in the years leading up to the Civil War. The South, being a minority in regards to population, began seeking ways to politically insulate itself from any move by the federal government which would challenge its status quo (the institution of slavery, in particular). In its efforts to defend its lifestyle, the South, including its religious institutions, became increasingly more conservative. The southern churches of national Protestant denominations separated from their northern counterparts one after the other in the 1840s. The South became the new "citadel of puritanism."[24] Culture and religion were "inextricably linked."[25]

The South's refusal to examine its status quo, particularly the institution of slavery, precipitated the Civil War. Hundreds of thousands of young men took up arms to defend the South from the northern aggressor. Despite valiant efforts and much bloodshed, the Confederacy lost the war. With the loss came a collapse of the white Southerners' "City of God," as plantations and farms were destroyed and slaves were freed. Adding insult to injury, northern politicians ran roughshod over the South while the industries of the North exploited the South and its resources.[26]

White Southerners, however, including Christians, refused to view their defeat in the Civil War as a disgrace. Instead, they continued to celebrate and uphold the memory of their former culture, an aristocratic, puritanical society in which white Southerners dominated black Southerners.[27] During Reconstruction, Southerners continued to hold to the individualism, piousness, and status quo which had characterized the pre-Civil War South. As one historian noted, such attitudes still prevail among some white Southerners to this day.[28]

Having been born and reared in the deep South, I can attest to the continued presence of the "Old South" mentality. There is a distinct southern "patriotism" among many Southerners which is often proclaimed through the display of Confederate flags and the not-so-rare bumper stickers which proclaim, "The South shall rise again." Such attitudes hearken back to the pre-Civil War South. Furthermore, among some Southerners, a thinly veiled contempt, if not downright hate, exists for anyone or anything northern. Racial prejudice and regional pride still run deep among some Southerners.

Religious life in the post-Civil War South also tended to hearken back to former pre-Civil War glories. The Second Awakening of the early 1800s had brought both evangelistic fervor and moral reform to the newly flourishing South. The revival preachers had largely been postmillennialists, which meant that they believed that an era of "peace, justice, and goodness" would precede the return of Christ. In light of such beliefs, the revivalists placed particular emphasis upon reforming society by denouncing such vices as profanity, card playing, and alcohol.[29] Over time, such moral stances became orthodox Christianity, for all practical purposes, in the South. This morality was based on a "presumed knowledge of absolute truth" which allowed "no room for adjustment." In other words, the moral norms which had arisen during the early 1800s were by then presented as gospel truth which could not be questioned.

Following the Civil War, southern Christians, not the least of whom were Baptists, continued to adhere to a gospel of moral purity.[30] In the wake of physical, visible destruction, southern believers clung to their religious heritage of the pre-Civil War era. This preoccupation with moral purity has been carried over to this day, as many Southern Baptists shun all profanity and refrain from the consumption of any alcoholic beverages, both actions being viewed as sinful. Some go so far as to also label card playing, shooting pool, and eating in restaurants that serve alcohol as sinful.

In 1880 an article in a Methodist newspaper reflected the opinions of many southern Christians, including Baptists. The article, which dealt with the issue of southern culture and religion, noted that the North and South were distinctly different: "The Southerner, as a matter of honor and principle, minds his own business, while the inborn nature of the Northerner is to meddle. The South is tolerant, courteous and refined . . . the North has a prying, inquisitive disposition, and is bent on bringing everyone to its way of thinking and doing." Furthermore, there is a "southside to churches . . . in the type of piety that prevails. . . . The North has been overrun with professional evangelists, whose methods and teachings have in many instances done harm." Also, northern believers are "apt to be essentially defective in the higher traits of Christian character . . . there is a spirit and practice, and a type of religion, that we should regret to see in our southern churches."[31]

Southern society and religion of the early 1800s meshed together to form a unique southern culture. Southern Baptists played a role in this intertwining of religion and society, as Baptists of the South oftentimes echoed or reinforced the societal norms of the South.[32] The unique southern religious-societal culture continued to exist during the post-Civil War years as Southerners sought to hold on to their past.

Now, at the dawn of the twenty-first century, Reconstruction is long past and the South has risen to a place of some importance and prominence in modern America. There is a southern pride in the current industrial and technological strength of the modern South, as well as a certain amount of pride in the South's and Southwest's large metropolitan cities such as Atlanta, Georgia, and Dallas-Fort Worth, Texas. Indeed, the nations of the world have taken note of the rise of the South, as evidenced by Atlanta's hosting of the 1996 Olympic Games.

Despite this remarkable success story of a region once destitute, Christians in the South, including Southern Baptists, tend to be conservative and have high standards regarding moral purity. The majority of Southern Baptists live in the states which comprised the Old South, and it should come as no surprise that the SBC, to this very day, is somewhat influenced and shaped by a genteel, southern culture that was forged in the early 1800s.

A NEW SOUTH GOD

The civil rights struggles of the 1960s proved to be a tumultuous time for Southerners and Southern Baptists. Radical change was in the air in the 1960s South, and these changes ran against traditional southern culture. Integration became the visible symbol of the changes which were sweeping the South, and many Southerners resisted the government's efforts to place black children with white children in public school classrooms, and efforts to allow blacks the same access to public places that whites had long enjoyed. Many Southern Baptist leaders saw the wisdom and rightness of integration, but many other leaders and laity reacted with fervor against any efforts designed to encourage the mingling of the races. When SBC leaders took a pro-integration stance, one lay leader from Louisiana spoke for many Southern Baptists when he accused the SBC of making "sinister maneuvers against Southern traditions."[33]

The civil rights movement served to pit Southern Baptists against Southern Baptists. While some churches opened their doors to blacks, others rewrote their constitutions to ensure that segregation would be enforced within their churches. Some churches split over the issue, and it was not uncommon for Southern Baptist ministers who spoke out for and welcomed blacks into their churches and homes, to be abused and alienated, or even receive death threats, from fellow Southern Baptist ministers.[34]

The civil rights movement, which marked the beginning of radical change in the South, also became the launching pad for a multitude of calls for change in the areas of social justice, equality, and progress. Leading the call for changes in Southern Baptist life were Southern Baptist college students of the 1960s and 1970s. The Baptist Student Union (BSU), Southern Baptists' ministry to college students on the college campus, provided a place for these questioning students to air their doubts and develop a faith within the context of a nation in upheaval. BSU students of the 1960s and 1970s challenged long-held assumptions about their world and traditional Baptist faith and practice, and the student department leadership at the Baptist Sunday School Board provided materials and resources for these searching students.

BSU students began taking particular interest in the problems of society, and many participated in a silent protest against the Vietnam War in 1968. The Home Mission Board noticed this trend, and responded by giving increased attention to Christian social ministries. Students, in turn, became further involved in social ministries through serving as summer missionaries at inner city missions, or giving two years of their lives to serve as US-2ers or Journeymen missionaries. These mission experiences confronted BSU students with poverty and cultural differences, which, in turn, expanded their horizons. As a result, Southern Baptist college and seminary students were envisioning progress and equality in their denomination and in their world.[35]

However, the winds of change were simply too much for many Southern Baptists. They attributed the social upheavals and the "sexual revolution" of the 1960s to be the result of society casting away the Bible. By the early 1970s, Southern Baptist ultraconservatives were adamantly promoting a strictly literal Bible and touting a return to "truth" in a crusade against what they perceived as liberalism within "modern" America and the SBC.[36] The New South had arrived, and it sent ultraconservative Southern Baptists scurrying back to recapture Old South norms and beliefs.

Even as Southern Baptist fundamentalists pitted themselves against the New South, with its focus on equality, social justice, and progress, they soon did embrace many of the technological advances which progress wrought. Through the power of television and modern marketing and advertising, fundamentalist Southern Baptist pastors now man the helm of some of the largest Southern Baptist congregations in the world. The message these ministers preach is Old South, but their packaging is overtly New South. Many mainline conservative and moderate Southern Baptist ministers, on the other hand, have openly embraced the campaign to establish social justice and equality among the world's citizens.

In the 1960s and 1970s, the SBC Christian Life Commission embraced integration and encouraged Southern Baptists to get involved in addressing social injustices such as peace, world hunger, and economic justice, along with traditional concerns about alcohol, gambling, and pornography. When the fundamentalists gained control of the CLC in the late 1980s, they immediately put social justice issues on the back burner and turned their attention almost exclusively to a hard-line, anti-abortion platform.[37] The fundamentalists' preference for enforcing moral purity over social justice points, once again, to the Old South and its moralistic crusade.

As the twenty-first century looms, Southern Baptists stand with one foot in the Old South and one foot in the New South. The trappings of the New South—the technological advances and innovations which now pervade the South—are embraced by both fundamentalist and mainline conservative and moderate Southern Baptists. However, while mainline conservatives and moderates have largely welcomed the New South ethic of social justice and equality alongside traditional moral concerns, fundamentalists have largely overlooked these new ethical concerns, and have instead focused almost exclusively on matters of "old" morality. Although the New South has made a lasting impression upon Southern Baptists, the Old South has arisen again. The resulting tug-of-war could last into the twenty-first century.

CHAPTER FIVE

The God of Exclusiveness

In the American judicial system, the defense and prosecution of any given criminal case seek to make presentations which will win jurors over to their particular view. Truth, in reality, oftentimes takes a back seat to persuasion in our nation's courtrooms. In a similar fashion, there are thousands of religions in our world, and each one proclaims to have "truth," whether in part or in full. As a result, many religious persons spend much time seeking to persuade others that their particular religion is, in fact, the one true religion.

Within the Christian community itself, various denominations claim to be the bearers of "truth," despite the fact that these "truths" are often at odds with one another. Although all Christians would most likely agree that God is "Truth," many denominations and individuals also seek to reserve certain "truths" for themselves.

One such example of a particular Christian denomination trumpeting the banner of exclusive truth is the Roman Catholic Church, which historically has maintained that the fullness of salvation can be found only through the Roman Catholic Church.[1] The centrally organized Catholic Church with its insistence upon absolute truth led to resistance among some believers, and from this Protestant "resistance" movement sprang, among other Christian groups, Baptists. In direct opposition to the Roman Catholic Church and the similar Church of England, Baptists crusaded for the right of each local church body to govern itself without interference from a central body or figure, such as the pope.

This independent mind-set, along with an aversion to any human religious authority outside of the local church, had the effect of creating a void in Baptist life in regards to ecumenical matters.[2] As a result of this non-ecumenical (as opposed to anti-ecumenical) stance, in 1833, New Hampshire Baptists formulated a confession of faith (known as the New Hampshire Confession of Faith) which made no mention of the universal Church.

Consequently, and not in the least bit ironically, this intentional omission gave unvoiced support to the view of some Baptists that they were true believers, while other Christians were not. The New Hampshire Confession went on to become very popular in the independently minded South, and became the most influential Baptist confession among Baptists of the South.[3] The implied claim to "exclusive truth" which the New Hampshire Confession voiced has made no small impact upon the SBC.

A BAPTIST GOD

In the 1820s and 1830s, Baptists of the South were preoccupied with the Campbellite controversy, an anti-missions, biblicist movement in Kentucky and Tennessee. Proponents of the movement decried the new Baptist emphasis upon missions, declaring that the Bible did not expressly give approval of local churches working together to support missionaries. Calvinistic beliefs also played a part in this missions backlash, as Baptists of strong Calvinistic backgrounds declared that since God had predestined those who would be saved, man's efforts in regards to spreading the gospel were useless.

Although the Campbellite controversy lasted for a number of years, resulting in the withdrawal of some Baptist churches from Baptist life, it did not destroy the Baptist denomination. The controversy, however, did lead to an effort to establish a Baptist identity and command Baptist loyalty in the midst of a time in which new Christian denominations were coming onto the scene. The New Hampshire Confession of Faith soon gained widespread recognition among Baptists of the South as the region's Baptist leaders sought to combat the Campbellites by firmly establishing a Baptist identity. Out of this charged atmosphere emerged a movement which went to extremes in trying to establish Baptist identity and maintain Baptist loyalty. The Landmark movement, as it came to be known, was characterized by its insistence, backed with revisionist history, that Baptists had the only true churches in the world.[4]

The Landmark movement itself seems to have directly started with one James Robinson Graves, a former Congregationalist. At about the age of twelve, Graves began questioning the proper mode of baptism. Concluding that only Baptist immersion was scriptural, he became a Baptist at fifteen. In turn, Graves came to be deeply influenced by his pastor, who had developed a strong defense against the teachings of the Campbellite movement. Despite possessing a "keen mind" and being a good speaker, Graves received no formal education, although he decided to pursue the ministry and, accordingly, became ordained to preach.[5]

An acquaintance of Graves described the pro-immersion advocate of the early 1840s. Graves was "a wild, thoughtless man . . . unscrupulous in his relation of facts." The friend also related how Graves told him he was a Baptist, while telling a neighbor he was a Presbyterian. This acquaintance of Graves certainly had doubts about the integrity of the young man, not knowing that he would become an important shaper of Baptist life.[6]

Despite these seemingly obvious shortcomings, Graves' ministerial career grew to the point that he was appointed assistant editor of the *Tennessee Baptist* in 1846, and senior editor in 1848. The Baptist paper soon became Graves' platform to preach his anti-alien immersion message—the belief that since Baptist immersion is the only true mode of baptism, all other baptisms are invalid. Although he met immediate opposition from many of his fellow Baptist ministers, Graves continued to proclaim his message through the Baptist paper.

In 1854 J. M. Pendleton, a pastor in Bowling Green, Kentucky, read some of Graves' anti-alien immersion publications. Pendleton, convinced that Graves was right, published a pamphlet urging that Baptists no longer exchange pulpits with ministers of other denominations (a common practice of the day). Pendleton espoused the belief that only Baptist ministers were true gospel ministers. The pamphlet used the world "landmark" in describing the truth of Baptist immersion, and Graves later picked up on this word, which soon became the title used to describe the controversial movement, a movement whose influence continues today.[7]

In 1857 Graves outlined his beliefs in a booklet entitled *A Statement of Landmark Principles*. In this little treatise, Graves declared that only Baptist churches were true New Testament churches, as evidenced by their practice of immersion, the biblical method of baptism. Graves located Baptist beginnings in the New Testament apostolic church, indicating (through a revisionist interpretation of church history) that the Baptist lineage had been passed on through the ages in the unbroken line of "repudiators of popery" (referring to the small Christian sects of ancient times which had opposed the Roman Catholic Church). As such, Graves rejected the notion that Baptists had arisen out of the Protestant Reformation. This "successionist" theory of Baptist history came to be a hallmark of Landmarkism. In declaring Baptists the sole possessors of religious and Christian truth, Graves declared that "unimmersed bodies of Christians are not churches," but merely "religious societies."[8]

The following year, Graves established a publishing board designed to compete directly with Southern Baptists' current national publishing agency. Graves' own pastor (Graves was not pastoring a church at this time), Robert B. C. Howell, who was opposed to the newly arisen Landmark doctrine, stood in defense of the national Southern Baptist publishing agency, and immediately came under the wrathful attacks of Graves. Later that year, Graves' church unanimously convicted Graves on a number of charges, including slandering the pastor, seeking to divide the church, attacking other Baptist leaders through the *Tennessee Baptist*, and speaking and/or publishing numerous lies. Graves was subsequently evicted from the church.

Undaunted, Graves and some of his loyal followers formed their own church, and Graves, still a popular leader among certain Baptist groups, set out to unseat Howell, the SBC president, at the 1859 SBC annual meeting. The messengers, however, dealt Graves and his followers a severe blow as they not only reelected Howell as president, but also refused to go along with the Landmarkists' proposal to dismantle the Foreign Mission Board. These actions slowed the progress of Landmarkism, and the distraction of the Civil War further hindered the movement.[9]

Nevertheless, Graves was not to be dissuaded. In fact, he remained editor of the *Tennessee Baptist* until his death in 1893, during which time he continued to espouse his Landmarkist views. His audience was expanded during this time when, for some years beginning in 1869, the *Tennessee Baptist* served as the state Baptist paper for Arkansas, Louisiana, and Mississippi, as well as Tennessee.[10]

In 1880 the combatant Graves published a small but important book, *Old Landmarkism: What Is It?* The work contained his same basic arguments about Baptists being the only true church, presenting again his falsely constructed church successionst theory to lend credibility to his argument. Graves also reiterated his extremist position regarding the primacy of the local church. This book, which received broad distribution, spread Graves' message wider than before.[11]

Not long afterwards, in 1885, Landmarkists again challenged the Foreign Mission Board on its right to send missionaries beyond the scope of the local church. From 1885 to 1893, Landmarkists pressed the "Gospel Missionism" movement, an effort to restore the right of local churches to send missionaries. The Landmarkists' efforts failed, but they did lead to the formation of a new Baptist denomination, the Baptist General Association, which is still in existence under the name of the American Baptist Association. The Landmarkists who formed the new organization were united in their opposition to "conventions," which they declared unscriptural. They also declared that the only true Christian churches in the world were landmark Baptist churches.[12]

With the formation of a new denomination and the death of Graves in 1893, the Landmark movement within the SBC was once again waning. In 1894 Landmarkists tried to gain control of the Baptist General Convention of Texas, but the Convention refuted these efforts until the usurpers finally left Southern Baptist life and formed a rival state convention, which eventually took the name of the Baptist Missionary Association.[13]

Landmarkists' final major attack upon the SBC began in 1896 and involved the Southern Baptist Theological Seminary, the SBC's only seminary at that time. William H. Whitsitt, who had become president of the seminary in 1895, had, since the 1880s, been an outspoken advocate of the view, grounded in historical fact (unlike Landmarkism), that Baptists had had their beginnings in the early 1600s. When he ascended to the seminary presidency and continued to publish his views of Baptist history, the Landmarkists, led by B. H. Carroll, dean of theology at Baylor University, and T. T. Eaton, pastor of Walnut Street Baptist Church in Louisville, Kentucky, and a trustee at Southern, immediately launched a campaign to oust Whitsitt from the presidency. Carroll and Eaton appealed to many ill-educated Southern Baptists who had previously embraced Landmarkism, and soon mounted a serious campaign against Whitsitt, who, in their opinion, was undermining Baptist distinctives. With the seminary faculty and trustees squarely behind Whitsitt, there evolved a long, drawn-out fight between the two sides. The Landmarkists were unable to lead the seminary to fire Whitsitt, but the controversy wore upon him so much that he voluntarily resigned in 1899 for the benefit of the seminary.[14]

Although the Whitsitt controversy was Landmarkism's final major gasp, Landmarkism is still alive today in Southern Baptist life. Only a few decades ago, one author, who was not an advocate of the successionist Baptist history theory, declared the likelihood that the majority of Southern Baptists believed in successionism.[15] That author's conclusion is interesting, although it may or may not be true. Even though I grew up as a Southern Baptist in a southern, rural, conservative community, I was not introduced to the successionist theory of Baptist history until I took a class in Baptist history during my college years. Furthermore, even most of the fundamentalists who now control the SBC do not advocate Baptist successionism. On the other hand, R. G. Lee, pastor of Bellevue Baptist Church of Memphis, Tennessee, during the 1960s, declared in writing that "all Christians today should believe that Baptists began their denominational life under the ministry of Jesus."[16] Yet, James Hefley, one of the leaders of the fundamentalist, inerrantist movement, has clearly and openly denied the validity of the Baptist successionism theory.[17]

However, in regards to baptism and the Lord's Supper in Southern Baptist churches, the Landmarkist influence is yet very pronounced to this day, particularly in rural areas. Many Southern Baptist churches declare that all non-Baptist Christians who join their congregation must be rebaptized—even if they were immersed in other Christian denominations. Likewise, many Southern Baptist churches do not allow non-Baptist Christians to participate in their observance of the Lord's Supper. These practices, which are direct holdovers from the Landmark movement, show no signs of dying out anytime soon.[18] A fellow seminary graduate who took a pastorate in a rural Southern Baptist church in the South recently lamented that the entire association in which he serves is Landmarkist. He did not agree with the Landmarkist traditions, but realized that these beliefs were so deeply entrenched that opposition to them would cost him his job.

What began as a reaction to a heresy within Baptist life led to the creation of a God who gave his stamp of approval only to Baptists—another heresy. The belief in a "Baptist God" appealed to many uneducated Southern Baptists of the nineteenth century, for it gave credibility and legitimacy to their faith. Although this heresy eventually led to a more widespread, objective, and historical examination of Baptist origins,[19] many Southern Baptists to this day serve a "Baptist God." More than a few Southern Baptists sincerely believe that Baptists have all the answers and are the only true Christian denomination.

AN ANTI-CATHOLIC GOD

Baptists emerged out of the Protestant movement against the Roman Catholic Church. The earliest Baptists declared that the spiritual hierarchy of the Roman Catholic Church was unscriptural, and they accordingly voiced their beliefs that each individual stands alone before God and is personally accountable to God. In essence, the early Baptists proclaimed a personal relationship with God, with Christ being the intercessor for each person. This belief in the "priesthood of all believers" became a hallmark Baptist belief. The early Baptist forefathers also rejected infant baptism, a longstanding Roman Catholic tradition.

The early Baptists loudly proclaimed their opposition to the Roman Catholic Church and its practices. Although the Protestant Reformation led England to denounce the Roman Catholic Church and establish the Church of England, the New World, thousands of miles from any known civilization, gave the early Baptist forefathers a place to physically separate themselves from the Roman Catholic Church and practice their beliefs in an autonomous local church within the framework of a personal relationship with God. In the New World, the Roman Catholic Church was but a distant memory as the early Baptists set out to proclaim and propagate their Christian beliefs.

Before long, however, the Catholic Church did establish itself in the New World as Catholics from Europe migrated to the Americas in search of a better life. By 1850 the Catholic Church had become the largest Christian body in the United States, a position which it holds to this day.[20] Although Baptists and Catholics never clashed as the Congregationalists (Puritans) and Baptists of New England did, their competing Christian ideologies did cause some friction. Baptists' consistent emphasis on local church autonomy, priesthood of all believers, personal salvation, and believer's baptism left virtually no room for common ground between the two denominations, in the minds of many. Furthermore, the independent mindedness of Baptists was not conducive to ecumenical dialogue between the two groups. The

New Hampshire Confession of 1833, with its notable absence of recognition of the universal Church, reflected the Baptist independent mind-set. Nevertheless, the early Baptist forefathers ardently campaigned for religious freedom for all Christians and all religions—including Catholics.

The Landmark movement served not only to deceive many Southern Baptists of the nineteenth century into believing that the Baptist faith was the only true faith, but also served to widen the gap between Baptists and other Christian denominations, including Catholics.[21] This chasm between Southern Baptists and Catholics was growing ever wider even as the Catholic Church claimed the title of largest Christian body in America.

An aversion to Catholics by some Baptists continues to this day. During John F. Kennedy's 1960 campaign for the presidency of the United States, many Protestants, including many Southern Baptists, rallied to oppose Kennedy because of his Catholicity.[22] Baptists' anti-Catholic nature was so well established by this time that it was widespread public perception that Baptists had led the broad religious opposition to Kennedy's presidential campaign.[23] In fact, by this time, many Southern Baptists believed that Catholics were not true Christians—that is, they were not "saved." Over the years, seemingly countless Southern Baptists, both ministers and laypeople, have adamantly insisted that a person cannot be both Catholic and "saved." This anti-Catholic prejudice owes much of its thrust to the Landmark movement of the 1800s.

Southern Baptists have been actively seeking to proselytize Catholics for a number of years. The mission boards of the SBC have routinely placed missionaries in Catholic-dominated communities and countries with the intent of evangelizing those who bear the name Catholic. The fact that many Roman Catholics are so in name only is a major reason for these efforts. Nevertheless, general anti-Catholic sentiment is widespread throughout the SBC, with fundamentalists in particular oftentimes getting caught up in the anti-Catholic agenda. In 1985, for example, the trustees of the Foreign Mission Board, for the first time in history, comprised of a fundamentalist majority, targeted Edward Taylor, a foreign missionary who refused to evangelize all Catholics because of his belief that some were already saved. Taylor resigned from the board rather than be fired by the trustees.[24]

Underlying the widespread anti-Catholic sentiment in Southern Baptist life is the fact that Baptists were birthed out of opposition to the Roman Catholic Church. Other factors include the prevailing Baptist emphasis on local church autonomy and personal salvation, and an exclusive Baptist claim to truth (inspired by the Landmark movement), which some Southern Baptists yet uphold. Many Southern Baptists simply cannot accept the premise that a Catholic can have a saving, personal relationship with Jesus Christ. Indeed, not all Catholics have a personal relationship with Christ—

but neither do all who bear the Southern Baptist name.

As a Southern Baptist minister in a college setting who has had the privilege and opportunity to work with a number of Catholic students, I can personally attest to the fact that a Catholic can have as deep a saving relationship with Christ as can a Southern Baptist. Unfortunately, as we hover on the verge of the twenty-first century, I fear that more and more Southern Baptists, spurred on by the current SBC leadership, are willing to generally declare all Catholics as "unsaved" without actually getting involved in the lives of individual Catholics to personally determine whether their judgmental conclusions are true or not.

Southern Baptist and Roman Catholic relations have taken on a new dimension in recent years. A recent agreement between some Southern Baptist leaders (namely, Richard Land of the Christian Life Commission and Larry Lewis of the Home Mission Board) and some Roman Catholic leaders recommended that Southern Baptists and Roman Catholics stop proselytizing ("sheep stealing") in order to work together to better effect certain social issues (i.e., a hard-line, anti-abortion stance) and religious liberty matters (i.e., bringing certain ultraconservative Christian views and beliefs to a dominant position in federal, state, and local governments).

Some very strong negative reactions arose from both theological camps in Southern Baptist life concerning this new development, and both Lewis and Land soon removed their names from the document. Some observers had called this agreement the most important religious document of this century. The statement, however, was not an official Southern Baptist position. Futhermore, there were strong indications that the real purpose of the Southern Baptist–Roman Catholic agreement was to put forth a united ultraconservative front on social and church-state issues, rather than to truly recognize and accept the legitimacy of one another's faith.[25]

As much as some would like to deny it, there is an air of superiority on the part of many Southern Baptists in regards to the spiritual state of their Catholic counterparts. Indeed, many Southern Baptists worship a god who does not give the time of day to Catholics. A painful irony to this observation is the numerous times in recent years the SBC has been referred to as the "Catholic Church of the South," a reference to the increasingly hierarchical, pope-like rule of the fundamentalist leadership of the SBC. The comparison, unfortunately, has some merit.

AN ANTI-ECUMENICAL GOD

While many Southern Baptists are staunchly anti-Catholic, even Protestant denominations, some of which share much in common with Baptists, are oftentimes looked upon with suspicion by Southern Baptists.

The Baptist practice of swapping pulpits with pastors of other Protestant denominations is not observed as widely now as it was in pre-Landmarkist days, for example.

In the nineteenth century, Southern Baptists, influenced by the Landmark movement, were prone to steer clear of working with other Protestant denominations. In the early 1900s, the faculty of the Southern Baptist Theological Seminary, led by president E. Y. Mullins, sought to work with other Protestant groups, including both Baptist and non-Baptist groups, for the advancement of the gospel. Although Mullins led Southern Baptists in establishing helpful ties with other Christian groups, the rising fundamentalist movement of the early twentieth century within the SBC, influenced by Landmarkists, ultimately forced Mullins to curtail many of his ecumenical activities.[26]

Although many individual Southern Baptist churches maintained their independent, uncooperative attitude towards other Christian groups, the SBC, as it became more centrally structured during the first half of the twentieth century, began to work quietly and sometimes indirectly with other Christian groups and organizations. This cooperation with other Christians, albeit limited in scope, reflected a mutual attempt to spread the gospel and propagate basic Christian ideals, beliefs, and convictions.[27]

The overall picture, however, is one in which Southern Baptists are generally not particularly enthusiastic about ecumenism. The idea of all Christians coming together to work for the advancement of the gospel has received little attention in Southern Baptist circles. Instead, Southern Baptists have consistently striven to maintain a distinct identity within the Christian world. Indeed, the independent, self-sufficient mind-set of Southern Baptists revealed itself in the launching of Bold Mission Thrust in 1977. Bold Mission Thrust is Southern Baptists' effort to carry the gospel message to every person in the world by the year 2000.[28]

Bold Mission Thrust, in many ways, sums up the exclusive mind-set of some Southern Baptists. In the midst of many Christian denominations, the SBC has undertaken a single-handed effort to proclaim the gospel to the world. For any single Christian group to take such an incredibly enormous task upon itself—especially a little-educated, predominantly white Anglo-American group rooted almost exclusively (numerically) in the American South[29]—reflects not only an isolationist, independent attitude towards other Christians, but also smacks of more than a little arrogance and self-righteousness.

Most unfortunately, many Southern Baptists have converted the God whom they worship into one who is preoccupied with Baptists to the exclusion of other Christian denominations. The Landmarkist movement has left its indelible, exclusive stamp upon mainline conservatives and moderates in Southern Baptist life, as evidenced in the fact that Bold Mission Thrust was instigated when mainline conservatives and moderates controlled the SBC. In all fairness, however, the conservative and moderate leadership which launched Bold Mission Thrust was, at the same time, involved not only in working with other Protestant Christian denominations on a number of fronts, but also dialoguing with other religions. When fundamentalists gained unprecedented control of the SBC, they quickly embraced Bold Mission Thrust, but took measures to halt productive dialogue with other Christian denominations, as well as non-Christian religions.[30]

In recent years some Southern Baptist leaders have declared that Bold Mission Thrust will not succeed without the help of other Christian denominations. Furthermore, the current SBC leadership, in an effort to inflate the perceived impact of the Foreign Mission Board, has focused more and more on baptismal statistics of overseas churches and organizations which Southern Baptist missionaries "relate to." In this instance, by associating with other evangelical groups, the Foreign Mission Board is polishing its image through counting many of the same "heads" that other evangelical groups are counting.

Thanks to the Landmark movement of the nineteenth century, throughout the 150-plus years of the SBC, there has been a tendency among many Southern Baptists to see Baptists as the one and only true Christian denomination. Out of this background arose a broad-based anti-Catholic and anti-ecumenical attitude within the SBC. Despite the efforts of some mainline conservative and moderate leaders to lead Southern Baptists into participation with the Church universal, the widespread independent and isolationist mind-set often found at the local church level has served to lead Southern Baptists to be champions of self-sufficiency, as opposed to co-laborers in God's larger vineyard. The legacy of the Landmark movement is visible in Bold Mission Thrust. Baptist supremacy, reflected in anti-Catholic and anti-ecumenical stances, was very much a part of the SBC when mainline conservatives and moderates controlled the reins, and has been taken to even further extremes under fundamentalist leadership.

The exclusive, denominational, self-centered attitude of the current fundamentalist leadership was voiced well by Adrian Rogers, a leading fundamentalist and past SBC president: "I believe the hope of the world lies in the West . . . the hope of the West lies in America . . . the hope of America is in Judeo-Christian ethics . . . the backbone of that Judeo-Christian ethic is evangelical Christianity . . . the bellwether of evangelical Christianity is the Southern Baptist Convention . . . as the Southern Baptist Convention goes, so goes the world."[31] That claims far too much.

CHAPTER SIX

The God of (Partial) Truth

In the early 1990s, Amy Grant, Christian musician and pop superstar, could be heard over the airwaves singing "Galileo," a song paying tribute to Galileo and his scientific proof regarding the earth's orbit, and to Christopher Columbus's subsequent discovery of the New World. Amy Grant can sing the praises of Galileo today because it is common knowledge backed by indisputable fact that the earth revolves around the sun. However, if the Roman Catholic Church of the seventeenth century had had its way, we might still believe that the earth is the center of creation.

For many centuries people did believe the earth was a still body. The Roman Catholic Church supported this traditional view on biblical grounds. Several biblical references could be interpreted to mean that the sun revolves around the earth (Josh. 10:13, Matt. 5:45, Eph. 4:26, etc.), and the Roman Catholic Church took such passages literally. When the astronomer Galileo scientifically challenged this traditional view in the seventeenth century, the Catholic Church, perceiving a threat to its long-held belief system, took Galileo to court and threatened to kill him if he did not recant. Although Galileo verbally recanted, he had set in motion a new period of scientific inquiry which would continue to fly directly in the face of long-held, cherished Christian beliefs.[1]

Galileo's work actually followed that of Copernicus, who initially aroused the wrath of Catholic leaders and Protestant reformers when he first theorized that the earth revolved around the sun, instead of vice-versa. The traditional belief at that time was that the earth was the center of the universe around which everything else revolved. Martin Luther blasted the "fool" Copernicus for trying to turn the science of astronomy on its head, noting that the Bible declared in Joshua 10:13 that the sun stood still, not the earth, indicating that the sun had been the one doing the revolving. Melanchthon, another Protestant reformer, had even harsher words for Copernicus, declaring, in essence, that Christians should believe without question what the Scriptures had to say regarding the relation of the sun and earth.[2]

Today we know the folly and foolishness of the Roman Catholic Church, as well as that of Luther and Melanchthon, regarding their views concerning the earth and the universe. However, Christians of the Middle Ages were seeped in long-held traditions which were established truths, never to be questioned. In their estimation, their belief system was ultimate truth, and could not be challenged. They claimed to rest their belief system upon the truths of Scripture, and thus felt themselves secure from any potential onslaught. The truth of the matter, however, was that their "certain truths" were no more than mistaken perceptions which scientific study was destined to shatter.

Modern science has been with us for several hundred years now, and is an integral part of modern culture. Despite this fact, many Christians continue to resist scientific truth, clinging instead to long-held, traditional teachings and understandings of Scripture. A widespread view in Christendom today claims that in those instances where science contradicts traditional understandings of Scripture, science is necessarily wrong. Anti-science advocates, like Luther and Melanchthon of several centuries ago, today contend that they are defending the Bible from false propositions put forth by science. The truth, however, is that oftentimes they are defending their traditional understandings of the Bible from new scientific understandings. It may come as a surprise that the Roman Catholic Church finally withdrew its condemnation of Galileo a few years ago at the hands of John Paul II![3]

Baptists, including Southern Baptists, have not been immune from this Scripture-science conflict. In two areas in particular, the fundamentalist faction within Southern Baptist life has mounted a vicious, prolonged attack upon science: these areas are the study of the earth's age (the framework for the theory of evolution) and textual criticism of the Bible. In their emotional, hard-hitting defense of traditional understandings of Scripture over against the scientific revelations concerning the earth's age and the rise of textual criticism of the Bible, fundamentalist leaders within the SBC have managed to muddle the issues to such an extent that they have won many mainline conservatives and moderates over to their point of view.

A TWENTY-FOUR HOUR GOD

The emerging fundamentalist movement in America during the early years of the twentieth century was built upon a literalistic view of Scripture. Darwin's theory of evolution, which called into question both the age of the earth (Christian tradition had long held the earth to be only thousands of years old) and the development of plant and animal species (the development of humans would be incorporated into evolutionary thought later), was first expounded in the mid-nineteenth century, and soon became one of the main targets of the fundamentalist movement. The aversion to this line of thinking was found in its opposition to the traditional, literal understanding of the Genesis account of creation. Fundamentalists within the Southern Baptist Convention, led by J. Frank Norris, had been stirring up trouble in Southern Baptist life during the 1910s, but when evolution rose to the forefront in 1921, the ultraconservative, fundamentalist movement gained momentum.

Through the early years of the twentieth century, Darwin's theory of evolution, though controversial in nature and rejected by many Baptists and other Christians, had not arisen as a major area of contention within Southern Baptist life. However, early in 1921, the ultraconservative Norris attacked a professor at Southern Methodist University for the professor's pro-Darwin stance. Several mainline conservative and moderate Southern Baptist leaders joined Norris, leading to the resignation of that particular professor. Flush with success, Norris then launched a campaign against Samuel Dow, a professor at Baylor University who had recently published a book through the university's press which did not openly and clearly condemn the theory of evolution. Norris, assuming the same mainline and moderate Southern Baptist leaders would join him in this campaign, was outraged when his former allies refused to take sides with him.

Norris, a well-known Southern Baptist, then resorted to slander and hate in his anti-evolution crusade, attacking not only Dow, but Baylor, Texas Baptists, any other Baptist professors and schools which did not take a clear anti-Darwin stance, and the SBC itself. Norris did succeed in forcing Dow's resignation despite the fact that Dow stated he was not an evolutionist. In 1926 Norris finally succeeded in leading messengers at the annual SBC meeting to pass a non-binding resolution (not an official declaration) denouncing evolution. Norris also succeeded in forcing Southern Baptist seminary and university presidents to sign the statement. Yet, even as Norris savored his triumph, he was accused of murder, and although acquitted, his influence among both fundamentalists and the larger Southern Baptist body declined greatly.[4]

One of Norris's chief opponents during the evolution controversy was E. Y. Mullins, Baptist statesman, theologian, and president of the Southern Baptist Theological Seminary. Mullins, who did not believe evolution posed a danger to Christianity, saw censorship as a bigger detriment to the cause of Southern Baptists than exposure to evolutionary principles. Mullins led the SBC in holding Norris in check until 1926, when Norris, with the support of a largely non-educated Southern Baptist constituency, managed to push through his anti-evolution resolution at the annual Convention.[5]

After the mid-1920s, the evolution-creation controversy in the SBC waned as Norris was discredited and the Great Depression began. However, the controversy never disappeared entirely, but instead lay dormant until the publication of *The Message of Genesis* in 1961 by Ralph Elliott, professor of Old Testament at newly established Midwestern Baptist Theological Seminary. In his book, Elliott focused on the meaning behind the Genesis account of creation, as opposed to focusing on the traditional, literal reading of the text. Elliott employed Old Testament historical-critical study methods, which had been used for decades by Christian scholars, in his examination of the Genesis creation account. However, certain fundamentalists within the SBC attacked Elliott as if he had dreamed up the whole matter himself, which, of course, he had not.

The timing of the publication of Elliott's book certainly had much to do with the controversy to which it gave birth. Some of Elliott's critics were students with ultraconservative backgrounds who questioned his use of long-accepted (but long-ignored in many Baptist circles) methods of biblical criticism. Other critics were area pastors who were harboring bitter disappointment that they had not been invited to be a part of the staff or faculty of the new seminary. Some were opportunists, and some simply were fundamentalists who, like the leaders of the Catholic Church of old, were easily threatened by any "new" idea which challenged long-held, traditional religious beliefs.[6]

A major controversy thus erupted as fundamentalist ultraconservatives rallied around the traditional, literal reading of the Genesis creation account and sought to eradicate any line of thought which appeared to conflict with their understanding of "truth."

The fundamentalists did manage to effect the removal of Elliott from the seminary's faculty, but the evolution-creation issue soon arose again with the Baptist Sunday School Board's publication of the first volume of *The Broadman Bible Commentary* in 1969. The author who wrote the commentary on Genesis used historical-critical methods in his evaluation of the meaning of Genesis, which helped lead to another fundamentalist backlash within the SBC.[7]

Although the commentary controversy of the early seventies is long past, the evolution-creation controversy continues to rage unabated in Southern Baptist life today. Many Baptist and non-Baptist fundamentalists, who have long denied any validity of the theory of evolution and modern understandings of the earth's age and development, continue to preach the necessity of believing in seven twenty-four-hour days of creation when reading the Genesis account of creation. They also commonly proclaim that the world is no more than ten thousand years old.[8] This is the traditional understanding of the creation account, and is a modern parallel of the pre-fifteenth-century traditional understanding of a flat earth which was the center of the universe. Like the Catholic Church of yesteryear, many fundamentalists today reject recent scientific discoveries and bend Scripture to their liking.

Furthermore, the twenty-four-hour, seven-day, ten-thousand-year creation understanding is yet so entrenched among much of Christendom that many non-fundamentalist Christians also hold to this traditional view.

As we approach the twenty-first century, overwhelming scientific evidence supports the view that the earth and the universe are billions of years old. As did the Catholic Church of old, today's fundamentalists are leading the way in resisting this scientific knowledge tooth and nail. These fundamentalists, who unswervingly insist upon a literal twenty-four-hour, seven-day creation (some to the point of resting their salvation upon this belief), are glossing over the fact that, according to the Genesis creation account, God did not create the sun and moon—the heavenly bodies by which we humans measure our twenty-four-hour days—until the fourth "day" of creation (Gen. 1:14-19). Furthermore, they seemingly ignore the fact that time is meaningless to an eternal God (Ps. 90:1-4). To presuppose that the "days" of the creation account must conform to man's standards—particularly when nothing existed by which to mark time, and man himself had not yet been created—is to bring God down from his heavenly throne in order to stuff him into a box with human confines. In reality, the Genesis creation account and the Bible itself are not in conflict with the modern understanding of an ancient earth.

As to the theory of evolution, it is just that—a theory. The concept of human evolution is only a part of evolutionary theory, and is a concept which is not proven and which does not have universal support among the modern scientific community. Many Southern Baptist fundamentalists (and non-fundamentalists), whose influence in this regard has spread throughout the SBC, rightly argue that evolution, and particularly human evolution, should be presented as no more than a scientific theory in our public school classrooms. However, many fundamentalists insist that their traditional, literal understanding of a twenty-four-hour, seven-day creation be taught as unquestioned fact.[9] The truth, however, is that the majority of Southern Baptists do not accept the literal, fundamentalist view of creation, nor do they subscribe to human evolutionary thought. Rather, they recognize humanity as being a unique, special, and direct creation of God, and plant themselves somewhere between "seven-day, twenty-four hour creationism" and full-fledged evolution.[10]

More than a few Southern Baptists rest the very existence of God, and thus their salvation, on the truthfulness of a literal twenty-four-hour, seven-day creation of the world. Subsequently, they insist that modern scientific understandings of the earth's development and age have no merit whatsoever. As were the Christians in Galileo's and Copernicus's day, these individuals are resting their faith on long-held, traditional, presupposed truths. There is a tendency to forget or overlook the fact that the central message of the Genesis creation account is that of God as Creator, with humanity being his unique and special creation. Bickering and arguing over the exact nature of the creative process serves to take one's eyes off the Creator while focusing on human reasoning and intellect.

Most, if not all, Christians and Southern Baptists would agree that God is the author and knower of all truth. However, when scientific advances and discoveries run amok of long-held, traditional beliefs which have become perceived truths, there is a tendency for the devout to deny God his sovereignty in order to preserve the status quo. For all practical purposes, far too many Southern Baptists this very day are worshiping at best a God of partial truth, and, at worst, a God of human reasoning, when it comes to the matter of the nature and understanding of our world and our universe.

A KING JAMES GOD

As the twentieth century draws to a close, biblical scholars have both older and more accurate Greek, Hebrew, and Aramaic manuscripts with which to work, and better exegetical tools with which to understand and contextualize Scripture. However, instead of welcoming these advances, many Southern Baptists fear them—some even going so far as to label new methods of scriptural research as the work of the devil.

The history of biblical criticism began during the first few centuries following Christ, when many learned biblical scholars interpreted Scripture through the use of allegory. In other words, they believed that the central messages of Scripture were often clothed in symbolic language. Although not all Scripture was to be taken literally, all Scripture did have a spiritual meaning.

Gradually, however, a typological view of the Bible came to replace the allegorical method. Advocates of this line of thought believed that Scripture as a whole and in part went beyond mere symbolism. Some typologists rejected certain books of the Bible for which they found no concrete meaning or purpose. Others, who did not go to such an extreme, grouped books of the Bible into categories of authority. One such biblical scholar of the sixth century, for example, divided the books of the Bible into works of perfect authority, moderate authority, and no authority.

The Catholic Church evolved into a model whereby it was recognized as having the authoritative interpretation of Scripture. The tradition of the Church became the standard by which Scripture was interpreted. The Church leaned more towards the longer-used allegorical method, although in the late Middle Ages the historical method (viewing the Bible as a historical document) began replacing allegorical interpretation of Scripture.

By the fourteenth century, Europeans were developing a critical approach in their efforts to recover the Greek and Latin classics. As the

Renaissance spread, humanist scholars began applying these same critical methods to the study of the Bible. Beginning with John Wycliffe in the 1300s, biblical scholars began going back to the biblical languages and publishing new translations of the Bible. Allegory was largely abandoned as the Reformation led to a more literal understanding of Scripture.

Modern critical interpretation of Scripture, rooted in the rationalism of the Enlightenment (which was characterized by belief in human reason, progress, and basic goodness), can be traced in its infancy to the 1700s as advances in science and technology led to the use of a critical scientific method in the study of historical documents, including the Bible. By the late 1700s, some biblical scholars were downplaying the supernatural within the pages of Scripture. Germany became the center of this "higher criticism" (looking beyond and behind the literal rendering of the biblical text), with some scholars going so far as to reject the historicity of Jesus.

Modern interpretation of Scripture has developed largely in response to challenges posed by such radical liberal criticisms of Scripture. In attempting to respond to such assertions in the nineteenth century, some biblical scholars began studying the history of the times, geography of the ancient world, religions of biblical days, archaeology, rabbinical literature and thought, and biblical languages. From these new methods of biblical study came "lower criticism" or "textual criticism"—the study of the immediate context of the biblical text and its canonicity (how it came to be accepted as Scripture). "Higher criticism," on the other hand, continued to look beyond the text itself, using rational logic and scientific methodology as the framework for examining Scripture.

In the mid-twentieth century, scholars began focusing more on the theology of the biblical writings (i.e., the central message which the biblical writers sought to convey), and in the 1970s the emphasis shifted to a literary approach (i.e., identifying common literary devices utilized during the era in which any given Scripture passage was composed) in studying the history of biblical traditions and the Bible as story.[11]

The net result of these advances in biblical studies has been a better understanding of Scripture, both of the actual text and the framework in which the text was composed. However, because modern biblical criticism moves beyond a mere traditional, literal understanding of the Bible, the whole of the Christian community has not welcomed these advances with open arms.

Although "lower criticism" has been embraced by many Christians, "higher criticism" has frequently been the target of attacks by many fundamentalist Protestant Christians, as well as some conservatives, including Southern Baptists. The fundamentalist movement of the late nineteenth and early twentieth centuries campaigned fervently against higher criticism, and modern fundamentalists, including those within the SBC, continue to wage war against the perceived evils of modern methods of biblical interpretation.

During the early twentieth century, J. Frank Norris, the well-known fundamentalist antagonist within Southern Baptist life, tried to arouse opposition to higher criticism by labeling it a German phenomenon. Since the United States was engaged in war with Germany during both World Wars, Germany was a natural scapegoat for the perceived evils of higher criticism.

The SBC of the early 1900s, being a more conservative body than most other Protestant groups, actually paid little attention as a whole to modern biblical interpretation. Even the "safer" lower criticism, that method of studying the text and its canonical history, was noticeably absent from Sunday School literature produced by Southern Baptists. Although considered the safer of modern biblical critical methods, lower criticism was disavowed by some fundamentalists of old, as do some of today's modern fundamentalists.[12]

Higher criticism did not find its way into Southern Baptist seminaries until the mid-1900s. The seminary in Louisville, Kentucky, was the first to propagate higher criticism in the classroom. Although higher critical methods of studying Scripture were being applied prior to the 1950s, the arrival of Professor Eric Rust in 1953 propelled higher criticism into the spotlight in Southern Baptist life. Rust, educated in England, was an open proponent of using modern scientific methods in the study of Scripture, and his open and unapologetic use of such modern biblical study methods did not win him any friends within the small but vocal fundamentalist faction of the SBC.

However, Southern Baptist professors as a whole maintained that although some laypeople would certainly be shocked by much of what was taught in theological circles, they felt it their duty to pass on the fruits of modern biblical research, albeit sometimes in small and incomplete doses, to their students and Southern Baptists in general. They were holding to the long-held Baptist doctrine of the priesthood of all believers, which advocates that each believer should be allowed to freely interpret Scripture through the guidance of the Holy Spirit, a task which is enhanced by a better knowledge of the Bible.[13]

Southern Baptist professors and graduates, despite oftentimes utilizing and advocating modern biblical research methods, tended to do so in a discreet and advantageous manner in order not to unduly upset the largely conservative (albeit not fundamentalist) constituency of the SBC. In fact, it was common practice for seminary professors to "feed" their audiences that which the audience wanted to hear. Outside of their professional setting, professors would basically be "backhanded" rather than "forward" about any of their personal views which might overly upset a given audience. Thus, modern critical research of the Bible reached the local churches of the SBC primarily in small, incomplete, calculated doses.

Ralph Elliott, former professor at Midwestern Baptist Theological Seminary, adopted Glenn Hinson's (who was church historian and former professor at Southern Seminary) use of the term "doublespeak" to describe how Southern Baptist seminary professors related to the wider Southern Baptist audience. That is, many professors, when speaking outside of academia, were in the habit of crafting some statements in such a way as to mean one thing to them, while sending a different message to their audience. In fact, Elliott claimed that he got into trouble over the publication of his *The Message of Genesis* because he did not try to cloak his personal beliefs and his acceptance of higher critical methods in "doublespeak."[14]

To understand the scope of the problem that modern critical study methods of the Bible pose in Southern Baptist life, one must bear in mind that a significant proportion of Baptists have historically been suspicious of education. Southern Baptists have historically been less educated than other major Protestant groups. Within the confines of Southern Baptist life, fundamentalists are far less educated than mainline conservatives and moderates. A recent survey revealed that among Southern Baptist clergy with higher education degrees, less than half of all clergy holding bachelors degrees, and a mere twenty-four percent holding masters degrees, were self-identified fundamentalists or fundamentalist-conservatives. Among laity, the gap was even more pronounced: of all Southern Baptist laity holding higher education degrees, only twenty-two percent of those holding bachelors degrees and thirteen percent of those holding masters degrees were self-identified fundamentalists or fundamentalist-conservatives.[15]

Higher criticism of the Bible, which is based on modern scientific methods, is viewed with suspicion in many Southern Baptist quarters, and opposed with ferocity by largely uneducated fundamentalists. Among the seminary-educated fundamentalist Southern Baptist ministers, many have obtained their degrees from non-Southern Baptist ultraconservative, fundamentalist seminaries which generally denounce modern biblical study methods.[16] Even today, many Southern Baptist ministers and future ministers seek a center of indoctrination as opposed to a well-rounded and informed education in their choice of an institution of theological higher learning.

Like the Catholic Church of old and the reformers Luther and Melanchton, many of today's fundamentalists within Southern Baptist life are threatened by modern scientific advances which challenge their cherished, traditional belief system. In fact, many fundamentalists are absolutely terrified of modern scholarly biblical research. They fear that modern biblical scholars, if not held in check, will wreak havoc and confusion upon Southern Baptist churches through their questioning of long-held, presupposed truths regarding the Bible.[17]

In fact, the current fundamentalist leadership of the SBC brazenly declares that widespread acceptance of modern biblical criticism within the SBC will bring the Convention to ruin. W. A. Criswell, fundamentalist

Baptist statesman and then pastor of First Baptist Church in Dallas, speaking at the Pastor's Conference prior to the 1985 SBC annual meeting, proclaimed that the acceptance of higher criticism and the championing of the principle of the priesthood of all believers by British Baptist leaders had led to a numerical decline among British Baptists. Declaring that if higher criticism were to come to permeate the SBC, Criswell claimed that the mission boards of the SBC would cease to exist because Southern Baptists would no longer see the need to send forth missionaries. He even declared that "no minister who has embraced the higher critical approach to the gospel has ever built a great church." In closing, Criswell pronounced that if Southern Baptists were to survive as a "people of God, we must wage a war against this disease (higher criticism) that more than any other will ruin our missionary, evangelistic, and soul-winning commitment."[18]

Criswell's sentiments, biased and misleading as they were, are generally shared by the current SBC leadership. The fact remains, however, that despite cries of doom and despair, the Catholic Church did not fall apart as it gradually embraced Galileo's scientific discoveries, nor did the Reformation die out when Protestants accepted Copernicus's theory of the true nature of the cosmos, upon which Galileo built.

The crux of the issue here is not higher criticism itself, but rather the search for truth. Virtually all Southern Baptists believe in the divinity of Jesus and the salvation which can be found only through him. However, advocates of theological higher education and modern criticism alike are dedicated to searching for a fuller understanding of truth within the framework of a God who sent his Son to save the world. In their search for truth, they are willing to follow wherever the search may lead, for their underlying assumption is that God is the source of all truth. Their presupposition is that humankind's finiteness limits the human understanding of truth. However, they believe that humanity should nonetheless search for truth in order to please God, while yet realizing that because of this finitude, humankind will never be able to fully comprehend all truth. Such a view clearly recognizes the limited nature of humanity over against the ultimate sovereignty of God.

Opponents of modern criticism are often critical of higher education— unless it is in the form of indoctrination. Such individuals are generally not concerned with the search for fuller truth, for they believe they already possess complete truth. The truth which they claim to possess is confined primarily to their own personal belief systems, which are based largely on cherished, traditional views of the world, of God, and of the Bible.

Baptists and Southern Baptists have traditionally allowed room for diversity underneath the umbrella of a divine Christ, the Son of God, who is the only avenue of salvation. In the face of a radically changing world in which cherished traditions and beliefs are falling by the wayside, some

Southern Baptists, usually identifed as fundamentalists, are insisting that a believer must adamantly subscribe to more narrow, minute doctrine in order to both be a "true" Southern Baptist and a saved Christian.

Indeed, the faith of many Southern Baptists would be dashed if it were proven—as modern biblical criticism advocates—that Moses did not write the entirety of the first five books of the Old Testament. The Mosaic authorship of these books is the cherished, traditional view—and unquestioned truth to some Southern Baptists. These same individuals would likely insist that Isaiah had to have written all of the book of Isaiah, that God created the world in seven, twenty-four hour days and that Jonah had to have been literally swallowed by a whale (despite the fact that many biblical scholars believe the story of Jonah to be an Old Testamant parable with a powerful message of truth, similar to the parables Jesus frequently told). The refusal of most fundamentalists to allow divorced men to serve as pastors, as well as the insistence that women should not be pastors, are just two more of a plethora of examples of fundamentalists seeking to weed out diversity in Southern Baptist life by enforcing stricter and stricter doctrinal parameters. The issue is not the beliefs themselves, but rather the insistence that these particular beliefs and viewpoints are the only correct and valid doctrinal understandings.

In the same fashion, more than a few Southern Baptists seem to rest their very salvation on the belief that the King James Version is the only accurate translation of the Bible. This version, though long used and cherished by Baptists and non-Baptists alike, is certainly not the most accurate biblical translation, as modern biblical criticism has clearly revealed. Nevertheless, the belief systems of some presuppose as truth that the King James Version is the most accurate translation—despite clear evidence to the contrary. Such a view places humanly perceived truth, in many cases, on a higher plane than actual truth. As such, God becomes subservant to humankind and his perceived truth.

Many of the current fundamentalist leaders of the SBC are more interested in defending their own belief systems, which are largely perceived truth, than in searching for God's fuller truth. Many apparently have not grasped the fact that God's truth exceeds the boundaries of human understanding and humanly perceived truths. Too many Southern Baptists are simply far too concerned with preserving the traditional, cherished, perceived "truths" which have been handed down to them, than to allow the possibility that God's truths may be different altogether. In the best case scenario, such an attitude replaces a sovereign God with a humanized god, and in the worst case scenario, it places the individual on a pedestal above God.

The folly of those who believe, as did the Catholic Church of old, that truth cannot exist outside of their own personal belief system is well illustrated by Adrian Rogers, fundamentalist pastor and past SBC president, who declared that if most Southern Baptists believe that pickles have souls, the Southern Baptist seminaries ought to teach that pickles have souls.[19]

The flagrant disregard for God's truth which the current SBC leadership is demonstrating is without excuse. To elevate and worship one's personal perceived "truth" above God's truth is irresponsible and self-serving. Practically speaking, such a mind-set robs God of his sovereignty. Yet, perhaps the most tragic fact is that the SBC, which for years virtually ignored new developments in the scientific community as well as in the realm of biblical scholarship, has created an atmosphere in which humanly perceived truth can so easily supersede God's truth, time and time again.

CHAPTER SEVEN

The Written God

Throughout the world, hundreds of millions of the devoutly religious believe that their religion's sacred Scriptures are free of any error. In the Muslim world, for example, several hundred million Muslims fervently believe that the Koran is free of all error in all matters it addresses. These Muslim fundamentalists, who outnumber the whole of Southern Baptists many times over, are so zealous in regards to their "perfect" Islamic Scripture that they will allow no argument, however factual it may be, to dissuade them from their beliefs. Although they find errors in the Holy Bible of the Christians, they find only perfection in the Koran. In fact, these devout Muslims exhibit so much confidence in the perfection of their holy Scriptures that they are willing to die for their beliefs with hardly a second's hesitation.

Muslim fundamentalists are only one example of a number of religious radicals in the world today. Many Christians would be quick to say that the perceived truth which these Muslims embrace is blinding them from the real truth. Yet, one has only to go back a few hundred years to find a Roman Catholic Church which was so adamant in its claim of full truth that it persecuted those such as Galileo who dared challenge the Church's teachings. In fact, one need look no further than the Southern Baptist Convention of today to see the working of Baptist fundamentalists who are so bent on preserving their perceived truth regarding the Bible that the real truth has been cast aside.

A LEATHER-BOUND DEITY

One of the hallmark principles of Baptists is the belief in the sole spiritual authority of the Bible, as opposed to human institutions or other holy books. The early Baptists championed this belief partially because they emerged from a Church which reserved spiritual authority unto itself.

Baptists have historically maintained that the Bible, as God's revelation to humanity (or the "Word of God"), is the final authority in matters of faith and practice. In this century, however, a vocal minority of Baptists, including Southern Baptists, have challenged this understanding of the Bible.

The Reformation led to a more literal understanding of Scripture. Baptists of yesteryear tended to subscribe to this literal understanding of Scripture. The earliest Baptists, emphasizing the final authority of Scripture in matters of faith and practice, eventually came to employ the term "infallible," which literally means "incapable of failing," as their manner of defining the nature of scriptural authority. The Second London Confession of 1689 was the first Baptist confession to actually use the term "infallible," although the concept had existed for several years. This early Baptist confession declared that Scripture was the "infallible rule of all saving Knowledge, Faith and Obedience."[1] The emphasis in regards to the infallibility of Scripture was reserved for spiritual matters. This belief in the spiritual infallibility of Scripture has been the standard Baptist and Southern Baptist view of scriptural authority since that time.

However, the escalation of the conflict between science and religion in the mid- and late-nineteenth century led some Protestants, including some Southern Baptists, to reevaluate this definition of biblical authority. Largely in response to scientific advances, such as Darwin's theory of evolution, which challenged cherished, traditional interpretations of certain biblical passages, a number of Protestants began extending the definition of biblical authority to include all areas of knowledge, as opposed to just the spiritual realm. In the very late 1800s, a new word used to define biblical authority began appearing on the Protestant scene: "inerrancy." This term was intended to convey a stronger degree of authority than "infallibility," and was liberally applied to all areas of knowledge on which Scripture touched. In essence, among some Protestants, the emphasis shifted from a Bible which was "incapable of failing" in regards to spiritual matters, to a Bible which was "free from error" in all areas of knowledge.[2]

Although only a minority of Protestants, including Southern Baptists, formally subscribed to this new view of biblical authority, "inerrancy" gradually grew in popularity throughout the first quarter of the twentieth century. The concept of inerrancy was birthed from within the framework of pre-twentieth century evangelical Christianity, which generally held to the plenary-verbal inspiration of Scripture (that is, the belief that God verbally dictated the Bible, word for word). Thus, the concept of a literal and "perfect" Bible was unquestioningly accepted by many nineteenth-century evangelical Christians, including many Southern Baptists. The theory of inerrancy was a systematic extension (perhaps culmination) of these underlying assumptions, yet the the theory per se was largely absent from Southern Baptist life until recent times. Now, radical views of inerrancy abound.

Those individuals who strictly adhered to this new "inerrancy" concept generally came to be known as the ultraconservatives, or fundamentalists, within Christianity. The fundamentalist faction of the SBC, although a small minority during the early twentieth century, became a major headache for the SBC. In fact, the fundamentalists, under the leadership of J. Frank Norris, prompted the mainline conservative-moderate SBC to formulate its first ever confession of faith in 1925, in which the article on Scripture declared the Bible to have "truth, without any mixture of error, for its matter" (a statement borrowed from the 1833 New Hampshire Confession of Faith). The word "matter" was intentionally vague and intended to be inclusive—it left room for mainline conservatives-moderates to interpret it to refer to the spiritual realm, but also allowed fundamentalists to interpret it in a broader sense, in an effort to promote harmony. In 1963, in the midst of a new controversy caused by the publication of Ralph Elliott's book, *The Message of Genesis*, fundamentalism prompted the SBC into reworking the 1925 statement in an effort to refute another fundamentalist uprising. The inclusive wording of the statement on scriptural authority was left intact.[3]

Despite the gradual rise of the minority fundamentalist faction within the SBC during the twentieth century, the term "inerrancy" did not actually become the buzzword that it is today until the 1976 publication of Harold Lindsell's book, *The Battle for the Bible*, in which the author incorrectly assumed that inerrancy had always been Southern Baptists' stance in regards to biblical authority. At this point Southern Baptist fundamentalists began rallying around the term and soon made it their battle cry in their "holy crusade" to take over the SBC. As it now stands, the fundamentalists, although still a minority in Southern Baptist life, have successfully used their "inerrancy" agenda in a political campaign to capture control of the SBC on the national level.

At first glance, the concept of an "inerrant" or "perfect" Bible seems quite appealing. Likewise, the hundreds of millions of Muslims who hold to the Koran as their "perfect" book of Scripture find the concept of a perfect religious document appealing—as long as that document is the Koran. In fact, if a worldwide vote were taken concerning which holy book is the one "perfect" book, the Koran would beat the Bible hands down as the one perfectly authoritative religious book.

The idea of a literal and perfect Bible has existed since the Reformation, and is of extreme importance to a minority of Southern Baptists. However, the concept of inerrancy, in its literal, most basic sense (that is, a Bible free from all errors of any kind—a perfect Bible), is a most dangerous and deceptive path upon which to trod.

To begin with, the concept of inerrancy is a non-biblical concept. Inerrancy, in both word and concept, is of human origin, not of biblical origin. The Bible does address matters of faith and practice in an authoritative manner, but it never claims to be without error in all matters. As such, the concept of inerrancy is imposed upon Scripture, not taken from Scripture. In fact, Jesus himself never referred to the Scripture of his day (the Old Testament) as inerrant, but rather pointed beyond Scripture to the heart of the matter, and ultimately to himself as the fulfillment of Scripture: "I am the way and the truth and the life. No one comes to the Father except through me" (John 14:6, NIV). Jesus pointed to himself, as part of the Godhead, as ultimate truth—not the physical, written words of Scripture.

Second, the concept of inerrancy was not born out of a systematic study of the nature of Scripture, but rather came into existence as a knee-jerk reaction against the rise of modern science in the mid-1800s. Princeton theologians gave birth to the concept of an inerrant Bible as they sought to ward off the perceived evil advances of science. In essence, the formulation of inerrancy, a modern doctrine which was birthed from within the framework of a literalistic, verbal-plenary approach to Scripture, was a goal-line stance by ultraconservatives to reposition the Bible's authority above that of science in all realms of knowledge (before the scientific age, science had been subjugated to traditional understadings of Scripture). This manuever of systematically positioning the Bible as a perfect and conclusive text in the field of science was a defensive move intended to preserve the "traditional" faith.[4]

Third, inerrancy, in its basic sense, transforms the Bible into a deity of its own. Baptists have long understood the Bible as the Word of God in that the Bible is recognized as the record of God's revelation to humankind. One Southern Baptist scholar used the word "relational" to describe this basic Baptist understanding of the Bible as the Word of God addressed (or directed) to the human race. As such, the Bible points not to itself, but to God through Christ. The concept of inerrancy, however, paints a picture of a Bible which is an end unto itself. As such, the Word of God, as bespeaking the Bible, becomes a "description" of the Bible itself, referring to the physical copy (the written words), as opposed to the conveyed message.[5] The result is the reduction of the Bible to an end within itself, rather than a "God-breathed" manuscript revealing the way for humankind to become righteous before a holy God (see 2 Tim. 3:16).

The ultimate formulation of employing the "Word of God" as a descriptive reference to the physical text of the Bible is crediting the biblical text itself with the attribute of perfection (the literal definition of "inerrancy")—a claim which the Bible never makes for itself, assumptions notwithstanding. Consequently, when the Bible as a physical document is upheld as perfect, it is placed on the same level as God. This becomes a problem, for a sovereign God (one who is above all, the "Supreme Being") can be a sovereign God only if his supreme, perfect state of being is unrivaled. In other words, if a leather-clad manuscript (or papyrus rolls, or clay tablets) comprised of words is bestowed with the label of perfection in all areas of knowledge (that is, it is credited with absolute supremacy), it serves to usurp the sovereignty of God, and itself becomes a humanly appointed god.

The concept of inerrancy, therefore, in its most basic sense (that is, the understanding of the Bible as being a perfect entity within itself), dethrones God Almighty and places a physical manuscript upon the now vacated throne. To advocate inerrancy in its most basic sense is to worship a twentieth century human understanding (albeit the extension of an older, traditional understanding of Scripture) of an ancient, divinely inspired document. One Baptist scholar defined inerrancy as "a condition that some human beings place on their willingness to accept the Bible as authority."[6] In essence, inerrancy places human understanding above both the Bible and God.

Lest the reader think to himself that no one, and certainly not a Southern Baptist, would nowadays have the audacity to knowingly usurp God in such a manner, perhaps a recent declaration from a Southern Baptist minister in a Southern Baptist pulpit would be enlightening: "You've heard it said that Jesus saves, but I'm here today to tell you that the Bible saves." Likewise, just prior to the 1980 annual SBC gathering, fundamentalist leader Paige Patterson openly complained that too many Southern Baptists were claiming Jesus Christ, over against the Bible, as their ultimate authority.[7]

A NON-EXISTENT GOD

Despite the fact that the logical corollary of inerrancy is Bible worship, the current leadership of the SBC proudly proclaims its belief in a perfect, inerrant Bible. Paige Patterson, a leading Southern Baptist fundamentalist and a chief architect in the fundamentalist takeover of the SBC, speaking on behalf of the new fundamentalist leadership of the SBC, declared in 1987 that fundamentalists were unwilling to stand before Christ on judgment day and declare that they had not opposed their fellow Southern Baptists who did not believe in an inerrant Bible.[8] The current president of the SBC declared that same year that inerrancy was a "question of Lordship."[9] A previous fundamentalist SBC president openly declared that an inerrant Bible is worth fighting for,[10] which is precisely what fundamentalists did in their takeover of the SBC. W. A. Criswell, well-known fundamentalist statesman, declared in 1985, "If we deliver the message of the inerrant Word of God, God will rise to meet us. . . . 'We shall not cease from battle strife, nor shall the sword sleep in our hand, till we have built Jerusalem in this fair and pleasant land.' God grant it!"[11]

In 1986 Adrian Rogers, a fundamentalist and then SBC presidential candidate, championing an inerrant Bible, ardently exclaimed that the entirety of Christianity hung on the virgin birth of Christ. "I wouldn't give you half a hallelujah for your chance of heaven if you don't believe in the virgin birth of Jesus Christ."[12] Although the virgin birth of Christ is a foundational doctrine, the New Testament plainly tells us that the whole of Christianity, and salvation itself, hinges only on the saving power of the cross and resurrection (1 Cor. 22-24, 2:1-2, 15:1-28). Two years later, in 1988, W. A. Criswell trumpeted his belief that anyone who admits that there are scientific errors in the Bible is committing blasphemy. Paul Pressler, leading Southern Baptist fundamentalist and cohort of Patterson, claimed that those who believe that "the original text of scripture can or does contain error" are theological liberals despite what they may call themselves.[13] The fundamentalist leadership is seeking to make the concept of inerrancy a litmus test for all SBC employees.[14] They have virtually completed their "purge."

A noted proponent of inerrancy summed up the fervor of inerrantists regarding their hypothesis of the nature of Scripture when he declared that he would have little respect for a God who allowed error to enter into the biblical text. Such a God would be "no God at all," and would not even be "worth knowing."[15]

The current fundamentalist leaders view themselves as holy crusaders ordained by God to weed out of SBC life any and all individuals who do not subscribe to their inerrancy hypothesis. Believing themselves to be bearers of absolute truth, they seek to force conformity on all Southern Baptists in regards to their agenda of a literal, inerrant Bible. These individuals, who subscribe to such a strict view of inerrancy that they classify the modern fathers of inerrancy (the authors of the 1978 Chicago Statement on Biblical Inerrancy, the current definitive statement regarding biblical inerrancy in the evangelical Christian world in this country) as liberals, have no interest in accommodating mainline conservative and moderate Southern Baptists into their elite group.[16]

Indeed, the current fundamentalist leadership has been so successful in promoting the term "inerrancy" in Southern Baptist life that a significant portion of Southern Baptists currently use the term to describe their view of biblical authority. However, there is an obvious disparity between the majority of Southern Baptists and the fundamentalist leadership regarding the definition of inerrancy, for over half of Southern Baptists who use the term "inerrancy" to describe their view of Scripture do not believe that Genesis is a book which has to be taken literally—whereas the current leadership is publicly adamant in their literal interpretation of Genesis. Thus, although fundamentalists have successfully introduced the term "inerrancy" into Southern Baptist life, and have led the way in its acceptance in the SBC, the typical Southern Baptist does not define the term "inerrancy" in the strict sense the fundamentalist leaders do.[17]

For all their battle cries and trumpeting of the inerrancy of Scripture, the fundamentalist leaders themselves do not actually believe that the biblical text they hold aloft is inerrant. As a matter of fact, despite all the emotion and fervor which they expend in advancing their cause, they do not really believe that any existing biblical text is actually free of errors. It may come as a surprise to some that the Bible which fundamentalists commonly hold aloft when declaring their belief in the inerrancy of Scripture is not error-free, in their own estimation. Much to the contrary, some fundamentalist leaders would, in reality, like to tear out certain Scripture passages from the Bible![18]

Instead of referring to the Bible when they speak of inerrancy (even though they use the word "Bible" when speaking of inerrancy), the current fundamentalist leadership of the SBC is in actuality referring to the long-destroyed, non-recoverable original Greek and Hebrew manuscripts. In other words, they are applying the term "inerrancy" to something which does not even exist![19]

As one Southern Baptist theologian asserted, we should not even be speaking of the inerrancy of the Bible, since inerrantists do not believe the Bible is inerrant.[20] Such an observation lends itself to the question of why inerrancy is so important to fundamentalists if the documents to which they are referring do not exist? To this question we could add, is "inerrancy" no more than an empty word if there is nothing tangible to which it can be applied? Is inerrancy in the least bit relevant to any aspect of the Christian life?

In essence, the current fundamentalist Southern Baptist leadership has been waging a war for control of the SBC under the banner of a modern, humanistic understanding of non-existent scriptural texts. What could be more deceiving? Or has the whole crusade been a well-orchestrated pretext which has served to cover up the true motives of the fundamentalists? Clark Pinnock, well-known Baptist inerrantist and a shaper of the 1978 Chicago Statement on Inerrancy, observed, while he yet embraced inerrancy, that the true agenda of Southern Baptist fundamentalist leaders is "to impose upon the Southern Baptist Convention a whole set of beliefs by force and not really a debate over inerrancy at all."[21] On the other side of the coin, non-inerrantist premier Baptist historian Walter Shurden has concluded that the inerrantist faction within the SBC has "demonstrated clearly that they are not interested simply in the nature and authority of the Bible but in imposing their interpretation of the Bible on others."[22]

Pinnock and Shurden, although coming from different theological backgrounds, in their penetration of the rhetoric of inerrancy, give us keen insight into the true goals of the leaders of the fundamentalist-inerrancy party. Inerrancy (albeit a will-o-the-wisp) may be the masthead of the new fundamentalist leadership of the SBC, but forced conformity and consolidation of power seem to be the real goals.

A HOLLOW GOD

Inerrancy is a humanly concocted assumption which pertains to ancient manuscripts that no longer exist. It is completely and utterly unprovable. The proponents of inerrancy are literally standing on empty space, as there is no shred of factual proof which substantiates their position.

However, the lack of even one ounce of substantial proof regarding inerrancy does not negate the fact that the fundamentalist-inerrancy party has taken over the SBC and is within short striking distance of a complete purge of the entire organization.[23] In fact, at this point, the fundamentalist-inerrancy leadership has virtually completed its hostile takeover of the SBC without causing major fragmentation of the Convention.[24]

Recognizing that the framework of the concept of inerrancy is based on wholly unsubstantiated human assumptions regarding Scripture, the hostile takeover the fundamentalist-inerrancy party effected is even more remarkable. In the old American West, the cowboys who slapped leather at high-noon in front of the O.K. corral made certain their six-shooters were loaded to capacity. The fundamentalist-inerrantists, on the other hand, strode out in the middle of the street and faced their opposition with an empty gun. Yet, they have managed to win the shootout.

As time passes, historians will certainly be able to explain more clearly the phenomenon of the fundamentalist-inerrantist takeover of the SBC. Clark Pinnock and Walter Shurden, who speak for a number of SBC observers, are adamant in their belief that inerrancy itself was, and is, nothing more than a ruse by the fundamentalist-inerrantist party in their quest for conformity and control. The inerrancy agenda was indeed an empty ruse, and the fundamentalist-inerrantist party won the "shootout" because they stole their opponent's six-shooter out of its holster before the gunfight. In other words, the current fundamentalist leadership of the SBC was successful largely because it placed a new label, "inerrancy," over the standard Baptist doctrine of the "infallibility" of Scripture and successfully hawked the "new" product as "old" Baptist tradition.

The definition of inerrancy is simply "without error." The inerrancy party uses the term to refer to non-existent manuscripts, which means their claims are both unfounded and unproven. In essence, therefore, they are focusing on a theoretical concept of certain non-existent documents which supposedly contain no errors, and would therefore be perfect in nature. Or does the inerrancy party actually hold to non-existent but perfect, error-free, original manuscripts of the biblical text?

Somewhat surprisingly, the truth is that the majority of foremost inerrantists, both Baptist and otherwise, do not believe that the now non-existent original biblical autographs were error-free and perfect in nature! Although they may proudly parade the term "inerrancy," they do not really subscribe to its actual, definitional meaning—"without error."

Some inerrantists may actually believe in inerrancy. The vast majority of the leaders of the inerrancy agenda both in and outside of Southern Baptist life, however, do not subscribe to true inerrancy.

Modern inerrancy leaders, both Baptist and non-Baptist, hang their hat on the 1978 Chicago Statement of Biblical Inerrancy of the International Council on Biblical Inerrancy (ICBI), the current definitive declaration of the concept of inerrancy. In the Chicago Statement, the ICBI expressly stated that, "We deny that biblical infallibility and inerrancy are limited to spiritual, religious or redemptive themes exclusive of assertions in the fields of history and science," and, "Scripture is without error . . . in all its teachings."[25]

These assertions by the authors of the Chicago Statement seem clear enough—their statements obviously express a belief in a Bible free of errors in all regards. Yet, the authors of the statement, later within that very document, openly acknowledge that the following things are found in the Bible: events related outside of chronological order, disagreement among the biblical writers concerning some numbers, differing accounts of the same event, incorrect quotations within Scripture regarding other passages of Scripture, etc. As such, the authors clearly contradict themselves by recognizing that errors within the Bible do indeed exist. However, the Chicago Statement contextualizes the above listing of obvious biblical discrepancies by declaring that such errors should not really be considered errors. In essence, the Chicago Statement exempts these errors from the theory of inerrancy by sweeping them under the rug through creative labeling.[26]

Thus, the Chicago Statement on Biblical Inerrancy, the hallmark of the current inerrancy movement, begs the obvious question: Is the theory of inerrancy real, or is it just a hollow notion? To declare that Scripture is completely error free, except for certain exceptions, is tantamount to stating that 2+2 always equals 4—except on Saturdays. Either 2+2=4, or it does not. Either the Bible (in its non-existent original manuscripts, as fundamentalists-inerrantists contend) is free of error, or it is not. An error is an error—despite the fundamentalist-inerrantist attempts at creative labeling. Are the fundamentalist-inerrantists expounding inerrancy? Apparently not, if the Chicago Statement is normative of inerrantist thought. It would be more accurate to say that the Chicago Statement advocates an error-free Bible—except where errors are found. Inerrancy is clearly not the correct word to describe such a view of the Bible.

As such, the term "inerrancy" is not merely misleading—it is plainly deceptive. The fundamentalist leaders who proudly claim to believe in an error-free Bible are simply blowing smoke. Led by the 1978 Chicago Statement on Biblical Inerrancy, they qualify their belief in inerrancy to such an extent that they actually discard inerrancy in practice. One little-known belief of "inerrantists" is their confirmation that only what the biblical writers intentionally taught in Scripture is inerrant. Inerrantists also believe that the biblical writers may have used incorrect and imprecise language. Likewise, they acknowledge that quotations of Scripture within the Bible are not always correct, but declare that these error-filled quotes should not be considered as errors. Inerrantists also acknowledge that the Bible contains teachings which obviously are not inerrant. Concerning the latter, some seek to explain away the discrepancies, while others conveniently ignore them altogether. Regardless, inerrantists as a whole refuse to label these errors as errors.[27]

In essence, many inerrantists say one thing but believe another. Their conclusions tend to contradict their public declarations—yet they continue as if no contradictions exist. In reality, some non-Southern Baptist inerrantists recognize that the term inerrancy is a false and deceptive term.[28] Southern Baptist fundamentalist-inerrantist leaders, however, have largely refused to face the music and own up to the contradictions of their professed agenda.

In 1985 the SBC voted to assemble a Peace Committee to identify the reasons behind the inerrancy controversy, with the goal of resolving the controversy before any more damage ensued. Although mainline conservative-moderates were supposed to be equally represented on the Peace Committee, it soon became clear that fundamentalists controlled both the committee and its direction. When the committee reported its conclusions to the SBC in 1987, the fundamentalists triumphantly claimed victory.[29]

The fundamentalist spin in the Peace Committee report was obvious. Claiming to speak for the majority of Southern Baptists, the fundamentalist-dominated report first declared, in regards to scriptural authority, that "most Southern Baptists . . . believe in direct creation of mankind and therefore they believe Adam and Eve were real persons."[30] This claim, in reality, is simply false. At the same time that the Peace Committee was in progress, a survey of Southern Baptists revealed that only slightly more than one-third (thirty-eight percent) of Southern Baptists insisted that the Genesis creation story had to be taken literally. Even more telling is the fact that only forty-four percent of inerrantists (that is, those who subscribed to the term "inerrancy") among the general Southern Baptist population believed that the Genesis creation account had to be taken literally![31] The fundamentalist-dominated Peace Committee's claim to speak for the majority of Southern Baptists in regards to the literalness of the creation account was simply a farce—they did not even speak for the majority of Southern Baptists who had come to embrace their own buzzword, "inerrancy!"

The truth is that the Peace Committee report did not speak for the majority of Southern Baptists, but for the minority, who by that point had gained political control over the SBC. Even at that point, however, the report was more of a summary of what the controlling fundamentalist-inerrantist party professed to the public, but not necessarily what the fundamentalist-inerrantist leadership believed.

Take, for example, the aforementioned pronouncement on the literal interpretation of the Genesis creation account. During the 1987 Ridgecrest Conference on Biblical Inerrancy (an event which emerged out of the milieu created by the Peace Committee but was sponsored by the six Southern Baptist seminary presidents), H. Edwin Young, leading fundamentalist-inerrantist, pastor of Houston's Second Baptist Church, and future SBC president, adamantly declared in a public statement that Adam and Eve were historical figures. Afterward, however, when pinned down by a reporter, he conceded that his literal interpretation of the Bible was only one of a number of responsible interpretations. When further pressed, he acknowledged that the creation story did not necessarily have to be taken literally. However, he adamantly insisted that interpretations other than his "don't belong in this conference."[32]

This incident regarding Young reveals the hypocritical mind-set and practice of much of the SBC fundamentalist-inerrantist leadership. Young's party claimed to speak for the majority of Southern Baptists in the Peace Committee report regarding scriptural authority. The claim was, and is, entirely false. To further compound the atrocity of this deception, the Peace Committee report did not, in reality, speak for the actual beliefs of the fundamentalist-inerrantist leadership. As Young revealed in the preceding statement, it spoke more directly for their ambitions to control the SBC under their own personal terms and conditions. Bear in mind that Young later served as president of the SBC.

If these facts would seem to point to a secret conspiracy by the current SBC fundamentalist leadership, other non-Baptist inerrantists would tend to agree. Clark Pinnock sounded a dire word of warning towards his fellow inerrantists, aimed directly at those inerrantists who proclaim one thing while believing another: "If we keep secret the manner in which we qualify the term, we give the impression to the general public that we hold a more unlimited inerrancy than we do, and for that reason cast dark suspicion upon fellow evangelicals whose actual view of the Bible may be very close to our own, and who differ from us chiefly in their desire to avoid the term inerrancy."[33] Pinnock's words cut to the quick of the matter. He feared a secret conspiracy on the part of some inerrantists to display a front to the public which is calculated to discredit others who are, in actuality, just as conservative as the inerrantists, but who refuse to play the inerrantists' word game.

Pinnock also touched on another insight by revealing, in his own estimation as an inerrantist, that, in truth, there is basically no difference between mainline evangelicals (i.e., mainline conservative-moderates in the SBC) and inerrantists. In fact, during the 1987 Ridgecrest Conference on Biblical

Inerrancy, Pinnock, when asked whether he was an inerrantist, responded in a very honest and forthright manner, when he declared, "I am and I'm not, because the thing is so ambiguous."[34] Pinnock admitted publicly what leading Southern Baptist inerrantists admit only privately—inerrancy is so "ambiguous" that defining it tends to refute the very notion of inerrancy.

Fundamentalist-inerrantists disagree in regards to the fronts which they display. Leading Southern Baptist fundamentalist-inerrantists, for example, according to their publicly declared stance on inerrancy, have pushed the modern fathers of inerrancy into the realm of "liberalism."[35] However, those same SBC fundamentalist-inerrantist leaders have themselves stepped into the realm of liberalism when they have moved away from their facades.

Adrian Rogers, leading Southern Baptist fundamentalist-inerrantist and former SBC president, like his comrades, is sometimes prone to say one thing but believe another. Although he champions a literal, inerrant Bible in public, he tends to contradict himself when things get personal, as he did when it was suggested to him that God had caused two bears to kill forty-two children, as is recorded in 2 Kings 2:23-24. Despite claiming to believe in a literal, inerrant Bible, Rogers disagreed with all major translations of the Bible, which indicate that God, at the request of the prophet Elijah, directed the bears to kill the forty-two children. Rogers tried to rationalize the text by declaring that the children in the passage were "teenage punks." Kenneth Chafin, a Southern Baptist conservative-moderate, noted that the term Rogers translated as "teenage punk" is the same term used in Isaiah 9:6: "For unto us a child (teenage punk) is born." Rogers went on to declare that the text does not say that the children ("teenage punks") were killed, despite the fact that the text indicates that they were indeed killed (in fact, massacred—some translations say that the boys were mauled, while others declare that the children were "torn" apart).[36] Rogers' public front and his private beliefs, in this instance, were worlds apart.

Taking into consideration that fundamentalists are now in control of the SBC, it is apparent that the fundamentalist-inerrantist leaders in Southern Baptist life have been successful promoters and advertisers of a theory of biblical inspiration built upon thin air. Tens of thousands of Southern Baptists have been taken in by the inerrantist propaganda. The private beliefs of those most fervently dispensing inerrantist dogma, however, reveal the falsity, deception, and hypocritical nature of their public agenda.

David S. Dockery, prominent Southern Baptist fundamentalist-inerrantist theologian, and academic dean of the Southern Baptist Theological Seminary, appears to have come closest to publicly acknowledging the ambiguity which surrounds the theory of inerrancy. In his *Doctrine of the Bible*, published by the Baptist Sunday School Board in 1991, Dockery outlined what he termed "Views of Inerrancy." He broke down the concept of inerrancy into five distinct and different "positions": 1) Naive inerrancy—

the belief that God verbally dictated the Bible to human writers; 2) Absolute inerrancy—the view that the Bible is absolutely true in all matters; 3) Balanced inerrancy—the belief that although the Bible is completely true in all that it affirms, some portions of Scripture may not be factually true in regards to science and history, with the explanation being that the writers were limited in their understanding; 4) Limited inerrancy—the view that the Bible is free from error in all matters regarding faith and practice; and 5) Functional inerrancy—the view that the Bible inerrantly accomplishes its purposes, with the factuality of any given passage of Scripture being secondary at best.[37]

As one takes note of these five "positions" of inerrancy, one can easily see that position one is worlds apart from position five. If inerrancy indeed embraces all five listed positions, the term is overtly ambiguous in the light of these differing and even contrasting stances which Dockery has defined as "inerrancy."

Dockery himself personally embraced position three as the definition that, in his opinion, is most faithful to the "nature and revelation of inspiration." He described "balanced inerrancy" as stressing "that what the Bible affirms is completely true, employing both a coherence view . . . and a correspondence view of truth at appropriate places." Dockery saw this view of inerrancy as recognizing the "diversity" (i.e., inconsistencies and mistakes—or errors—within some passages), but seeking to "harmonize" these discrepancies. He maintained that this "base of inerrancy" is necessary to "maintain an orthodox confession of Christian truth." Furthermore, from within the context of "balanced" inerrancy, he defined "inerrancy" as meaning that "when all the facts are known, the Bible (in its autographs, that is, the original documents), properly interpreted in the light of the culture and the means of communication that had developed by the time of its composition, is completely true in all that it affirms, to the degree of precision intended by the authors' purpose, in all matters relating to God and His creation."[38]

Dockery's statements were certainly well thought out in regards to the meaning of inerrancy as he embraced the term. However, his definition rubbed against the grain of the actual definition of the term inerrancy ("without error" or "errorless") because he left room for error in the biblical manuscript within the context of ancient human writers who had a limited understanding of the functioning of the world in which they lived. Concerning this possibility, Dockery dismissed any such errors in the biblical manuscript which may have resulted from incomplete knowledge on the part of the writers by asserting that such errors are not actually errors.

Although Dockery's reasoning was sound, the fact that he made room for errors in the first place (whether they are subsequently explained away or not), means that his definition of the term "inerrancy" actually turns upon the term and shatters it. In other words, "inerrancy" is not a fitting term for a view which leaves room for errors, even if the errors are promptly glossed over through systematic reasoning and/or creative labeling. Some contemporary inerrantists are now acknowledging this fact.[39]

In fact, an analysis of Dockery's five "positions" of inerrancy reveals that positions three, four, and five "turn upon" the very term "inerrancy," simply because varying degrees of room are left open in which errors in the biblical manuscript may exist. A more appropriate definition of these three "positions" in regards to biblical authority would be the historic Baptist term of "infallibility" (i.e., "incapable of failing"). "Infallibility" uplifts the truthfulness of the biblical manuscript without getting caught up in the distraction of trying to impose perfection or quasi-perfection upon all of the minute details of the physical contents or microscopically analyzing discrepancy-prone passages dealing with non-religious matters.

If Dockery had presented his above definition of biblical authority to a mid-nineteenth-century Baptist or Southern Baptist audience, he would have most likely presented it under the auspices of biblical "infallibility," for the concept of biblical "inerrancy" per se did not yet exist. However, Dockery seems to have held up "inerrancy" as the norm for Southern Baptists, as evidenced by the fact that he used the term to include stances on biblical authority which clearly make room for errors within the biblical manuscript, while making no mention of "infallibility," despite the fact that "infallibility" is the manner in which Baptists and Southern Baptists have largely understood scriptural authority for several hundred years. In reality, "inerrancy" has been a popular concept of biblical authority in Southern Baptist life only since the late 1970s.

While upholding inerrancy in Southern Baptist life, Dockery seriously downplayed the historically dominant role of scriptural "infallibility" in Southern Baptist life. Regarding infallibility, Dockery stated that "some contemporary scholars want to apply the term infallible only to the message of the Bible to avoid the affirmation that the Bible is also truthful in matters relating to history, geography and related matters." Dockery labeled this as the "revised" meaning of infallibility, and insisted that the "classical" meaning refers to all subject matter in the Bible, as opposed to just spiritual matters.[40]

The "classic" meaning of infallibility is, in fact, just the opposite of that to which Dockery attributed it. The Second London Confession of 1689 and the Philadelphia Confession of 1742 set forth the classic Baptist view of biblical infallibility when they tied infallibility only to matters pertaining to spiritual faith and practice—no mention was made of peripheral subject matter, contrary to Dockery's assertions.[41] In fact, no major Baptist confession to this day (with the exception of some confessions of Landmark and fundamentalist Baptist denominations) has ever expressly declared the absolute truthfulness of Scripture in all subject matter, or has used the term "inerrancy" to denote or describe the nature of biblical inspiration or authority.[42]

In effect, Dockery, in his breakdown of inerrancy into five distinct positions, has pushed aside and misrepresented the concept of infallibility in order to force that which would normally be construed in terms of infallibility underneath a very generous umbrella of inerrancy. In reality, however, positions three, four and five (balanced, limited, and functional inerrancy), by Dockery's definitions, which leave varying degrees of room for error in the biblical manuscript, beg to differ with the very term "inerrancy." In his efforts to establish inerrancy as the Baptist norm, Dockery seems to have pushed inerrancy beyond its actual boundaries into the area of infallibility, a fact which he has not seemed to recognize.

Dockery's first two inerrancy positions (naive and absolute inerrancy) are the only two of his five which actually remain faithful to the basic postulate of the term inerrancy (i.e., "without error"). These two positions simply make no room for error in the biblical manuscript. Dockery has not been willing to embrace these two positions,[43] perhaps indicative of his unwillingness to move into the true inerrantist camp. Furthermore, the current fundamentalist-inerrantist leaders, although paying public lip service to a truly "error-free" Bible, have not moved into the true inerrantist camp, according to their own private, less-publicized view of Scripture.

These observations regarding the misuse of the term "inerrancy" and the hesitation (perhaps unwillingness?) of leading Southern Baptist fundamentalist-inerrantists to move squarely into the true inerrantist camp (public displays notwithstanding) bring us to the question: Is the inerrancy agenda of the self-proclaimed Southern Baptist fundamentalist-inerrantists simply a hollow facade which has been employed as a front to divert attention from some larger fundamentalist scheme? Considering the fact that most inerrantists, including Southern Baptist inerrantists, are not inerrantists in the true sense, are there, in actuality, any significant doctrinal difference between fundamentalist-inerrantists and mainline conservative-moderates? If the doctrinal differences are indeed minimal, why are Southern Baptist fundamentalist-inerrancy leaders so adamant in pushing their agenda that they are not backing off even in the face of having caused unprecedented division in America's largest Protestant body?

Clark Pinnock seems to have peeled back the layers of deception several years ago when he, as a non-Southern Baptist analyzing the state of the SBC, declared that what was really going on was "an attempt to impose upon the Southern Baptist Convention a whole set of beliefs by force and not really a debate over inerrancy at all."[44] Pinnock pointed to a thirst for power as the underlying motivation of the leaders of the fundamentalist-inerrantist camp in the SBC:

> It seems a crying shame to me that a world class evangelical (and successfully evangelistic) denomination like the Southern Baptist

Convention—the great preponderance of whose members by all accounts hold fast to the everlasting gospel of Jesus Christ according to the Scriptures—should be embroiled in a bitter and painful struggle ostensibly over the theory of biblical inerrancy and how tightly it should be drawn and defined. Christians have never agreed on the details of this belief, yet that has never before prevented them working together in the defense and proclamation of the gospel. Why should it now?

The tragedy is compounded by the fact that it is also unnecessary. For if we take the Chicago statement as the definition of what inerrancy signifies (and what other definition is there of such authority and stature?), we find the large majority of Southern Baptists able to find room under its generous provisions. Its version of inerrancy . . . scarcely poses much of a problem to the essentially conservative Southern Baptist moderates. . . . It causes me to wonder—has the Enemy cooked up a fight among God's people to try and prevent them [from] posing the threat to this dark kingdom which the denomination does, in fact, represent when it is unified?[45]

Likewise, Fisher Humphreys, a Southern Baptist theologian, questioned the very existence of "inerrancy" in and of itself: "I myself am unable to understand how sophisticated, qualified inerrancy . . . differs substantially from non-inerrancy."[46] Humphreys was well aware that inerrancy as qualified by the Chicago Statement is not true inerrancy at all.

As such, the very existence of the theory of biblical inspiration known as "inerrancy" is called into question—not just by non-inerrantists, but by some professed inerrantists as well. Inerrancy is an unprovable, humanistic, non-scriptural concept of biblical inspiration which imposes itself upon non-existent manuscripts. Some leading Southern Baptist fundamentalists give public, verbal allegiance to this theory—but in private probably none actually subscribes to inerrancy proper. If they did, however, they would, in effect, be making an idol or even a god out of the non-existent original autographs of the Bible.

In its qualified sense, as put forth by the 1978 Chicago Statement, inerrancy no longer means "inerrant," for biblical errors are recognized. Since leading Southern Baptist fundamentalist-inerrantists hold to inerrancy in its qualified sense (despite public advocacy of inerrancy in its true sense), it would seem that the current SBC battle is being waged over theological terminology as opposed to theological substance.

An incident at Midwestern Baptist Theological Seminary illustrates this point. Recently, fundamentalists, for the first time in history, gained majority control of the trustee board of Midwestern. Most of these fundamentalists openly advocate inerrancy. In October 1993, Midwestern theology professor Wilburn Stancil was recommended to the trustees for tenure. Stancil, an avowed conservative, affirmed his belief in the authority of the Bible as the Word of God, but declined to use the term "inerrancy" to describe his view of Scripture. The fundamentalist trustee board immediately lunged at him. One trustee, speaking for many others, righteously declared that "people don't use the term inerrancy because they don't believe the Bible." Doubtless, this righteous crusader did not realize that he was condemning Jesus as well, for Jesus never used the term inerrancy, and by this trustee's reasoning, Jesus therefore did not believe the Bible.

At least one fundamentalist trustee did speak up for Stancil, however. This lone trustee declared that "even though we use different words, we believe the same thing." Midwestern president Milton Ferguson also spoke up in Stancil's defense with some pointed language: "I urge you to get beyond your terminology. Lay aside whether he speaks kindly of inerrancy or is friendly to current leadership. He believes more about the Bible than some folks who call themselves inerrantists."

In the end, however, the hard-line fundamentalist-inerrantists overwhelmingly denied Stancil tenure by a vote of twenty-four to nine—mainly because he would not use the proper terminology.[47] Theological substance was, in fact, pushed aside by concern for theological terminology. Tragically, Stancil is only one of many conservative Southern Baptists who have been brusquely pushed aside by fundamentalist, inerrantist bullies because they refused to bow down to the bullies and use the "correct" terminology. However, the most tragic fact of all is that Jesus himself would have failed this "theological terminology" test.

In the "holy crusade" carried out under the banner of inerrancy within the SBC, the substance of inerrancy has taken a back seat to the use of the term itself—perhaps because there is actually no real substance to the public inerrancy agenda which many Southern Baptist fundamentalist leaders are espousing.

A REVISIONIST GOD

Unfortunately, crusaders of a modern view of scriptural authority, characterized primarily by humanistic understandings of a divine manuscript, have brought the SBC to the brink of possible self-destruction. The current situation of the SBC is reminiscent of the Roman Catholic Church of yesteryear, which insisted that their human understandings of Scripture were absolutely correct, and that the earth could not possibly revolve around the sun, because "the Bible said so." The old-time traditional understanding of

Scripture as being an unquestioned literal authority in all matters was the forerunner of modern "inerrancy" of Scripture. It was just such arrogant insolence, in the name of championing the faith, on the part of the Roman Catholic leadership that led to the Protestant Reformation. Five hundred years later, the Southern Baptist fundamentalist leadership has come full circle.

What rationale is there behind this blind pursuit of implementing a humanistic understanding of scriptural authority throughout the SBC? Many observers would attribute the underlying issues as a self-centered drive for control and power, which was much the same reason the Catholic Church of yesteryear spent so much time and effort in squashing dissenters.

The desire for power and control drives many good people to do unethical and ungodly things. For the Catholic Church, it was death at the stake for dissenters. For the communist regimes of old, it was wholesale slaughter of dissenters. For the current SBC regime, it is the gradual forced removal of all who disagree.

Oftentimes, when a transition of leadership takes place from one center of power to a radically different center of power, revisionist thought is employed as a method of leading the constituency into acceptance of the new power structure. The Catholic Church did not have to worry about revisionist thought—Roman Catholic leaders were simply trying to retain the power they had long possessed. Communist regimes, however, did feel the need to employ a propaganda campaign (in the form of revisionist history) in order to elicit loyalty from constituencies who were accustomed to much different forms of government. The current fundamentalist leadership of the SBC has likewise employed a revisionist history of biblical authority in an effort to lead Southern Baptist masses to accept the new power structure which they have enacted.

The Bible has long been the sole written spiritual authority for Southern Baptists, so it is no surprise that the new power brokers have wrapped their revisionist history and doctrine around the Bible. The key concept used in this revisionist campaign has been the propagating of an "inerrant" Bible, a good-sounding but misleading term.

The understanding of biblical authority and interpretation which is now espoused by the current fundamentalist leadership of the SBC is presented in such a way as to seek to lend legitimacy to the new power structure. Furthermore, it is designed to try to cloak modern, humanistic understandings of Scripture underneath the guise of solid, historic Baptist doctrine.

The 1978 Chicago Statement on Biblical Inerrancy has been the launching pad for the fundamentalist leadership of the SBC. The chief fallacy of the Chicago document is the open door it extends for a plethora of biblical errors to exist, stated intentions otherwise notwithstanding. Thus, the very foundation upon which the fundamentalist leadership has anchored itself is of little substance and questionable merit when it comes to upholding the word "inerrancy." Still, fundamentalist leaders have busied themselves in recent years in constructing a revisionist version of Southern Baptist understandings of Scripture in order to give credibility to their agenda.

The Baptist Faith and Message of 1963, a slight reworking of the 1925 document by the same name, is the only formal doctrinal confession that Southern Baptists have ever issued. Even so, the Faith and Message was carefully clarified with the understanding that it was a "consensus" of beliefs and carried no "mandatory authority." This document affirmed the high view of Scripture which Baptists have historically upheld, noting that Scripture is "truth, without any mixture of error, for its matter." This statement was intentionally left ambiguous in regards to whether it referred to matters of faith and practice alone, or matters in all realms of knowledge. Historically speaking, Baptist confessions regarding biblical authority have confined themselves to matters of faith and practice. However, the fundamentalist leaders of the SBC have departed from this historical stance, and have striven to convince Southern Baptists at large that such a view has never been the normative Southern Baptist stance. Their campaign has been remarkably successful.

To begin with, the fundamentalist leadership was not satisfied by the Baptist Faith and Message alone. In a nutshell, in their minds, it left too many loose ends flopping around. Subsequently, when they gained enough of a foothold within the SBC, they quickly set out to "flesh out" the Faith and Message to their liking. As they did so, they declared over and over again that they were championing what Southern Baptists had always understood the Faith and Message to say. Far too many Southern Baptists, unschooled in the historic faith and doctrine of their own denomination, were soon easily convinced by the smooth-talking newcomers.

Championing the Chicago Statement on Biblical Inerrancy as the normative Christian and Baptist view of biblical authority, fundamentalist power brokers set out to fashion additional Southern Baptist confessions of faith which would champion their own personal opinions.

In all candor, much of what the Chicago Statement declares is normative Christian and Baptist doctrine. Where it falters, however, is the attempt to impose the modern concept of bibical "inerrancy" upon the historic Christian understanding of Scripture. While it is true that many Christians throughout the ages have viewed the Bible as a perfect document in all respects, many others, including millions of Southern Baptists throughout the past several hundred years, have understood the Bible to be fully authoritative only in matters of faith and practice.

The fundamentalist leaders of the SBC first began formally putting forth their personal opinions in semi-creedal statements of faith in the 1987 Peace Committee Report. This report did not accurately reflect what the majority of Southern Baptists actually believe (or even what many of the fundamentalist leaders truly believe), despite claims to the contrary. However, it did serve to give some legitimacy to the concept of inerrancy within Southern Baptist life, which was what it was designed to accomplish. The truth about inerrancy—its unbiblical, humanistic basis—was never mentioned within the document.

Six years later, in 1993, fundamentalist leaders further solidified their doctrinal grip upon the SBC with the publication of the results of a presidential "Theological Study Committee," drafted as a doctrinal statement—"a reaffirmation of major doctrinal concerns set forth in the Baptist Faith and Message of 1963." This misleading document was built upon the Chicago Statement and the Peace Committee Report, and was designed to further legitimize the concept of biblical inerrancy within Southern Baptist life. Once again, the truth about biblical inerrancy was omitted.

The "Theological Study Committee" document is a telling indication of how the fundamentalist leadership of the SBC has revised historic Baptist understandings of biblical authority. The opening statement immediately dictates the direction of the document. "In every generation, the people of God face the decision either to 'reaffirm the faith which was once delivered unto the saints' (Jude 3) or to lapse into theological unbelief. Precisely such a challenge now confronts the people of God called Southern Baptists." The opening sentences declare that the new fundamentalist leaders of the SBC are champions of historic Baptist beliefs, and that to resist their leadership will be tantamount to losing one's Christian faith. Despite the obvious duplicity and falseness of such conclusions, this theme is woven throughout the entire document.

The second paragraph states, "We must also pass on to the rising generation the fundamentals of the Christian faith and a vital sense of our Baptist heritage . . . toward a new consensus rooted in theological substance and doctrinal fidelity."

Several paragraphs later, the document states: "We seek to clarify our historic Baptist commitment to Holy Scripture . . . affirm our commitment to these great theological tenets since they are assailed, in various ways, by subtle compromise, blatant concession, and malign negligence." In truth, some Southern Baptists do twist and distort Scripture in a very liberal manner. However, few have distorted Scripture more than have the current fundamentalist leaders of the SBC.

The Theological Study Committee document simply reveals that it is more propaganda than substance. A faltering attempt is made to uphold inerrancy as the historic Southern Baptist position on biblical authority, but only one SBC leader prior to 1979 is quoted as using the word "inerrancy" in his description of the Bible. In truth, few national Southern Baptist leaders prior to 1979 used the term inerrancy to describe their view of Scripture.

The document is simply an effort to give a formal blessing upon the new direction and leadership of the SBC. Although there is some theological substance in the document, the numerous half-truths and innuendos therein reveal it to be a pathetic attempt to revise Southern Baptist history to suit the personal preference of those now in control of the SBC. In this document, the Bible itself takes a backseat to human opinions.

Tragically, one of the greatest casualties of the fundamentalist takeover of the SBC has been the Holy Bible. Fundamentalist leaders are not content to let the Bible speak for itself, but are bent on forcing their humanistic understandings, based on personal opinions, upon Scripture. To compound this atrocity, they have cloaked themselves in a false understanding of Baptist heritage and doctrine, all the while seeking to force this deceptive agenda upon the Southern Baptist populace.

In the world of Christendom, some doctrines are crucial and unchanging. However, when Christian leaders build upon the basics of the Christian faith and began devising their own personal doctrines regarding Scripture and imposing them by force upon others (whether the doctrines themselves have merit or not), they are in danger of likening themselves unto gods. Likewise, when the Bible is upheld as a perfect written entity in and of itself, it is in danger of becoming a god.

Most Christians in this world have good intentions. However, good intentions are meaningless in the Christian life if one's personal agenda is self-centered as opposed to God-centered. Doubtless, many may have trouble distinguishing between a self-centered agenda and a God-centered agenda. However, God's agenda is found in the Bible. Scripture speaks for itself. It is not always easy to understand in its minute details, but it is not designed for us to impose our humanistic understandings over it. Indeed, when the Bible is reduced to modern human formulas that claim to answer all questions, Scripture takes a backseat to humanistic whims, and God's agenda is trampled underneath the feet of human agendas.

CHAPTER EIGHT

The Political God

Baptists and Southern Baptists have historically championed religious liberty and the separation of church and state. Having been severely persecuted at the hands of a state-controlled church, Baptists have worked ardently to make certain that federal and state governments do not officially sanction one religion over against another.

The fervor with which Southern Baptists have championed the principle of the separation of church and state has somewhat dissipated within Southern Baptist Convention life, however. As Southern Baptists moved from a persecuted minority to the religious majority within their region, they became the establishment, as opposed to the outcasts. As long as the leadership of the SBC remained in the hands of mainline conservative-moderates, Southern Baptists, mindful of their days of persecution, continued to take the strong stance that church and state should remain as separate entities. The current fundamentalist leadership, however, has seemingly forgotten Baptist persecution of long ago, as they now seek to politically exert their influence not only over the SBC, but also over the United States government and other religions, to the point that their heavy-handedness is moving ever closer into the realm of persecution of others.

In years past, the SBC, under the control of mainline conservatives and moderates, had, at times, been involved in secular politics, but was typically not the victim of organized political activity expressly designed to speak for and lead Southern Baptists as a whole in a particular direction in regards to theological and/or political ideology. Individual Southern Baptists were oftentimes involved with secular politics, however.

The Protestant fundamentalist movement of the 1920s, which included a small minority of Southern Baptists, sought to force some state governments to sanction and mandate the fundamentalist view, shared by many Southern Baptists who did not use the term fundamentalist, that the teaching of evolution was wrong, immoral, and unbiblical. These early fundamentalists tried to convince the government that only biblical creation should be taught in public school classrooms.

Although the SBC leaders did not go along with these efforts of the fundamentalist faction, this was an example of some individual Southern Baptists seeking to use the vehicle of secular politics to achieve "spiritual" ends. This effort to force the secular government to impose (that is, mandate) a particular theological viewpoint upon the general populace was in direct violation of the Baptist principle of separation of church and state, a principle which was designed to keep any religious group from forcing its theological opinions upon all others (as the Puritans had previously done to Baptists).

Although prayer and Bible reading had long been popular in our nation's public school systems, such activities were not "mandated" by the federal or state governments, although these activities oftentimes received encouragement and approval from the government. The school system of that day and prior was thus partially "Christianized," despite the existence of the First Amendment. Many Protestant Christians had come to feel that they, in effect, owned exclusive rights to the nation's public school system.

In the late 1920s, many Southern Baptists, on both the national and local level, crusaded against United States presidential candidate Governor Albert Smith, who was running for office on an anti-prohibition platform. The anti-Smith campaign, which cut across denominational lines, was presented primarily as a moral crusade, rather than a theological battle.

Likewise, in the late 1950s, many Southern Baptists on the local level banded together in an effort to defeat presidential candidate John F. Kennedy, whom they opposed because of his Roman Catholicism. The anti-Catholic mind-set of many Southern Baptists was the driving force behind this foray into national secular politics.

In the early 1960s, the SBC went on record as supporting the Supreme Court's decision to ban government-sponsored (that is, government-approved) prayer in public schools. Southern Baptists, led by mainline conservatives and moderates, declared that government-sponsored prayers both infringed upon the religious liberty of those religious groups who were not represented in the prayers, and cheapened prayer by making it no more than general, formal utterances. In this instance, the SBC was speaking out for the long-held Baptist belief in the separation of church and state. This stance was an affirmation that government had no right to show favor to one particular religion over against another. In essence, it reinforced the Baptist belief that secular governmental politics should not impose upon religious practice by favoring one religion over against others.

In regards to the Supreme Court decision on prayer, some Christians at that time and later have charged that God has been taken out of the public schools. Indeed, the move away from open Christian prayer approved (albeit tacitly) by the government served to lead many Christians into believing that they had lost control over the nation's public school systems. In truth, Christians did lose, through this process, the favored status they had had within the public school system. However, Southern Baptist leadership of that time rightly pointed out that neither God nor prayer could be taken out of the public school system, since God was not constricted by legislation, and those students who so desired were (and are) free to pray in school whenever they chose to do so.[1]

In the 1970s, Jimmy Carter, a Southern Baptist layman from Georgia, ran for the presidency of the United States. He received much support from individual Southern Baptists in his successful bid for the oval office. During his term in office, he openly worked with Southern Baptist leaders to help further advance Southern Baptist mission efforts.[2] Carter, however, did not seek to use his presidential powers to show political favoritism to any particular ideology or theology within Southern Baptist life.

In effect, individual Southern Baptists, like other American citizens, have historically taken personal interest in politics insofar as they have sought to support candidates and policies which they deemed in agreement with their civil and/or Christian beliefs. Until recent years, however, the SBC has not actively sought to align itself with a particular party within secular politics.

The late 1970s marked a turning point in the interaction between politics and the SBC as fundamentalist Southern Baptists, long a minority in Southern Baptist life, turned to internal politics in their effort to gain control of the SBC. The beginning of the fundamentalist siege of the SBC marked the first time in Southern Baptist history that a particular group in Southern Baptist life turned to organized, political machinery in an effort to gain control of the SBC for the express purpose of forcing their personal theological ideology upon the Convention.

At the same time, leading Southern Baptist fundamentalists were aligning themselves with the Republican Party on the national American political scene. By the time fundamentalists had secured control of the SBC in the 1980s, they had successfully secured the help of secular political leaders in the Republican Party to help push forward their fundamentalist moral-religious agenda upon the whole of America. By the end of the 1980s, flush with their victory over the SBC and having gained considerable influence within the Republican Party, a number of the SBC fundamentalist leaders had developed ties with advocates of "Reconstructionism," the espousal of a complete overthrow of democracy and installation of a government based on literal Old Testament laws ("theocracy"), as outlined largely in the book of Deuteronomy.

In one decade, the long-held Baptist emphasis on separation of church and state had, for all practical purposes, been undermined by the new fundamentalist leadership who had gained control of the SBC by astute political maneuvering in a manner never before witnessed in Southern Baptist life. The swift and thorough success of the minority fundamentalist faction within SBC life and on the national, secular political scene was testimony to their political skill and acumen. However, the anti-Baptistic political tactics which the fundamentalists employed have left the SBC reeling.

AN UNETHICAL GOD

During the 1970s, the small fundamentalist faction within the SBC was hungrily eyeing the agencies of the Convention. Paul Pressler, a fundamentalist Baptist and Texas judge, spent many years analyzing the structure of the SBC, seeking to find an Achilles' heel. He discovered the weak point of the Convention—the appointive powers of the presidency—in the 1970s, and in early 1979 put his plan into action as he stumped around the country speaking to groups of fundamentalist Southern Baptists and enlisting them as infantrymen in a crusade to change the course of the SBC to an ultraconservative direction.[3]

The initial battle cry of the fundamentalist crusaders, under the leadership of Pressler and Paige Patterson, then president of Criswell Center for Biblical Studies in Dallas, Texas, was loud proclamations of "liberalism" in Southern Baptist seminaries.[4] Since that time, dozens of professors have been "forced" into early retirement and hounded from their positions. However, it should be noted that as of this date, the fundamentalist leadership, despite oft-repeated charges, has not fired a single Southern Baptist seminary professor on the charge of liberalism, despite the fact that fundamentalists have been on a liberal "witch-hunt" during the last fifteen years.[5] This fact alone demonstrates the empty charges and duplicity of the leaders of the fundamentalist faction.

By June of 1979, it was well known that Pressler and Patterson had been working hard to muster voter support for a fundamentalist assault upon the SBC. The Pressler-Patterson faction, months prior to the Convention, fervently began circulating charges of liberalism in SBC seminaries, while announcing their intention to see that the next president of the SBC be an inerrantist. At this time, inerrancy was not a well-known term in Southern Baptist life.

During the pre-Convention meetings, Pressler, Patterson, and well-known Southern Baptist fundamentalists W. A. Criswell, pastor of First Baptist Church, Dallas, Texas, and Adrian Rogers, pastor of Bellevue Baptist Church in Memphis, Tennessee, along with others, turned up the heat in their accusations of liberalism and their championing of inerrancy. SBC leaders, sensing trouble brewing, made pleas for unity. When the votes were tallied, however, Rogers, the handpicked candidate of the Pressler-Patterson faction, won the SBC presidency. In all likelihood, his personal popularity (he was well known around the SBC as a good preacher) assisted his winning the presidency. The Pressler-Patterson faction had their man in office, and they never looked back.

The 1979 annual SBC meeting set the stage for the years to come. Pressler, having been charged with political strategizing to control the outcome of the meeting, adamantly denied putting together an "organized effort" to get his agenda pushed through the 1979 Convention. The messengers attending the Convention were not fooled, however, and passed a resolution, aimed at the Pressler-Patterson faction, deploring overt political activity in regards to pushing a particular ideological agenda. Pressler once again denied any political actions. However, Porter Routh, chief executive officer of the SBC Executive Committee for more than a quarter-century, openly voiced his concern about the "methodology of a secular political machine" used at the Convention. Lee Porter, registration secretary, noted that many messengers had been bused in by the Pressler-Patterson forces in what he called an unprecedented "get-out-the-vote" effort.

An even darker side of the Pressler-Patterson politicking machine was revealed during the 1979 Convention. Rogers won the election by only 163 votes, and his victory will always be clouded against the backdrop of numerous voting discrepancies and irregularities. In the fundamentalist get-out-the-vote drive, ethics were by and large thrown out the window. Some churches registered more than their legal limit of messengers. Some pastors registered for their full allotted number of church members even though the members were not in attendance. Some messengers registered themselves twice. One pastor admitted to registering for his entire family, including his children, even though they were not present. One messenger personally marked eleven presidential ballots and turned in all of them, and Paul Pressler himself was illegally registered as a messenger.[6] If the truth were known, Rogers may not have actually won the presidency. In any case, organized politicking of an unethical nature had suddenly surfaced in SBC life, and the Convention would forever be affected by this new and sinister development.

The fundamentalist political machine was in motion, and nothing, it would turn out, could stop the machine, as fundamentalists would win every presidential election through 1995. Each fundamentalist president named only individuals who toed the party line to positions on agency trustee boards and committees. They refused to accept any compromise in their crusade to capture the SBC.

In 1982, fundamentalist James T. Draper, Jr., was elected to the SBC presidency. He promptly declared, "God wanted me to be president of the Southern Baptist Convention." When long-time SBC leaders presented a motion to depoliticize the position of the president, Draper would not hear of such an idea. Instead, he declared that he was seeking to be a peacemaker in the midst of the controversy, and sounded as if he wanted to make overtures to the majority mainline conservative-moderates. However, his actions betrayed his words, as he refused to appoint mainline conservative-moderates to positions of leadership.[7]

The political maneuvering continued. Mainline conservatives and moderates began recognizing the fundamentalist machinery as just that. In 1984 Southwestern Seminary president Russell Dilday warned of "a powerful machine, computerized, national in scope and aimed at control of the democratic processes of this convention." That same year, Roy Honeycutt, president of Southern Seminary, revealed that fundamentalists were trying to tear down Southern by enlisting "campus subversives" and trying to entice students as spies.

By 1985 some mainline conservatives and moderates, recognizing the seriousness of the fundamentalist assault, were themselves involved in political maneuvering in an effort to break the fundamentalist stranglehold. Both factions were busing in messengers by this point. Fundamentalists continued firing volleys at Southern Baptist seminaries, charging rampant liberalism. Baptist Press, the news agency of Southern Baptists, was also attacked as being slanted against the fundamentalist agenda.

Once again, the fundamentalists emerged with the upper hand as they won the presidential convention behind candidate Charles Stanley. And once again, they continued to throw ethics out the window in the heat of their political conquest. Lee Porter, registration secretary, noted that he had received "numerous" reports of bogus ballots being distributed outside the Convention center before the session began.[8] Furthermore, when mainline conservatives and moderates managed to turn back fundamentalist nominations to key posts, Charles Stanley abused his presidential power by deviating from standard, clearly defined procedure and violating the bylaws of the Convention in brushing aside this small victory which the mainline conservatives and moderates had rightly won.[9] Several conservative-moderates subsequently sued the SBC over these violations when the SBC Executive Committee refused to reverse Stanley's faulty rulings.[10] Although those who filed suit had a concrete basis for their accusations, in May 1986, a U.S. district judge sided with the SBC, stating that secular courts had no jurisdiction over internal church matters.[11]

By 1990, through their continued heavy-handed, less-than-ethical political agenda, the fundamentalists had largely won control of the SBC. Although mainline conservative and moderate leaders pointed out that God surely had not been honored through such deception, dishonesty, rigidity, and downright arrogance on the part of fundamentalist leaders, they were nonetheless outcasts, having been pushed out of the SBC by the "secular political machine" that Porter Routh had warned of a decade earlier.

Fundamentalist James T. Draper, commenting on the ruthlessness of fundamentalists before he pitched his tent in their camp, noted that the fundamentalist "feels he has a corner on truth and the rest of the Christian world is groping in error . . . uses the Bible as a club with which to beat people over the head, rather than a means of personal strength and a revealer of God . . . is virtually always negative and condemning." Draper also noted that fundamentalists are intolerant of others' opinions to the point of writing them off as "sinister and heretical." Fundamentalists, according to Draper, are bigots, prejudiced, unfair, and unfamiliar with love and compassion. Furthermore, they display "hatred, bitterness and condemnation" towards those whom they do not like.[12] One is left to wonder how Draper could have been lured into becoming part of the very group that he so strongly condemned.

The tactics and the mind-set of the "secular political machine" which fundamentalists employed in their takeover of the SBC are easy to discern to anyone who is willing to open his or her eyes. The origins of the tactics used by the fundamentalists are equally clear to theologian Clark Pinnock, who, while yet an avowed inerrantist, declared that the fundamentalist takeover "causes me to wonder—has the Enemy cooked up this fight among God's people to try and prevent them [from] posing the threat to his dark kingdom which this great denomination does, in fact, represent when it is united?"[13]

A FALWELLIAN GOD

Following the withdrawal of J. Frank Norris from Southern Baptist life in the 1930s, fundamentalist Baptist churches, including some former SBC churches, began coming together to form their own fundamentalist conventions. In 1950 the largest of these groups, the Baptist Bible Fellowship, was formed. Today, it has some three million members within its churches.

In the 1960s, as the United States was in the midst of the civil rights struggle, a rising star in the Baptist Bible Fellowship condemned Christian involvement in secular politics. His name was Jerry Falwell.

By the late 1970s, however, Falwell had changed his mind about politics. Partly in response to what he perceived as Jimmy Carter's liberalism, Falwell launched the now famous Moral Majority, an organization dedicated to using the secular political arena as an avenue to force fundamentalist Christian beliefs upon the entire nation.

By the time he launched the Moral Majority, questions existed about his integrity. In 1973 the U.S. Securities and Exchange Commission charged Falwell's church with "fraud and deceit" in the issuance of $6.5 million worth of unsecured church bonds. The court eventually had to place the church's finances under the control of five businessmen handpicked by the court. Falwell has also long been accused of soliciting funds under the guise of raising money to feed starving children in third-world countries, then turning around and using the money for other purposes. For example, his "Liberty Missionary Society," which was launched about the time of the founding of the Moral Majority, appealed for funds to help "thousands upon thousands of small children . . . dying from starvation and malnutrition in refugee camps around the world. . . ." Falwell qualified his soliciting, noting that feeding starving children in refugee camps was only one of several projects to which money raised would be applied. He seemed to spell out his intent when he declared that ministering to starving people required feeding them first. However, when the projected $2 million budget for the Missionary Society was published, not one penny was earmarked for buying food for starving children or adults, while almost twenty-five percent of the budget was dedicated to construction projects at Falwell's Liberty College.[14]

The year 1979 marked three very significant events for both Falwell and Southern Baptist fundamentalists. The Moral Majority was founded, and Southern Baptist fundamentalists began their unprecedented political crusade to wrest control of the SBC from mainline conservatives and moderates. These two events were melded together by the fact that Charles Stanley, a leading Southern Baptist fundamentalist, pitched his tent with Falwell by becoming Falwell's partner in founding the Moral Majority. This third significant event would prove to have profound, lasting implications for the SBC

Stanley himself had been an independent, fundamentalist Baptist for much of the 1970s. By the late 1970s, he had ascended to the pastorate of First Baptist Church of Atlanta, a nominal Southern Baptist church. His leadership soon brought controversy to the congregation, resulting in the exodus of several hundred church members. Nevertheless, Stanley prospered in Atlanta, partially because of the successful television ministry which he had developed, following in the footsteps of Falwell's highly successful television ministry. In light of his background, it was certainly no surprise that Stanley teamed up with Falwell in the formation of the Moral Majority.[15]

Thus, as the fundamentalist takeover of the SBC began, Falwell was not only sympathetic with Southern Baptist fundamentalists; he was in cohorts with them—or perhaps vice versa. Joe Barnhart declared that "Southern Baptist fundamentalists have followed Jerry Falwell's politics and interpretation of Scripture almost blindly."[16] One study done in 1981 revealed that Falwell, thanks to his television programs, was the most popular preacher among Baptists in eighteen states. His call for "old-time religion" made an impression on many Southern Baptists. He incessantly pitched his newly founded Moral Majority and his fundamentalist, right-wing political stance through his television programs, and they made an impact upon many of those individuals in SBC life who tended toward fundamentalism.[17]

Southern Baptist fundamentalist leaders were certainly aware of Falwell's grassroots appeal to some Southern Baptists.

Southern Baptist fundamentalist leaders and Jerry Falwell worked hand-in-hand during the early years of the controversy, although they did so rather discreetly at first. By 1985, however, with victory in sight, SBC fundamentalist leaders became more open about their ties with Falwell. Charles Stanley, close cohort of Falwell, was running for the SBC presidency in 1985. Falwell openly endorsed Stanley, warning that the SBC would split if Stanley did not win the election.[18]

By this point, Falwell was becoming a regular speaker at evangelism conferences sponsored by Southern Baptist fundamentalists. He also began running feature articles on SBC fundamentalists in his independent *Fundamentalist Journal*. Furthermore, by this time, the vast majority of Southern Baptist self-identified fundamentalists were of the opinion that Falwell's Moral Majority was a good organization which was standing up for Christian principles in the secular political arena. Interestingly enough, the minority fundamentalist faction in SBC life was almost unanimously united around the platform of a personality who was characterized by questionable ethics and heavy secular political involvement.[19]

Even as Falwell was openly becoming the "outside" leader and hero of the Southern Baptist fundamentalist movement, he denied any intention to merge the Moral Majority with the SBC.[20] Nevertheless, mainline conservative and moderate Southern Baptists were fearful of some attempt to bring Falwell into the SBC fold. Their fears were confirmed when, in 1988, current fundamentalist SBC president Jerry Vines announced that he liked Jerry Falwell so much that if he lived in Virginia, he would attend Thomas Road Baptist Church (Falwell's church). Thomas Road is an independent Baptist church, and Vines' remarks caused no little furor. Vines' stated preference for an independent Baptist church over against a Southern Baptist church while he occupied the presidency of the SBC sent chills through mainline SBC conservatives and moderates.[21]

By now, Southern Baptist fundamentalist leaders were unabashedly working alongside Falwell. Bailey Smith, fundamentalist and former SBC president, declared that he liked Falwell because the independent Baptist had the right enemies (referring to mainline conservatives and moderates, whom they considered to be liberals). In 1989, speaking at the SBC Evangelism Conference, Falwell declared that the SBC was "the hope of Bible-believing Christians everywhere." Falwell and SBC fundamentalist leaders were united for the common cause of turning the SBC into a fundamentalist body.[22]

In the summer of 1990, after another presidential loss, mainline conservative and moderate Southern Baptists by and large turned away from trying to regain control of the SBC. The fundamentalist victory over the SBC had been sealed. In October 1993, H. Edwin Young, recent fundamentalist president of the SBC, and Jerry Falwell cohosted a Bible conference, called "Building Bridges to Bible-Believing Churches and to a Lost World," at Montrose Baptist Church in Rockville, Maryland. Young skipped the inauguration of fundamentalist Jerry Rankin to the position of Foreign Mission Board president, the first fundamentalist elected to that crucial position, in order to co-host the Bible conference with Falwell.

Following the two-day meeting, Falwell declared that more cooperative efforts, such as Bible conferences and crusades, were ahead for independent fundamentalist Baptists and Southern Baptists. Then Falwell made a stunning but not unexpected announcement: "I would say we're a couple of years away . . . but I don't think there's any question that we're heading toward some major mergers that will probably surprise a lot of people." According to Falwell, he and Southern Baptist fundamentalist leaders were already making plans that were leading to a merger. Paige Patterson recently declared, "We keep on hoping and praying that Uncle Jerry will come our way." Perhaps not insignificantly, in 1994 at least seven of the thirty-five trustees of Falwell's Liberty University were prominent Southern Baptist fundamentalists, including Bailey Smith and Jerry Vines, former SBC fundamentalist presidents.[23]

Many mainline conservative and moderate Southern Baptists are horrified at the thought of merging with Jerry Falwell's independent Baptists. Yet, such a merger may be only a matter of time—and a short period of time at that. The fundamentalist leadership of the SBC has already distorted and twisted what it means to be a Southern Baptist. Now they appear ready to virtually do away with any semblance of Southern Baptist identity in order to fully implement their fundamentalist agenda. It may not be too far off base to charge that Southern Baptist fundamentalist leaders have turned their allegiance to a Falwellian god.

A REPUBLICAN GOD

Another very significant event which occurred near the beginning of the fundamentalist effort to capture the SBC was the 1980 election of Ronald Reagan as president of the United States. Fundamentalist (and many conservative) Christians, led by the newly formed Moral Majority, united behind presidential candidate Ronald Reagan during his campaign. In the election, many conservative Southern Baptists joined fundamentalists in abandoning their support of fellow Southern Baptist Jimmy Carter, whom they had come to view as a liberal. They accused Carter, who was a faithful churchgoer and lay leader, and who had greatly helped Southern Baptist mission efforts, of quoting from unacceptable Christian theologians, being a social drinker (ironically, the fundamentalists supported Bush in 1988 and 1992, despite the fact that he drank alcoholic beverages on more than just social occasions), and of promoting liberal political policies.[24] Southern Baptist fundamentalists switched loyalty to Reagan, a divorced, non-Baptist Christian who was not a regular churchgoer during his presidency, and who will long be remembered for his lack of integrity.

Reagan, in fact, courted fundamentalist Christians during his campaign. This wooing on the part of Reagan led Southern Baptist fundamentalists into getting involved in partisan politics as never before.[25] Reagan tailored his message to appeal to fundamentalist Christians who were concerned about a society which they believed to be in moral bankruptcy. Many fundamentalists, and not a few conservatives, took the bait—hook, line, and sinker.

Following the election of Reagan, fundamentalists further allied themselves to Reagan and the Republican Party by buying wholesale into Reagan's policies. Reagan, in turn, seemed, at least, to champion certain causes which were in line with the fundamentalist agenda of a moral cleansing of America. The fundamentalists believed they had found a powerful ally (indeed, the most powerful human ally) for the part of their agenda which had to do with moral purging. They believed Reagan to be one of them, although some political analysts believed Reagan was trying to simply keep their votes more than anything else. In any case, not long after Reagan's election, fundamentalist television evangelists, such as Jerry Falwell and Pat Robertson, were packaging the Republican right-wing party line in the name of Christianity, in effect blurring the lines between secular right-wing politics and Christianity.[26] Under Reagan, a civil religious movement was suddenly under way in America.

The Religious Right, which included many Southern Baptist fundamentalists, soon mirrored Reagan's policies in its stated agenda. In 1982 Reagan stated that he was opposed to abortion with no exceptions. Almost immediately, Southern Baptist fundamentalist leaders turned their attention to abortion and began trying to lead the SBC to take a stronger stance against abortion (at this point, SBC messengers had previously reaffirmed resolutions opposing abortion in principle, but acknowledging that there were a few legitimate reasons for some abortions to be performed).

Also in 1982, Reagan announced his intention to present a constitutional amendment which would bring government-sponsored prayers back into public schools. The Baptist Joint Committee and many mainline conservative and moderate Southern Baptists quickly voiced opposition to the proposed amendment, citing the long-held Baptist view of separation of church and state.

Southern Baptist fundamentalists, however, embraced Reagan's prayer proposal. In fact, Reagan invited Southern Baptist fundamentalist architect Paul Pressler, Southern Baptist religious right activist Ed McAteer, and

Dorothy Patterson (wife of Southern Baptist fundamentalist ringleader Paige Patterson) to a White House ceremony concerning the proposed prayer amendment.

What followed this White House caucus was something unprecedented in Southern Baptist history. Fundamentalists quickly began preparing to bring the prayer issue before the annual SBC meeting in New Orleans. When Pressler was asked if he was orchestrating such a move at the New Orleans Convention, he quickly denied any such plans: "I have no agenda— I never have." Pressler, like many other fundamentalist leaders, was becoming well known for his tendency to publicly deny his true intentions.

During the Convention that year, a fundamentalist-supported amendment asking SBC messengers to go on record as supporting Reagan's proposed prayer amendment was passed. A month later, the White House acknowledged that Reagan staffers had worked with Southern Baptist fundamentalists to push the amendment through SBC committees and have it passed on the floor of the Convention. Morton C. Blackwell, a Reagan special assistant, had been appointed to work with Ed McAteer, a Southern Baptist fundamentalist who was a leader of the newly emerged Religious Right, to formulate strategy and ensure implementation of the Southern Baptist amendment supporting Reagan's proposal. In other words, the Reagan administration directly helped SBC fundamentalists in leading Southern Baptist messengers at the annual Convention to voice support for Reagan's policies. Never before had Southern Baptist leaders allowed a sitting United States president to orchestrate the political direction of the SBC.

Shortly thereafter, Southern Baptist fundamentalists returned the favor to Reagan when Ed McAteer and Pat Robertson voiced support for the constitutional prayer amendment before the Senate Judiciary Committee. The Reagan administration and Southern Baptist fundamentalist leaders were clearly in cohorts, and mainline conservatives and moderates were understandably worried about the future of the separation of church and state.[27]

In 1984 Ronald Reagan was up for reelection, and once again fundamentalist Southern Baptist leaders made unprecedented voyages into the realm of secular politics. They, along with other fundamentalist Christian leaders, moved into an arena that had previously been the domain of the secular government—the registration of new voters. In many cases, local fundamentalist churches provided voter registration forms in the church, and took up the forms in their offering plates. The intent was to register individuals who would vote for Republican candidates, whom fundamentalists portrayed as representing "traditional family values." Ronald Reagan endorsed these efforts. Fundamentalist James Draper hosted a reception for Republican presidential hopeful Pat Robertson during the 1987 annual SBC meeting.[28]

In 1985, during the fundamentalist-controlled Pastors' Conference prior to the annual SBC meeting, the air was filled with patriotism as preachers proclaimed the need for a spiritual and moral revival. An enormous American flag was stretched across the speaker's platform. In the midst of the festivities, a message of greeting was read from the Reagans. In 1986, following the fundamentalist victory in that year's presidential election at the annual SBC, a letter from president Reagan was read to the messengers. In the letter, Reagan commended Southern Baptist fundamentalists, declaring his support for the new fundamentalist direction of the SBC.[29]

Southern Baptist fundamentalists continued their cozy relationship with the Republican administration as Reagan handed the reins over to George Bush in 1988. Paul Pressler reputedly had had family connections with Bush for many years. In 1982 Bush had spoken at the SBC Pastors' Conference prior to the Convention, urging Southern Baptists to support the newly formed Religious Right.[30] Southern Baptist fundamentalists supported Bush in the presidential elections of 1988 and 1992.

By the late 1980s, fundamentalists had largely succeeded in shaping the Christian Life Commission into an agency which mirrored Republican right-wing policies, something unprecedented in Southern Baptist life. New fundamentalist Christian Life Commission (CLC) director Richard Land was a former staff advisor to Republican Governor Bill Clements of Texas. Some fundamentalist leaders within the CLC actually opposed Land as being "too political." Furthermore, under Land's directorship, the CLC began touting the Religious Right's claim that Thomas Jefferson never intended for the First Amendment to be construed as being a "wall of separation" between church and state. The CLC has apparently ignored the fact that Jefferson himself clearly used those very words to describe the First Amendment, and that such was the view of the early Baptists who ardently campaigned to have church and state separated—because they had suffered intense persecution at the hands of a state church.[31]

Further indicative of the Republican influence within the CLC was the 1989 hiring of a full-time CLC employee stationed in Washington, D.C., to help direct the right-wing agenda of the agency. The employee so hired had previously been a full-time employee of the United States House of Representatives Republican Study Committee.[32]

Also in 1989, fundamentalist (and former Southern Baptist) Pat Robertson, following his unsuccessful bid for the United States presidency in the Republican primaries in 1988, formed the "Christian Coalition." The Christian Coalition has largely taken over where the now defunct Moral Majority left off. Robertson, whose questionable ethics in regards to the use of funds solicited for his various ministries have gotten him into trouble with the Internal Revenue Service on several occasions, has lined his Christian Coalition solidly behind the right-wing of the Republican Party. The Coalition, which supported Bush in 1992, actively seeks to get fundamentalist Christians elected to all manner of political posts—local, state, and national. The Coalition is well-known for its efforts to sneak candidates into office—"stealth campaigning"—through quiet, undercover political maneuvering. Coalition-supported candidates virtually always run on Republican tickets.[33]

In 1992 SBC president H. Edwin Young and former SBC president Adrian Rogers openly supported the Christian Coalition's distribution of some forty million copies of the "Christian Coalition Family Values Voter Guide" to fundamentalist and conservative churches and individuals across the nation. Although the voter guide stated it was "non-partisan" in nature, it was designed to lead readers to vote for Bush. The Democratic Party loudly denounced this so-called "non-partisan" voting guide.[34]

Many will also remember the prominent role Christian fundamentalists played in the Republican Convention of 1992. Furthermore, in 1992 SBC president Morris Chapman invited Vice-President Dan Quayle to address the annual SBC meeting, in what amounted to an election rally for Bush and Quayle.[35]

Not surprisingly, George Bush's defeat in the 1992 presidential election did not sit well with the Christian Coalition. With the White House solidly in the hands of the Democratic Party at that point, some long-time political observers believed the Christian Coalition had become even more galvanized in its determination to work from within the Republican Party to force the nation to bow down to their vision for a "moral" America. When Republicans gained control of both houses of Congress in the 1994 elections, the Religious Right, including the fundamentalist leaders of the SBC, quickly embraced the goals and agenda of the Republican Congress, and—for all practical purposes—elevated House Speaker Newt Gingrich, a Southern Baptist congressman of harsh words and questionable integrity, to the status of hero.

Southern Baptists, like all other American citizens, have a responsibility to vote their conscience in national political elections. Nevertheless, in the past, the SBC had not actively attempted to recruit a particular national political party to aid it in championing a certain ideology within Southern Baptist life, nor had it attempted to use a particular national political party to force a narrow-minded theological ideology upon the general American populace.

Now, however, many current Southern Baptist fundamentalist leaders are actively seeking to use political means to control the theological ideology of both the SBC and the United States of America. In effect, Christian fundamentalists, who once shunned secular politics, are now attempting to use secular politics to enact their agenda not only within their churches, but within the nation as a whole. Many Southern Baptist fundamentalists have turned their back on Baptist heritage and have boarded this bandwagon.

Wayne Flynt, head of the history department of Auburn University and a specialist in southern history and religion, noted that it is "difficult now to distinguish between Southern Baptist leadership and the right-wing of the Republican Party."[36]

A RECONSTRUCTIONIST GOD

A growing movement within the Religious Right advocates the removal of the democratic system in America and the replacing of democracy with theocracy—that is, a national government based on the laws of God as outlined in the Old Testament. This movement is known as the Reconstructionist movement, and a number of Christian fundamentalist organizations advocate Reconstructionism. Several are dedicated to implementing theocracy in America.

The Institute for Christian Economics, based in Tyler, Texas, is the foremost organization dedicated to the implementation of theocracy in America. Headed by Gary North, the institute publishes books and seeks to positively promote the Reconstructionist view. Yet, there is not much positiveness about the type of government North and his institute want to see implemented in America. If North and his fellow Reconstructionists were to have their way, democracy would be abolished in favor of a theocratic government based on Old Testament laws. Government would enforce laws which would be overtly religiously based. Many offenses, ranging from blasphemy to homosexuality to adultery, would be grounds for the death penalty. The government Christian Reconstructionists claim to want would be based on fear, as opposed to the grace and love of God.[37]

Christian Reconstructionists represent the far extremes of Christian fundamentalists. Only a small percentage of fundamentalists openly espouse such views. Nevertheless, the movement is gaining momentum among fundamentalists, including Southern Baptist fundamentalists.

Paul Pressler, architect of the Southern Baptist fundamentalist movement, has indicated an openness to Christian Reconstructionism. In 1985 or 1986, he gave an interview to Gary North, the leading Christian Reconstructionist in the country. In this interview, which came to be known as the "Firestorm Chats," Pressler openly revealed how he had plotted to wrest control of the SBC from mainline conservatives and moderates.[38] Pressler's association with North in regards to this interview, as well as the gloating nature of Pressler's remarks about the fundamentalist triumph in the SBC, bodes ill in the eyes of mainline conservative and moderate leaders.

In 1988, prior to the SBC meeting in San Antonio, fundamentalist leaders, as was their custom, were busy making attacks upon the "liberals" (that is, all those who did not agree with them) who were opposing their agenda. In the midst of this mudslinging, Winfred Moore, the conservative-moderate candidate for the SBC presidency in 1988, joined the fracas by distributing a brochure linking Paige Patterson, Pressler, and other Southern Baptist fundamentalist leaders to Christian Reconstructionism.[39] Although fundamentalist leaders to this day have not openly identified themselves with Christian Reconstructionism, there is concern among mainline conservative and moderate Southern Baptist leaders that more and more fundamentalists are sympathetic to this extremist movement.

Pat Robertson, fundamentalist and former nominal Southern Baptist, ran for the presidency of the United States in 1988 with the support of present Sunday School Board president and former SBC president James T. Draper.[40] Robertson owns and operates Regent University, which he proudly touts as the nation's "only accredited, Bible-based law school." A number of Regent professors are openly involved with the Christian Reconstructionism movement.[41]

One recent trend in a number of local Southern Baptist churches is the infiltration of the idea that the concept of the separation of church and state is a myth. Many Southern Baptist laity do not know much about Baptist history, and therefore may be unaware that Baptists have always steadfastly held to separation of church and state because of the horrendous persecution the earliest Baptists had to endure at the hands of church-controlled state governments in Europe and colonial America. The SBC Christian Life Commission is compounding this problem by seemingly denying the validity of the historical Baptist understanding of the concept of church and state.

One resource in current circulation which portrays the separation of church and state as a myth is a video entitled *The Myth of Separation*, by David Barton. Some Southern Baptists seem to have been taken in by Barton's glib video, which is comprised largely of half-truths, distortions, and simple lies. Those who may have been taken in by the video doubtless are unaware of Barton's shady background and his total lack of academic credentials in regards to either history or law. However, even more alarming are Barton's ties to the Christian Reconstructionist movement.[42]

The Christian Reconstructionist movement is a very dangerous, albeit behind-the-scenes, political movement which runs counter to the teachings of Christ and his gospel of forgiveness, grace, and love. It would be premature at this point to charge that current Southern Baptist fundamentalist leaders are wholesale advocates of this movement. However, it does appear that Christian Reconstructionism is making inroads into Southern Baptist life largely because of the fundamentalist agenda which has been forcefully imposed upon the SBC.

As the SBC moves beyond its 150th anniversary, it finds itself involved in secular politics as never before. Our Baptist forefathers, who suffered mightily at the hands of "Christian" state governments, would roll over in their graves if they knew of the secular political involvement of current SBC leadership. Likewise, the founders of the SBC would be horrified at how our current Convention has been torn apart by internal partisan politics structured along the lines of minutely "correct" theology and terminology.

Politics has most certainly been a part of the SBC over the years—any large organization such as the SBC is subject to some internal politicking. The SBC political structure, in years past, has been able to accommodate divergent viewpoints while maintaining a focused vision on missions, evangelism, and education. However, the fundamentalist onslaught upon the SBC which began in 1979 was an unprecedented attempt to use political means to force a narrow, minority ideology upon the SBC. Now that this new political ideology has become the status quo in SBC life, a new vision has emerged—a focus on discharging those individuals and discarding those practices and policies which do not toe the party line as espoused by the fundamentalist leadership. Missions, evangelism, and education have taken a back seat to the politics of theological and political correctness.

CHAPTER NINE

The Pharisaic God

The Gospels reveal that Jesus, while on earth, was constantly struggling with the Jewish religious leaders of that day. One of these religious groups which pitted itself against Jesus was the Pharisees, middle-class "laymen" who were committed to strict obedience to Jewish law. They were the Jewish ultraconservatives (or fundamentalists) of Jesus' day.

The Pharisees were organized into small brotherhoods or fellowships, and were related to the Jewish synagogues. In effect, the synagogue was a Pharisaic institution. The Pharisees were committed to obeying the Jewish law as interpreted by the scribes. The scribes, who were devoted to interpreting and applying the written law, produced a second body of law designed to complement the law as given by God in the Old Testament. The Pharisees were intent on obeying both the written law of God and the new law as interpreted by the scribes. Indeed, for practical purposes, the Pharisees were more devoted to the legalistic traditions of the scribes than to biblical law.

In the Gospels, Jesus criticized the Pharisees repeatedly. His criticisms were generally leveled against them in four areas: 1) their tendency to substitute their traditions for the revealed will of God, 2) their lack of compassion, 3) their contempt for the common people who did not obey the law as carefully as they did, and 4) their failure to practice what they preached. In other words, Jesus criticized the Pharisees for their legalism, unkindness, self-righteousness, and hypocrisy.[1] The Pharisees responded to Jesus' criticisms by having him crucified.

Today, "pharisaic" is a term sometimes used to describe Christians who reflect the same tendencies of the Pharisees of Jesus' day. Historically, the term has generally been used to refer to ultraconservative or fundamentalist Christians who are overly legalistic in their beliefs and practices.

In Baptist life, the ultraconservative leaders of the Campbellite and Landmarkist movements of the 1800s could accurately be referred to as "pharisaic." These individuals grabbed onto certain issues and viewpoints and proceeded to build rigid theological systems upon matters which were not of primary importance.

In the early twentieth century, Southern Baptist fundamentalist J. Frank Norris sought to transform the Southern Baptist Convention into a body which mirrored his own narrow, legalistic viewpoints and beliefs. Although Norris was eventually tossed out of SBC life, his influence is still alive today in the current SBC fundamentalist movement.

Within the context of mainstream Baptist and Southern Baptist life, Baptists have often been looked upon by other Christians as being legalistic—pharisaic, even—in regards to their strict adherence to certain moral codes. Many have long identified Baptists as Christians who do not drink, dance, or play cards. Indeed, some Baptists to this day, particularly those in rural areas, continue to disavow many social activities such as dancing, playing cards, and going to movies. Many Baptist schools of higher education still forbid dancing on campus. Such views can be traced back to the influence of the Second Great Awakening of the early 1800s.

These strict moral codes often associated with Baptists are only part of a larger picture. Historically, Baptists and Southern Baptist leaders have largely refused to be legalistic or pharisaic regarding theology. Baptists (with the exception of the fundamentalist Baptist bodies which have arisen this century) have shunned creedalism throughout their entire history, preferring to adopt various "confessions of faith" which serve as non-binding guidelines for Baptist faith and practice. The strong adherence to the concept of soul competency has kept the SBC from trying to impose conformity among Southern Baptist agencies, churches, and individuals—until recently.

The new fundamentalist leaders of the SBC have made no bones about their intention to forcefully impose rigid, legalistic theological viewpoints upon Southern Baptist agencies. There have even been recent decrees from fundamentalist leaders that those individual "liberal" Southern Baptists who do not believe as the fundamentalists do should leave the SBC.[2]

Most fundamentalists seem to conveniently ignore the fact that Jesus was a radical liberal in the Jewish religious world of his day. His liberal religious beliefs and practices eventually led the ultraconservative Pharisees to have him crucified. Some parallels between the Pharisees of Jesus' day and the current Southern Baptist fundamentalist leadership should raise warning flags among all Southern Baptists.

A LEGALISTIC GOD

In 1973 future Southern Baptist fundamentalist James T. Draper declared in explicit language that fundamentalists "stand condemned" by their "own dogma." The fundamentalist "has a strange mixture of biblical truth and traditions and customs. Like the Pharisees in Jesus' day, he preaches tradition and custom with the same vigor and authority as he does the written Word of God." Furthermore, in regards to theological legalism among fundamentalists, Draper noted that fundamentalists had no use for anyone who did not agree with their viewpoint.[3]

Ten years later, Draper, then an avowed fundamentalist, lived up to his own definition of fundamentalism as theological legalism. As SBC president, he made the unprecedented suggestion that the SBC issue creedal decrees. He advocated the stating of certain principles which Southern Baptists would be forced to subscribe to, or else leave the SBC. In effect, Draper believed that Southern Baptists should openly subscribe to his own fundamentalist beliefs. He was afraid that if parameters are not set, the people will be free to "believe anything they want." Draper, who once criticized fundamentalists for not allowing freedom of thought, is now himself trying to do away with freedom of thought.[4]

The 1987 decrees of the fundamentalist-dominated SBC Peace Committee were used effectively to bring theological legalism upon Southern Baptist agencies. Claiming that they spoke for the majority of Southern Baptists (despite the fact that they had not bothered to take a single survey), the fundamentalist majority on the Peace Committee declared that Southern Baptists believe in a literal Genesis creation account, the traditional authorship of biblical books, all biblical miracles as supernatural events, and the full historical reliability of historical narratives (down to the minute details) recorded in Scripture.[5]

The majority of Southern Baptists, in fact, do not agree with all of the above statements, although many do subscribe to them. Furthermore, a number of SBC fundamentalist leaders privately do not agree with their own Peace Committee declarations. Still, fundamentalists proceeded to force these particular legalistic interpretations upon SBC agencies. Such actions reflected more of an interest in traditional understandings of Scripture than in the Scripture itself, and subsequently hearkened back to the Pharisees of New Testament days.

Following the Peace Committee report, fundamentalists celebrated the fact that they had "settled the issue of the Bible."[6] In other words, they had successfully forced their own legalistic interpretations of Scripture upon the SBC under the false guise of speaking for the majority of Southern Baptists.

To go outside the parameters set by the current fundamentalist leadership is to incur the wrath of the fundamentalists. The Pharisees of Jesus' day were so legalistic in following their interpretation of the law that they would not minister to a sick man on the Sabbath. When Jesus had the audacity to defy them by performing just such an act, the Pharisees immediately began plotting to put Jesus to death (Mark 3:1-12).

Like the Pharisees of old, SBC fundamentalist leaders have set their own legalistic agenda based upon a particular interpretation of Scripture. For example, divorced individuals cannot be appointed as missionaries by the fundamentalist-controlled Home Mission Board.[7] While others are condemned for being divorced, fundamentalist superstars Charles Stanley and Joel Gregory, the former separated from his wife, the latter divorced, have largely been treated with kid gloves by their fundamentalist brethren.

The fundamentalist-controlled Foreign Mission Board broke a financial covenant with Rushlikon Baptist Seminary in 1991 when board trustees perceived that Rushlikon had stepped outside of acceptable theological boundaries. Trustee Joel Gregory had no reservations about breaking the sacred covenant the board had had with Rushlikon simply because the seminary did something which was outside of his legalistic parameters.[8]

Fundamentalist leaders are also dogmatic in their legalistic insistence that women should not be ordained into the ministry. Fundamentalist hero W. A. Criswell was asked, "What if a woman believes she has been called to minister?" Criswell replied, speaking for God: "Well, she has made a mistake."[9] It is indeed a tragic day in Southern Baptist life when a Southern Baptist leader presumes to know absolutely the very mind of God on such matters which are not clearly spelled out in Scripture.

Criswell's statements evidence the fact that fundamentalist leaders have gotten so wrapped up in their legalistic declarations that they have stripped God of his sovereignty and placed him in a little box of their own making. A god who cannot call a woman to ministry is not the all-powerful God. Yet, the fundamentalists have chosen a small, legalistic god over against the sovereign God. Furthermore, they are so intent on preserving their version of god that they will not let anyone sidetrack them.

As the Jewish Pharisees plotted and carried out a plan to kill Jesus because he stepped outside of their legalistic boundaries, so the current SBC fundamentalist leadership has spent the past seventeen years carrying out their agenda of purging SBC agencies of those employees who dared to openly oppose their legalistic personal beliefs. Could it be that many of the current fundamentalist leaders of the SBC serve the same small, legalistic, self-serving god which the Pharisees of two thousand years ago served? It might not be inaccurate to say that the fundamentalist leaders of the SBC have sacrificed their roles in the Kingdom of God on the altar of their own egos.

AN UNKIND GOD

The Gospels reveal to us that Jesus was a man of compassion. When the Pharisees caught a woman in the act of adultery, they were ready to kill her by stoning, in accordance with their interpretation of the law. Knowing of

Jesus' compassion, they brought the woman before him, seeking to entrap him into openly disobeying the law.

Jesus did indeed have compassion on the woman, refusing to condemn her. However, he did not play into the bloodthirsty Pharisees' hands. Rather, he put the burden of condemnation upon them, stating that whoever was without sin should go ahead and cast the first stone. The Pharisees, once cocky, slowly began to slink away into the night following Jesus' invitation and the words he slowly wrote in the dirt (John 8:1-11).

The current fundamentalist leadership of the SBC, like the Pharisees of Jesus' day, tend to have a lack of compassion when it comes to dealing with their own brothers and sisters in Christ who do not think as they do. Ironically, in the seventeenth and eighteenth centuries, the Puritans showed no compassion towards the upstart Baptists. Jail terms, whippings, and beatings were the ways in which Puritans dealt with Baptists. Now, one segment of the Southern Baptist family is busy persecuting those who do not agree with them. Verbal and political abuse have replaced physical abuse, but the effect is the same.

James Draper, before he joined the fundamentalist camp, noted that fundamentalists use the Bible "as a club with which to beat people over the head." Draper declared that fundamentalists are condemned for their bigotry, prejudice and unfairness. Furthermore, fundamentalists are unfamiliar with "love and compassion." Instead, their attitude is one of "hatred, bitterness and condemnation."[10] When Draper made these observations, he probably never suspected he would one day embrace the very group which he condemned.

In earlier years, the mainline conservative-moderate leaders of Southern Baptist life, although not openly embracing the mind-set of the minority fundamentalist faction within the SBC, accommodated the fundamentalists. Several, including W. A. Criswell, served as SBC president from the 1950s through the 1970s.

The current fundamentalist leaders, however, have displayed no desire to accommodate mainline conservative and moderate leaders, although these leaders represent the majority of Southern Baptists. In fact, fundamentalist SBC leaders have shown unveiled hostility and disgust toward their Southern Baptist brothers and sisters who dare to differ from them.

The fundamentalist-controlled SBC Pastors' Conference, held each year just prior to the annual SBC meeting, has, in recent years, been reduced to a platform for openly bashing "liberals" (i.e., those Southern Baptists who do not subscribe to the fundamentalist agenda). Mainline conservative and moderate Southern Baptists have been berated as "snakes" and "cancers." One of W. A. Criswell's terms for those who do not agree with him is "skunks." It seems to matter little, if any at all, that the persons whom Criswell and other fundamentalists are referring to are followers of Christ.

By the late 1980s, with the SBC solidly in fundamentalist hands, the fundamentalists' open disdain of dissenters was plainly showing itself in the annual Conventions. In 1990 the fundamentalists' mockery of dissenters reached new heights. Newly elected fundamentalist SBC president Jerry Vines taunted mainline conservatives and moderates who did not support the fundamentalist agenda, ridiculing their pastors and churches. Many mainline conservatives and moderates, following the 1990 SBC, vowed never to attend another annual SBC meeting.[11]

Mainline conservatives and moderates, even in the midst of the current controversy, have attracted to their ranks a number of individuals who hold theological views identical to those of fundamentalists. Mainline conservatives and moderates continue to welcome persons with differing theological viewpoints—while the fundamentalist leaders of the SBC have coldly shut their doors on all who disagree with their agenda. As James Draper declared, fundamentalists condemn all who dare to disagree with them.[12]

Jesus showed compassion on sinners. The current fundamentalist leadership has failed to show compassion for their own brothers and sisters in Christ, and they appear unlikely to change anytime soon. In this regard, the fundamentalists have modeled themselves after the Pharisees, instead of reflecting the attitude of Christ. One is led to wonder: if the fundamentalists refuse to show compassion for their many Southern Baptist Christian brothers and sisters who do not agree with their agenda, are their oft-repeated declarations of their compassionate concern for the lost (that is, those who do not know Christ as Savior) anything other than hot air? Can one have compassion for a lost sinner if he or she does not have compassion for committed followers of Christ?

At one point in his ministry, Jesus warned his disciples, "Be on your guard against the yeast of the Pharisees" (Matt. 16:6, NIV). Would the Son of God say the same thing today about the current fundamentalist leadership of the SBC?

A Baptist journalist pointed out that although the fundamentalist leadership insists on an "inerrant" Bible, they "frequently give no evidence of so much as an elementary understanding of Jesus' emphasis on the primacy of love of neighbor as the fulfillment of the law and prophets."[13]

A SELF-RIGHTEOUS GOD

Webster defines "self-righteousness" as "piously or smugly convinced of one's own righteousness." Unfortunately, churches harbor many self-righteous individuals. Self-righteousness does not constrict itself to Christians or Southern Baptists of any particular persuasion, but those who claim to possess "all the answers" tend to perhaps gravitate towards self-righteousness more than others.

James Draper once noted that fundamentalists feel they have "a corner on truth and the rest of the Christian world is groping in error." Fundamentalists leave "no room" for those who believe differently than they do. Any beliefs which contradict those of the fundamentalist are labeled as "sinister and heretical." In fact, the fundamentalist "is sure that he is the only true follower of Jesus Christ."[14] Draper's condemnation of fundamentalism was pointed.

A Baptist journalist noted that the current fundamentalist leadership is "comfortable with power, prestige, and privilege."[15]

Jesus said, "For I tell you that unless your righteousness surpasses that of the Pharisees and the teachers of the law, you will certainly not enter the kingdom of heaven" (Matt. 5:20, NIV). And, "Be careful not to do your 'acts of righteousness,' before men, to be seen by them. If you do, you will have no reward from your Father in heaven" (Matt. 6:1, NIV). The Pharisees were well-known for their pretensions of righteousness in their acts and attitudes.

Religious individuals must always beware of the danger of becoming self-righteous. Baptists, whether conservative-moderate, or fundamentalist, are no exception. However, it does appear that the current SBC fundamentalist leadership has become the standard-bearer of self-righteousness.

The fundamentalist-controlled SBC Peace Committee, in its 1987 report, claimed to speak for the majority of Southern Baptists, when, in fact, it did not.

Former fundamentalist SBC president Adrian Rogers brazenly declared that if most Southern Baptists believe pickles have souls, Southern Baptist seminaries should therefore teach that pickles have souls.[16]

In the 1985 SBC Pastors' Conference, fundamentalist W. A. Criswell denounced Southern Baptist seminary professors as infidels. Criswell was of the opinion that professors at Southern Baptist seminaries who did not agree with what he viewed as the basics of the Christian faith should be fired and replaced by those who did agree with him.[17] Furthermore, Criswell took it upon himself to speak for God by declaring that any woman who feels she has been called to the ministry is flatly "wrong."[18] In 1961 Criswell had resigned from Baylor University's Board of Trustees because the university would not bow down to his personal theological beliefs.[19]

Paige Patterson, architect of the fundamentalist takeover of the SBC, while admitting that most theologians and biblical scholars in the world do not think that the denial of inerrancy is a sufficient reason to classify someone as a liberal, nonetheless insisted on describing non-inerrantists as liberals.[20] In 1985 he, claiming (falsely) that "ninety percent of the Southern Baptist people are on our side," declared that he wanted to control three of the six Southern Baptist seminaries. He claimed that such a split was a "generous" offer.[21] We now know that Patterson's generous offer was a smoke screen, for fundamentalists openly sought control of all six seminaries. In

1992 Patterson was rewarded for his role in the fundamentalist takeover by being named president of Southeastern Seminary.

Paul Pressler, Patterson's Texas cohort in engineering the capture of the SBC, has long wanted his views presented well in Southern Baptist seminaries and colleges, but not opposing views.[22] Several years ago, when a large percentage of the faculty at Southwestern Seminary signed a statement supporting President Russell Dilday, who was actively opposed to the fundamentalist takeover, Pressler refused to believe that the faculty had acted voluntarily. Not believing that the faculty would voluntarily support the conservative-moderate Dilday who openly opposed him, Pressler charged Dilday with manipulating faculty members.[23]

SBC fundamentalist leaders, seeking to validate their inerrancy agenda, have tried to portray Southern Baptists as being inerrantists from their beginnings. James C. Hefley, an intellectual leader of the SBC fundamentalist faction, righteously declared that Southern Baptists have always held to the inerrant view of Scripture which fundamentalists are currently championing.[24] Hefley seemed to conveniently ignore the fact that the theory of inerrancy per se had not been put forth when the SBC was founded, and that the term "inerrancy" was very rarely heard in SBC life until the late 1970s. Furthermore, when Hefley elevated the founders of the SBC, while noting that they assumed that the original texts of the Bible were without error,[25] not only did he make a generalization that has only partial merit;[26] he completely overlooked the fact that those early founders also believed in slavery and defended it with Scripture. If the current SBC fundamentalists are truly champions of the views which the founders of the SBC held, as Hefley maintained, then fundamentalists should be openly embracing slavery. The truth is that neither fundamentalist nor conservative-moderate Southern Baptists hold to the Bible in the same manner as did the founding fathers of the SBC.

Although the fundamentalist party leaders are quick to declare publicly their belief in inerrancy, many have privately expressed beliefs which run counter to their public declarations. In light of this fact, the rhetoric which the fundamentalist leaders oftentimes parade in self-righteous fashion points, perhaps, to a desire to win the approval and favor of (and/or power over) others, rather than to the state of their heart in relation to God.

In recent years, fundamentalist SBC presidents have made clear their desire that those Southern Baptists who do not embrace the new fundamentalist direction of the SBC should leave the Convention. In essence, they have declared that those Southern Baptists who do not agree with them are not welcome in SBC life. Never before have those who led the agencies of the SBC been so arrogant as to openly request that all those who disagree with them should pack their bags. Diversity, which was an integral part of Southern Baptist life, is no longer acceptable to the new SBC leadership.

Just how self-righteous has the current fundamental leadership of the SBC become? The words of fundamentalist Nelson Keener may give something of an insight into this question. In an article in the *Fundamentalist Journal*, Keener stated: "Fundamentalists seldom, if ever, regard the criticism or evaluation of non-Fundamentalist Christians as worthy of consideration because these critics are not 'of us.' We are seldom self-critical."[27] When one considers that the current SBC fundamentalist leadership has repeatedly refused to even acknowledge conservative-moderate offers of compromise,[28] much less words of criticism, Keener's words speak all the louder.

A HYPOCRITICAL GOD

A hypocrite is one whose actions contradict his or her words. Unfortunately, our Christian churches are full of hypocrites, and Southern Baptist churches are no exception.

Hypocrisy is certainly not limited to any one group of Christians or Southern Baptists in regards to the theological spectrum. Fundamentalist J. Frank Norris insistently attacked the SBC in the 1920s in an effort to bring the Convention to doctrinal purity (as he defined it), but his methods and his personal life were far from being pure and above reproach. In 1928 it was discovered that Clinton S. Barnes, mainline conservative treasurer of the Home Mission Board, had embezzled almost one million dollars from the board. This, along with the stock market crash and the Great Depression, put the entire SBC on the edge of bankruptcy.[29] Furthermore, the tendency of many Southern Baptist seminary professors, including many whom the current fundamentalist leadership have labeled as liberals, to use "doublespeak" (that is, purposely not revealing their true beliefs and viewpoints when addressing some audiences) has already been noted. While this latter instance may not be outright hypocrisy, conservative-moderate Ralph Elliott seemed to indicate that it is at least in the ballpark.[30]

Finally, on the local-church level, hypocrisy seems to favor no particular group of individuals over against another. Numerous are the persons who attend church on Sundays but "live for the devil" throughout the week. Numerous also are those who both attend church and live "rightly" throughout the week, but who are ultimately more interested in "having their way" than being open to the Lord and his leading.

Although not confined to a particular theological mind-set, there does appear to be a tendency for hypocrisy to thrive among those who proclaim to hold to the most rigid, inflexible belief systems.

Consider the Gospels. The fiercest opposition which Jesus met on earth was from the Pharisees, the ultraconservative Jewish religious leaders of his day. Jesus did not have kind words for the Pharisees and their hypocrisy:

"Why do you break the command of God for the sake of your tradition? . . . You hypocrites! Isaiah was right when he prophesied about you: 'These people honor me with their lips, but their hearts are far from me. They worship me in vain; their teachings are but rules taught by men" (Matt. 15:3, 7-9, NIV).

"Do not do what they do, for they do not practice what they preach" (Matt. 23:3, NIV).

"Woe to you, teachers of the law and Pharisees, you hypocrites! You shut the kingdom of heaven in men's faces. You yourselves do not enter, nor will you let those enter who are trying to.

"Woe to you, teachers of the law and Pharisees, you hypocrites! You travel over land and sea to win a single convert, and when he becomes one, you make him twice as much a son of hell as you are" (Matt. 23:13-15, NIV).

". . . Woe to you, teachers of the law and Pharisees, you hypocrites! You give a tenth of your spices—mint, dill and cummin. But you have neglected the more important matters of the law—justice, mercy and faithfulness. You should have practiced the latter, without neglecting the former. You blind guides! You strain out a gnat but swallow a camel.

"Woe to you, teachers of the law and Pharisees, you hypocrites! You clean the outside of the cup and dish, but inside they are full of greed and self-indulgence. Blind Pharisee! First clean the inside of the cup and dish, and then the outside also will be clean.

"Woe to you, teachers of the law and Pharisees, you hypocrites! You are like whitewashed tombs, which look beautiful on the outside but on the inside are full of dead men's bones and everything unclean. In the same way, on the outside you appear to people as righteous but on the inside you are full of hypocrisy and wickedness" (Matt. 23:23-28, NIV).

"You snakes! You brood of vipers! How will you escape being condemned to hell? Therefore I am sending you prophets and wise men and teachers. Some of them you will kill and crucify . . ." (Matt. 23:33-34, NIV).

If we are to believe Jesus, the Pharisees of that day were anything but servants of God. Likewise, the history of Christianity is littered with ultra-conservative leaders who claimed to worship God, but whose allegiance was primarily to laws and traditions, and thus led lives of hypocrisy. Copernicus and Galileo nearly lost their lives at the hands of church leaders who were more interested in the traditions of men than in God's truth.

The current fundamentalist leaders of the SBC, by simple virtue of the fact that, unlike Southern Baptist statesmen before them, believe they have a corner on the truth (as Jimmy Draper noted[31]), are prone to hypocrisy. They might not have mastered the art of hypocrisy quite as well as the Pharisees (and it would certainly be unfair to call them "sons of hell"), but their hypocritical tendencies have manifested themselves over and over.

W. A. Criswell, longtime fundamentalist leader within the SBC, has for decades charged that Southern Baptist seminaries are liberal because the professors embrace higher biblical criticism. Among other charges, Criswell and his fundamentalist allies have repeatedly contended that these "liberal" professors explain away many of the miracles of the Bible through the use of higher criticism.

In 1985, during the SBC meeting in Dallas, Ted Koppel of ABC interviewed Criswell and Cecil Sherman, SBC mainline conservative-moderate leader, live in Dallas on the news program *Nightline*. The issue of "liberal" Southern Baptist scholars arose during the interview. Sherman quoted from a "liberal commentator" who denied the biblical account of the waters of the Nile River turning to blood during the time of God's plagues upon Egypt (Exod. 7:14-24). The scholar Sherman quoted from explained away the miraculous nature of the biblical account by declaring that the red clay lining the banks of the river turned the water red, thus making it appear to be blood.

Criswell would normally have sided with Sherman in condemning any liberal scholar who dared deny the literal biblical account of the plague. Indeed, for years Criswell had been hounding Southern Baptist professors who advocated such liberal understandings of Scripture. However, this time Criswell did not denounce the liberal scholar whom Sherman quoted, because that liberal scholar was Criswell! The "liberal" commentary which Sherman had quoted from was the *Criswell Study Bible*, and the "liberal" teaching concerning the plague upon the Nile River was none other than that of W. A. Criswell. Sherman had effectively revealed the "liberal" Criswell's hypocrisy before a television audience of millions.[32] Furthermore, Joel Gregory, formerly Criswell's right-hand man at First Baptist Church, Dallas, recently stated that Criswell's main concerns are power and money, rather than spiritual matters.[33]

Today, thanks largely to the fundamentalist takeover of the SBC, the SBC Cooperative Program, the unified plan of raising money for SBC agencies, including the mission boards, has been on a financial roller coaster. The fundamentalist leadership, during recent years, has begun a concentrated crusade to convince Southern Baptists to increase their giving through the Cooperative Program. However, many mainline conservative and moderate Southern Baptists are only too well aware that SBC fundamentalists have been giving far less to the Cooperative Program than they have. Fundamentalists are grousing because mainline conservatives and moderates are leading more and more churches and state Baptist conventions to bypass the fundamentalist-controlled Cooperative Program—a practice which fundamentalists utilized when mainline conservatives and moderates operated the SBC.[34] While fundamentalists plead for more money, the ship they have captured springs more and more leaks under their leadership.

Current SBC fundamentalist leaders proclaim their allegiance to an "inerrant" Bible, but their actions and attitudes reflect a different understanding of Scripture. Former fundamentalist Edward Carnell noted that fundamentalism, "in its fervent quest for doctrinal purity appears to neglect a long list of New Testament teachings, notably, forgiveness, Jesus' willingness to use broken reeds and smoking flax in his kingdom, Paul's emphasis on reconciliation in helping weak and slow believers, John's lessons on love, *koinonia*, and above all the New Testament's teaching that grace is ascendant over law." Carnell continued, "Fundamentalism's chief characteristics are legalism, exclusiveness, rancor, arrogance and pride."[35] Carnell pointed out that although fundamentalists fervently claim to subscribe to biblical inerrancy and a belief in "all" the Bible says, their actions say otherwise.

In fact, despite their outward righteousness, the fundamentalists' tendency towards dishonesty and misuse of ethics is well-known. Grady C. Cothen, former president of the Baptist Sunday School Board, has documented scores of instances of fundamentalists' lying, distorting the truth, slandering others, being dishonest, showing contempt towards those of differing opinions, being deceptive in words and actions, and displaying an open attitude of combativeness.

The intrigue and underhandedness surrounding many of the actions taken by fundamentalists which Cothen documented would make good fodder for a made-for-TV movie: attempts to subvert seminary students, character assassinations, unholy politicking, threats, book burnings, a secretive meeting behind locked doors guarded by off-duty police officers, deceit, lies, cheating—the list goes on and on.[36] Indeed, the SBC fundamentalist leadership seems bent on putting forth a false notion of who they are and what they are about. When one looks beyond the front and penetrates the deception, the words "integrity" and "Christ-like" are hardly applicable to the actions of the fundamentalist leadership as a whole.

New Testament Pharisees, if we are to believe Jesus, were instruments of the devil more than they were servants of God. Their ultraconservative theology did not keep them from turning away from God. Their legalism, lack of compassion, self-righteousness, and hypocrisy spoke more loudly than their pretense of correct doctrine. Jesus saw through their thinly veiled pretenses and condemned them for their ungodliness.

To say that the current fundamentalist leadership of the SBC is in the same boat as the Pharisees whom Jesus condemned again and again might be a bit of an overstatement—maybe. However, as the fundamentalists tighten their grip on the SBC, it would appear that they are descending further and further into the Pharisaic mentality—the same mentality which ignored many of the teachings and proclamations of the Son of God in a passionate crusade to push God aside in order to better serve themselves.

CHAPTER TEN

The Organizational God

The Southern Baptist Convention has existed as an organization for over 150 years. Much has changed since the formation of the SBC in 1845. The current leadership of the SBC, for example, does not openly defend slavery on biblical grounds, as did the founding fathers.

On the other hand, much is still the same. The founding fathers of the SBC felt it their Christian duty to lord it over their black brethren. Likewise, the handful of SBC leaders who call the shots today feel that it is their Christian duty to cast from their midst any who do not believe as they do. As the old saying goes, the more things change, the more they remain the same.

In many respects, the SBC has grown remarkably throughout its century and a half of existence. Many Southern Baptists today, including this author, are apt to declare that God has used Southern Baptists in a mighty way to spread his kingdom in our nation and around the world. Indeed, statistics would tend to lend credibility to this claim. Southern Baptists are the largest Protestant body in the United States. The SBC has more missionaries on the field than any other Protestant denomination. Southern Baptists are scattered all around the United States and throughout the world.

And yet, has God really blessed the SBC? Have we as Southern Baptists even come close to that which God desires of us? Have we really been the kingdom people God has desired us to be? Has God's hand been upon the SBC in a special sense?

The SBC was born because many white Baptists in the South did not want to give up the right to keep blacks in bondage. We oftentimes try to gloss over the issue, but the fact remains that if Baptists in the South had not been so adamant about their "biblical right" to own slaves, the SBC would not have come about in 1845—in fact, it may have never been born.

Just how much could God have blessed a group of Baptists who united to form a new convention largely because of their racism and prejudice against people of a different skin color? The answer may not be what some people want to hear.

Tragically, that sordid past is not all behind us. Many white Southern Baptists to this day are prejudiced towards blacks.

As the fledgling Convention grew, its leaders and its people proudly proclaimed the Bible as their sole authority in matters of faith and practice. However, at the same time they largely ignored advances in biblical scholarship which were giving the Christian world new insights into the written Word of God.

Could God have truly blessed a people who professed to hold to his written Word, yet were indifferent toward learning more about his Word? Indeed, many Southern Baptists are, to this day, unconcerned with gaining new insights from the Bible which contemporary scholarship affords us.

The growing SBC has been marred with controversy from the beginning, and the controversy which engulfs it now threatens to cause physical division among Southern Baptists. Can God really work through a group of Christians who have constantly been in conflict with one another, and who now are turned more inward than outward?

As the SBC grew into the largest American Protestant group in the mid-twentieth century, arrogance began to creep into its midst, to the point where Southern Baptist mainline conservative-moderate leaders led the Convention to take upon itself the task of preaching the gospel to every person in the world. Since that time, the current fundamentalist leadership has taken arrogance to new heights in their crusade to rid the SBC of all who do not believe as they do. Can God bless a group of Christians whose leadership has been and remains immersed in a degree of arrogance?

The faults of the SBC, past and present, are numerous and are by no means minor offenses. Yet, statistically, when compared to other Protestant Christian bodies, the SBC has had outstanding numerical and financial success in its endeavors. How much of this success can actually be attributed to God, however? Could it be that if Southern Baptists had really been able to focus on God and his purpose, God may have been able to touch our nation and our world through Southern Baptists in ways we cannot even imagine?

In truth, it is quite possible that much of the success which the SBC has enjoyed can be attributed to the effective and efficient operation of the organization itself. Indeed, the SBC as an organization is an impressive entity. The SBC employs—or supports—several thousand full-time missionaries in both the United States and on foreign soil. The SBC operates the largest seminaries in the world. It has a publishing agency which publishes tens of millions of pieces of literature each and every year. In short, the SBC is a large, diversified, worldwide corporation.

The SBC arrived where it is today by leading local Southern Baptist churches to collectively pool a portion of the tithes to fund the agencies of the national SBC. Although this concept of directing a portion of offerings from local churches to the national organization is certainly not unique to Southern Baptists, the SBC has perhaps utilized this method more efficiently and effectively than any other major Protestant body.

The SBC did not arrive at its current state overnight. In fact, the Cooperative Program, the actual funding plan of the SBC, was not put into place until 1925. Much groundwork had previously been laid, however, as national SBC leaders prior to 1925 had stressed the importance of missions and evangelism and had sought to help local Southern Baptist churches catch a vision of what their collective efforts could accomplish. Indeed, perhaps the period of Reconstruction in the South, that time after the Civil War when Southerners sought to recover from their defeat and reestablish their identity, helped move local Southern Baptist churches toward more cooperation in an effort to establish a regional identity and vision in the wasteland which was the South.

SBC leaders desired to see the national organization grow. The diversity which had long characterized Baptists, as shaped by the long-held Baptist distinctives of soul competency, the priesthood of all believers, and local church autonomy, lent itself to establishing and developing of a national organization which was autonomous and based on voluntary cooperation from the local-church level. The more flexible and open an organization, the larger has been its potential for growth and accomplishment. The SBC most likely owes much of its past success to its willingness to accommodate diversity and constant efforts to keep everyone's attention focused on common goals, such as missions and evangelism.

Southern Baptist church historian Bill Leonard argued that the holding together of the national organization became the overriding priority of SBC leadership. Leonard called the old establishment's ability to accommodate the minority, extremist fundamentalists, without allowing them to take control, the "Grand Compromise," which turned out to be a fatal weakness.[1]

Indeed, the mainline conservative-moderates who long operated the SBC tended, at times, to place the good of the institution above all else. William Whitsitt resigned from the presidency of the Southern Baptist Theological Seminary at the close of the nineteenth century in order to preserve the integrity of the seminary. Southern Baptist mainline conservative-moderate leaders sought to accommodate, but not give in to, the minority fundamentalists during the 1920s (the Norris controversy), the 1960s (the Elliott controversy), and the 1970s (the *Broadman Bible Commentary* controversy). In the Norris and Elliott controversies, Baptist leaders came together to issue confessions of faith intended to appease the fundamentalists, while at the same time re-acknowledging the non-creedal nature of Southern Baptists.

Steering a course between the extremes, and thus holding together the diverse constituency of the organization became more and more of a priority as the years passed and the agencies of the SBC grew larger and larger. As long as the glue held, the SBC continued growing and expanding. The glue, by and large, was missions and evangelism.[2]

The success of the SBC is evident. We are left to speculate on the reason behind the success, however. Has it been the direct blessing of God? Or has it primarily been orchestrated by the denominational leaders who built the organization into what it is today through careful planning and cultivation? The answer undoubtedly lies somewhere between the two.

Interestingly enough, the current controversy within the SBC has highlighted the degree to which Southern Baptists have become entrenched with their national organization. Although this is a testimony to the effectiveness of the past mainline conservative-moderate leaders who sold the Convention idea to local churches, it is also indicative, perhaps, of the danger of loyalty to an organization supplanting loyalty to Christ.

Fundamentalist Southern Baptist churches for years gave little support to the Cooperative Program, for they considered the SBC and its national leadership to be too liberal. Even to this day, with fundamentalists in full control of the SBC, fundamentalist churches are well-known for their token support of the Cooperative Program. However, fundamentalists are finally beginning to increase their support through the Cooperative Program.

Mainline conservatives and moderates have long been big supporters of the Cooperative Program and of SBC agencies (fundamentalists, by contrast, have historically been negatively critical of these agencies until recently). Support of the SBC as an organization has been firmly entrenched within mainline conservative and moderate churches for several decades. This mainline conservative and moderate loyalty to the SBC and the Cooperative Program has played, and is playing, a very vital role in the current SBC controversy.

Although the 1979 SBC presidential election marked the first overtly political effort by a faction within SBC life to get "their" man elected, most mainline conservatives and moderates were initially unconcerned about the fundamentalist political victory. The events of 1979 raised some eyebrows among a few mainline conservative-moderate Southern Baptists leaders, but no backlash was forthcoming that year.

Following the 1980 SBC meeting in which fundamentalists again used organized politics to get their candidate elected, some conservative and moderate leaders in SBC life did begin worrying about where the Convention was headed. Cecil Sherman, longtime SBC denominational leader who was at that time pastoring in Asheville, North Carolina, took the initiative to call together key conservatives and moderates to discuss this new development in the SBC and seek ways to correct what was taking place. Sherman subsequently led the way in establishing a resistance effort to the fundamentalist encroachment. Although not really wanting to resort to politics, the group Sherman spearheaded decided such a move was necessary in order to effectively answer the fundamentalist siege of the Convention. Despite the fact that the handful of mainline conservative-moderate leaders who followed Sherman in this effort managed to put together a good, effective network, fundamentalist leaders continually managed to wage a more effective, cohesive campaign. Consequently, mainline conservatives and moderates were unable to turn back the fundamentalists in the annual presidential elections.[3]

Sherman, in retrospect, has identified a number of factors which hindered the mainline conservative-moderate response to the fundamentalist takeover. To begin with, mainline conservatives and moderates were, for the most part, appalled by the idea of open participation in partisan politics. Many believed taking political action against their brothers and sisters in Christ would be unchristian. Fundamentalists, on the other hand, had no qualms about using politics to achieve their goals.

Second, Sherman contended that mainline conservative-moderates were unable to demonstrate effective leadership in countering the fundamentalist siege. Thirdly, mainline conservative-moderates were put at a disadvantage in that, although they were conservative, they were more "liberal" than the fundamentalists, a fact which fundamentalists exploited quite well. Mainline conservative-moderates were not helped by the fact that they were constantly being called "liberals" by the new fundamentalist leadership. Furthermore, their embracing of the term "moderate" to describe themselves was probably more of a hindrance than a help because the term itself was not forceful or "moving."

The last two factors which Sherman listed as contributing to the hindrance of the mainline conservative-moderate response to fundamentalists were the hesitation of many SBC agency heads to act upon their personal convictions, and the refusal of many influential preachers to come public with their personal convictions.[4]

These latter two factors demand closer attention. Sherman, who worked closely with many Convention agency heads during the 1980s as the controversy escalated, provided some interesting insight into the reaction of these mainline conservative-moderate denominational leaders in regards to the fundamentalists' power grab.

In the early years of the controversy, Sherman noted that mainline conservative-moderate denominational leaders were uncertain about which direction to pursue. He recounted a conversation with long-time SBC Executive Committee head Porter Routh in which Routh discouraged him from taking any action against the fundamentalists. Calling Sherman a novice, Routh blithely declared that "we (denominational leaders) can handle these people. The pendulum will swing back." Later, Russell Dilday, president of Southwestern Seminary, told Sherman the same thing.

At the same time, some denominational leaders, such as Foy Valentine of the Christian Life Commission, Jimmy Allen of the Radio and Television Commission, and Duke McCall of Southern Seminary, quietly supported the blossoming conservative-moderate counter-movement.

By 1984 the sinister nature of the fundamentalist political machinery was plainly evident, and denominational leaders, by and large, joined together to assist the conservative-moderate counter-movement in combating the fundamentalist encroachment. Dilday, Roy Honeycutt, newly elected president of Southern Seminary, and Randall Lolley, president of Southeastern Seminary, took the lead in an effort by SBC denominational leaders to turn back the tide of fundamentalism. Sherman identified 1984 and 1985 as the most effective years of the conservative-moderate counter-movement.

However, in 1986, with fundamentalist pressure mounting, Sherman recounted how the seminary presidents in particular caved in to the fundamentalists through issuing the now famous "Glorieta Statement." The Glorieta Statement threw open the door for fundamentalism, a minority, extremist mind-set long existent only on the fringes of SBC life, to establish itself firmly in the seminaries. In order to "save" the seminaries from destruction, the presidents had chosen to accommodate the extremists.

Instead of saving the seminaries, however, the presidents had sounded the death knoll for academic freedom and integrity. Since the signing of the Glorieta Statement, fundamentalists leaders have purged dozens of solidly conservative professors from the seminaries (largely through hounding them out of their positions), hijacked four of the six seminaries, and have the other two safely in their grasp. Integrity, academic freedom, and the unhindered search for truth within the classroom are rapidly becoming a thing of the past. Sherman viewed the Glorieta Statement as a major turning point in the controversy.[5]

Sherman noted that many influential Southern Baptist preachers did not openly follow through on their personal convictions during the mounting years of the controversy. Although these mainline conservative-moderates were silent supporters of the conservative-moderate counter-movement, they refused to align themselves publicly for various reasons. Some did not want to endanger the prestige they enjoyed. Others were afraid going public would hinder their future options in regards to church placement. In short, the possible threat to career and family hindered many from openly supporting the conservative-moderate counter-movement.

Summing up his argument for why the conservative-moderate counter-movement lost the battle, Sherman declared:

> Moderates did not have enough moral energy to win. We could not bring ourselves to use moral language to describe our cause. Truth was butchered. We said nothing. Good people were defamed. We

were silent. Baptist principles were mangled and Baptist history was replaced, rewritten. All the while, teachers who could have written about the problems of calling the Bible inerrant, did not. And preachers who could have called us to arms said nothing. The want of moral energy was the undoing of the Moderate movement.[6]

Sherman expressed eloquently what has been discussed among mainline conservative-moderates many times over. Denominational leaders and other influential mainline conservatives and moderates did not, by and large, publicly act on their consciences. Southern Baptist sociologist Nancy Ammerman further expounded on Sherman's observations by noting that while the denominational leadership waffled, the fundamentalists, in their campaign to take over the SBC, effectively cast mainline conservative-moderate leadership in a negative light by repeatedly labeling them as "liberals." Although such charges were false and misleading, the tactic helped the fundamentalists sow seeds of distrust among many Southern Baptists in regards to their denominational leaders.[7] Ammerman's observations highlighted the dishonest and deceptive nature of the fundamentalist leadership, as well as the gullibility of many Southern Baptists.

One of the biggest ironies of the controversy is the fact that during the fundamentalist takeover of the SBC, which has drastically altered the life and function of the Convention, many mainline conservative-moderate leaders were busily seeking to preserve the SBC which they had known for so long, rather than publicly following their consciences. The Glorieta Statement issued by the seminary presidents was a prime example of how institutional SBC life was placed above private convictions. The seminary presidents went against their consciences and caved in to the demands of the fundamentalists in an effort to salvage the seminaries. They were not the only ones who did so, however.

The same tune is being played today. Even at this point beyond the takeover, many employees of Southern Baptist agencies who have privately expressed dissagreement with the fundamentalist leadership have chosen to remain offically silent, rather than risk their jobs.

. An outside observer of Southern Baptist life might wonder why so many mainline conservative-moderates have placed a higher priority on the survival of their denomination than following their own Christian consciences. Institutional loyalty is high among many mainline conservative-moderates. Many good, strongly committed Southern Baptists have left the SBC and joined other Christian bodies. Others have chosen to stay in Southern Baptist life and publicly keep their mouths bridled about their personal convictions.

The reasons for such an attitude are varied. Many have been Southern Baptists all their lives, and are second, third, or fourth generation Southern

Baptists. To leave Southern Baptist life would mean leaving behind a heritage, a family, and a large part of one's Christian identity. Any decision in life which involves such a high sacrifice is a tough decision to make.

Others, though opposed to the fundamentalist coup, have decided to stay put and keep quiet because they feel that the controversy is distant and will have no effect on their local churches. A survey taken in the late 1980s revealed that the majority of mainline conservative-moderates did not believe the controversy would affect their local churches.[8] Many Southern Baptist pastors in particular have this attitude.

Yet others are simply ambivalent about who leads the SBC. These local churches and their leaders have been trained over the years to give a portion of their income through the Cooperative Program of the SBC, but in effect, the national organization is out of sight and out of sound—other than as a place from which to order Sunday School and other church literature.

A fourth reason many mainline conservative-moderates are remaining loyal to the SBC, despite their intense disagreements with the current leadership, is the fear that the great missionary enterprise of the SBC will be destroyed if conservative-moderates pull out of the Convention. This fear of hurting the missionaries may well be the single most important reason. In this instance, the high mission-mindedness of the Southern Baptist people may have turned out to be an ally for the fundamentalist cause.

Quite frankly, the missionary force of the SBC is in danger. Recent financial cutbacks at the mission boards directly affected the missionaries on the field. The fundamentalist leadership of the SBC is charging that the kingdom of God will be hurt if Southern Baptists do not start giving more money to the boards. The truth, most likely, is that the current leaders of the SBC have already destroyed much of the kingdom work of the SBC through their unethical and ungodly actions. SBC missionaries have made great strides for the Lord, but to maintain that God can only win the world to himself through the SBC mission boards (as some fundamentalist leaders have insinuated) is both naive and egotistical. In some respects, the SBC missionaries, at this point, are being used as blackmail at the hands of the current fundamentalist leadership. Thus far, the ploy appears to be working, simply because many Southern Baptist missionaries are doing a good kingdom work, and Southern Baptists are sensitive to that fact.

For these reasons and more, many mainline conservative-moderate Southern Baptists have chosen, thus far, to muzzle their personal convictions and consciences in order to remain a part of national Southern Baptist life. Now that the chips are down, the "need" to stay a part of the Southern Baptist family has thus far won out over the cries of the conscience.

The decisions thus made are not hard to understand when placed in context. The Southern Baptist machinery has been gradually put into place, bit by bit, over a period of time. Loyalty to the machinery was secured through tireless efforts and the passage of time. It became second nature for local churches to support the SBC through the Cooperative Program. After all, the Cooperative Program funded thousands of missionaries and financed an evangelistic Baptist witness around the nation and the world.

Fundamentalists never controlled the machinery until the takeover. In fact, they largely shunned the Cooperative Program while mainline conservative-moderates were becoming more and more loyal to the SBC way of doing missions and evangelism. Now that they have maneuvered their way into controlling the machinery, fundamentalists have kept the trappings while rewriting the ground rules. Stan Hastey, a leader in the conservative-moderate movement, acknowledged that the fundamentalists have proved adapt at governing the "complex structure" of the SBC. He even declared that the transformation of power has been "remarkably smooth."[9]

The fact that fundamentalists have preserved the basic trappings of the SBC machinery has thus far averted a mass exodus of mainline conservative-moderates from SBC life. The machinery has continued to function without completely faltering in mid-stride, and the masses are prone to focus more on the external appearances than on the new motor under the hood which now drives the machinery. Far too many who do not like what is under the hood have probably, to this point, chosen to politely look the other way. Some have pushed aside convictions and ignored conscience in jumping aboard the new bandwagon. Others have grumbled, but not loudly.

Thus, at this point, loyalty to the SBC machinery seems to have so far prevented the wholesale destruction of the SBC. Many mainline conservative-moderate pastors, missionaries, denominational employees, and laity silently squirm under the new fundamentalist leadership, but nevertheless continue to stay a part of the national SBC family.

In 1988 R. Keith Parks, then president of the SBC Foreign Mission Board and a supporter of the conservative-moderate cause, nevertheless was bound by loyalty to the SBC. Parks pleaded with the Southern Baptist Alliance, an organization of conservative-moderates which was actively seeking to distance itself from the fundamentalist-controlled SBC, not to do anything which would drain money away from the Cooperative Program which financed the work of the Foreign Mission Board. Parks stated, "I am still convinced we can support what is going on, regardless of where you are in the political spectrum."[10]

Four years later, Parks resigned from the presidency of the Foreign Mission Board rather than compromise his integrity. Following his resignation, he quickly became the leader of the Cooperative Baptist Fellowship's mission enterprises. The same man who had so adamantly supported the SBC Cooperative Program a few years before had now disavowed the Cooperative Program and was heading an alternative Southern Baptist missions organization. Today, there are many conservative-moderates who are now standing where Parks stood in 1988.

An extremist minority has completed a takeover of America's largest Protestant group without arousing strong, united opposition from the majority. The time to mount unified opposition to the hostile takeover has come and gone, some would say. That opposition never fully materialized, and now those who could have acted have largely resigned themselves to outward submission to the new national leadership.

The SBC has survived the hostile takeover largely intact—thus far. The very organization which mainline conservatives and moderates labored so long and tirelessly to build has now entombed the convictions and consciences of many of their rank and file.

One is left to wonder: are many Southern Baptists more concerned with being Southern Baptists than following Christian convictions? Indeed, is being part of the national Southern Baptist family more of a priority than speaking up for the truth—at least for practical purposes? Are many mainline conservative-moderate Southern Baptists so convinced that God's hand has been upon the SBC that they are willing to look the other way while current national leaders muscle through their self-centered, personal agenda?

These dangers are very real for many mainline conservative-moderate Southern Baptists. Although consciences may scream out against those who, through the use of deceit and ungodly methods, now control the SBC, the thought of departing from the SBC is not easy to digest. However, more and more Southern Baptists are choosing not to remain silent any longer as accomplices to the deception and prideful arrogance of those who now control the SBC machinery. Just as the slavery of the black race which characterized the early years of the SBC was wrong and sinful, so also is the slavery of the human mind, spirit, and conscience which today's SBC leadership has instigated.

Perhaps now is the time for all mainline conservative-moderate Southern Baptists—and this includes the majority of Southern Baptists—to ask themselves whether their allegiance is primarily to God or to the SBC.

Jesus said, "No one can serve two masters" (Matt. 6: 24, NIV). When one chooses to muzzle one's God-driven conscience and convictions for the sake of something human or material, God is no longer master.

For some individuals, remaining a part of national SBC life, all the while taking a bold stand for truth, may be the direction God would lead. Taking such a stand certainly entails risk; yet following God's leading is far more important than self-preservation. For others, breaking away from the SBC may be where God is leading. Hopefully, God will call many within SBC life to take a bold stand for truth, for the SBC, despite its current humanistic agenda, could one day return to being a body used mightily by God.

CHAPTER 11

The Future: Hope or Despair?

One of my favorite movies is *The Mission*. The movie tells the story of several Jesuit priests and their work among a South American Indian tribe in the untamed jungles of eighteenth-century South America. Having made great strides with the natives, the Jesuits suddenly find themselves confronted by their own Catholic Church, which has become a pawn of the colonial empires vying for control of South America. When the Catholic Church gives its consent for the tribal missions to be closed, and the natives killed if necessary, the Jesuits must decide whether to submit to the will of church leaders or hold true to their convictions.

After much agonizing deliberation, the Jesuits make their choice. In the face of a murderous government-led army supported by church leaders, the Jesuits side with the tribal natives whom they have led to Christ. To a man, the Jesuits resist the orders of their church in a heroic climax. One resists through peaceful protest, while the others take up arms. In the end, they all die, along with the natives.

The blood-letting aside, there is a parallel between the situation of the Jesuits in *The Mission* and that which many mainline conservative-moderates in the Southern Baptist Convention are now facing. On the eve of the twenty-first century, many mainline conservative-moderates have been, and are now, agonizing about what they should do in the face of the hostile takeover of the SBC. For many, silent submission to the fundamentalist leadership of the SBC amounts to pushing aside God-driven convictions. On the other hand, to openly pit oneself against those now in authority poses an enormous risk in terms of career and prestige for many national leaders and local Southern Baptist ministers. For laity, the risk often primarily involves the forsaking of long and deep roots. For all who do not like the new direction of the SBC, it is a choice of submitting to a known evil, daring to venture into the unknown and the unchartered waters of which the Cooperative Baptist Fellowship has only recently emerged as the fledgling flagship, or straddling the fence as long as possible.

As the twenty-first century looms ahead, the future of Southern Baptists and the SBC has never been more uncertain. The next five to ten years will be extremely crucial years. Yet, those years are shrouded in uncertainty.

Both fundamentalist and mainline conservative-moderate leaders are now speculating on what the future holds. In truth, neither faction possesses a crystal ball. The only certainty at this point is that the SBC is rapidly heading towards deeper fragmentation. The full nature and extent of this further fragmentation has yet to come into focus.

THE FUNDAMENTALIST VISION FOR THE FUTURE

When Paul Pressler and Paige Patterson launched the fundamentalist campaign to capture the SBC, they cast themselves and their fellow fundamentalists as heroes of the "old-time" faith trying to save the SBC from the clutches of liberalism. They had been commissioned by God to resurrect the dying SBC. They constantly pounded home the line that if the "liberals" were removed from Southern Baptist life, God would be able to place his hands upon the SBC as never before. Fundamentalist leaders envisioned the "turnaround" of the SBC as being the beginning of a great American revival.[1]

Pressler, Patterson, and their cohorts conveniently ignored the fact that Southern Baptists have always been considered one of the most conservative Protestant Christian bodies in America. They believed that an ultraconservative stance was necessary in the face of a radically changing world. Then they appointed themselves to carry out their personal agenda which they championed as being the will of God. Criswell embodied this arrogant attitude when he declared, during the 1985 SBC Pastors' Conference, that "if we deliver the message of the inerrant Word of God, God will rise to meet us. . . . 'We shall not cease from battle strife, nor shall the sword sleep in our hand, till we have built Jerusalem in this fair and mighty land.' God grant it!"[2]

In the early and mid-1980s, fundamentalists were waxing eloquently about how the SBC would become a mighty instrument for God if they were able to gain control of the national agencies. In 1986 fundamentalist writer James Hefley published a book, *The Truth in Crisis*, in which he predicted what would happen should the fundamentalists win control of the SBC.

Hefley predicted that once SBC agencies were purged of their liberal leadership, the Cooperative Program "could take on new vigor."[3] As it turns out, Hefley was dead wrong. Since 1990, when the leadership of the conservative-moderate counter-movement conceded defeat to the fundamentalists, Cooperative Program receipts have been on a roller coaster ride.[4] Although fiscal 1995 witnessed a temporary reversal of the downward trend,[5] the SBC is yet in financial decline overall as more and more state conventions reduce their funding of the SBC. Indeed, the only immediate hope for reversing the downward spiral lies with the fundamentalist churches which in years past have given little or no support through the Cooperative Program. The temporary upswing in receipts in fiscal 1995 testifies that perhaps some of those churches are beginning to lend more support through the Cooperative Program, now that the SBC is solidly in fundamentalist hands. However, the question which has yet to be answered is whether increased support from fundamentalist churches can offset potential decreased support from more and more conservative-moderate churches (from both the local level and the state convention level), the latter of which comprise a majority of the churches within the SBC.

Hefley also predicted that national baptism statistics would rise under fundamentalist leadership as fundamentalists put more emphasis on revivalistic and soul-winning techniques from "old-time religion." Once again, Hefley was wrong. The number of baptisms in Southern Baptist churches has declined since the SBC has come under fundamentalist control. By December 1993, the fundamentalist leadership of the SBC was frantically scrambling to find ways to reverse the downward trends in baptisms.[6]

Fundamentalists had also long declared that if they could gain control of the six Southern Baptist seminaries, the seminaries would become stronger and healthier as bastions of inerrancy. In fact, when fundamentalists scored a coup at Southeastern in the fall of 1987, the seminary promptly crashed and burned. By the end of the following school year, one-third of the faculty and over one-half of the administration had resigned. Student enrollment dropped drastically. Enrollment during the fall of 1989 was half of what it had been in the fall of 1987.[7] By the fall of 1991, the number of full-time students enrolled at Southeastern had dropped to about a third of the full-time enrollment prior to the beginning of the fundamentalist takeover of the SBC.[8] Although Southeastern's enrollment has risen somewhat since 1991, the numbers in late 1993 still remained far below 1987 levels.[9] Some fundamentalist leaders have expressed the belief that when the seminary becomes fundamentalist enough, the students will come. In fact, with fundamentalist architect Paige Patterson now having been at the helm of Southeastern for several years, student enrollment has begun to grow, although many incoming students are not Southern Baptists.

In addition to a mass exodus of students, Southeastern saw its alumni contributions drop to a trickle. Former graduates clearly do not support the new fundamentalist direction of the school, and their withdrawal of contributions has negatively impacted the financial well-being of the institution.[10]

In 1989 the Southern Association of Colleges and Schools put sanctions upon Southeastern in light of the improper administrative changes that the fundamentalist trustees had made in their takeover.[11] Only recently has the association revoked its sanctions against Southeastern.¹²

In 1993, Southern Baptist Theological Seminary, after being harassed and assaulted for years by fundamentalists, finally came fully under fundamentalist control through the elecction of fundamentalist R. Albert Mohler to succeed Roy Honeycutt as president.¹³ Immediately, enrollment at Southern dropped.¹⁴ In 1994 fundamentalists removed conservative Russell Dilday as president of Southwestern Baptist Theological Seminary, and replaced him with someone who would carry out their wishes. In 1995 fundamentalists appointed their own man to the presidency of Midwestern. In all three of these institutions, enrollment is down and many remaining students are dissatisfied. The continued downward enrollment has been such a serious problem that SBC leaders, in some recent years, have been evasive (and some would charge misleading) in their reporting of enrollment statistics.

Paige Patterson, chief architect of the fundamentalist movement, has long envisioned what glorious heights the SBC would obtain under fundamentalist control. With inerrantist fundamentalists in control, he envisioned a time of evangelism, revival, and growth. He envisioned an SBC which has "integrity" (never mind that he and his cohorts displayed very little, if any, integrity during their takeover of the SBC).¹⁵ Yet, with each passing month, prospects of revival and growth in the SBC are dimming, despite the fact that the fundamentalist leadership continues forecasting a rosy picture ahead, and manipulates statistics to try and paint a picture of vibrancy. Furthermore, numerous eyewitnesses indicate that the so-called revivals of 1994-95 which began in Texas were of far less significance than what the fundamentalist-controlled Baptist Press portrayed them to be.

In short, the fundamentalist vision of a vibrant, growing SBC has not materialized. Instead of taking on new life, the SBC has started wilting under fundamentalist control. The Convention is in unprecedented decline, both financially and numerically, publicity "spins" notwithstanding. Furthermore, despite fundamentalist leaders' claims in recent years that they are governing the SBC through a mandate, the fact remains that the vast majority of Southern Baptists do not describe themselves as strictly "fundamentalists" (eighty-nine percent), and at least two-thirds do not support the fundamentalist agenda.¹⁶ The SBC ship is slowly sinking at the hands of the minority fundamentalist leadership, as the leaders desperately man the buckets while putting on a good face.

THE MAINLINE CONSERVATIVE-MODERATE VISION FOR THE FUTURE

Whereas fundamentalists have long pictured a day when they would have control of the SBC and subsequently take the Convention to glorious new heights, mainline conservative-moderates are still trying to bring their future vision of Southern Baptist life into focus.

The old vision of a unified SBC reaching out in the name of Christ to a lost and dying world was trampled underfoot during the fundamentalist takeover. The fundamentalist vision of reaching new heights in evangelistic and missions efforts is not being achieved despite statistical manipulation and a heavy spin on what is reported to the public.

Mainline conservative-moderates, at this point, are united only in the fact that they disagree with the ideology and methodology of the fundamentalist leadership. What they have done with those disagreements has, in the past, been disjointed. Some have kept their opinions to themselves for fear of reprisal, while those who have expressed their displeasure have done so in varying degrees.[17]

Several new structures, in addition to the Alliance of Baptists and the Cooperative Baptist Fellowship (CBF), have arisen from the ranks of those mainline conservative-moderates who have been vocal about their disagreements with the new fundamentalist leadership. New theological institutions and programs, such as the Baptist Theological Seminary at Richmond, the George W. Truett Theological Seminary at Baylor University, and the School of Theology at Mercer University have emerged. A new Baptist ethics agency (the Baptist Center for Ethics) and a new Baptist publishing house (Smyth and Helwys) have been born and are thriving in their infancy. A national Baptist newspaper (*Baptists Today*), a national Baptist press association (Associated Baptist Press), and a new Baptist historical society (the Whitsitt Baptist Heritage Society) have also been founded by disenfranchised mainline conservatives and moderates. These mainline conservative-moderates who have openly opposed the fundamentalist infringement upon the SBC have made concrete efforts to uphold and champion historic Baptist principles and beliefs even as fundamentalists have been working to turn the SBC away from long-held Baptist principles and beliefs.

Mainline conservative-moderate resistance to the fundamentalist takeover is just now beginning to focus its vision primarily on the recently formed CBF, an organization dedicated to carrying on the Great Commission through a distinct Baptist perspective devoid of the fundamentalist mind-set. Birthed in 1990, and officially organized the following year, CBF is quickly becoming the single rallying point around which openly disenfranchised mainline conservatives and moderates are gathering. Although CBF is still in its infancy, and the vision which is being brought about through this organization is still being clarified, it has become clear that CBF is the vehicle through which a new Southern Baptist vision is being realized.

Longtime Southern Baptist conservative-moderate leader Cecil Sherman recognizes that the future of mainline conservative-moderates lies with the Cooperative Baptist Fellowship. "I am hopeful for CBF. I think that fragile infant carries Baptist ideas . . . out of the old SBC and out of the Moderate movement; it is CBF that now is our best hope."[18]

The overriding purpose of CBF is missions and evangelism in the name of Christ. However, CBF focuses on missions in a more balanced, inclusive manner than does the current fundamentalist leadership of the SBC. The political and theological correctness which pervades the SBC is not present in the CBF. CBF seeks to stand upon the Bible itself, and not upon manmade presuppositions about the Bible (such as strict inerrancy). CBF is pointing Southern Baptists back to their Baptist heritage in such matters as the priesthood of all believers, separation of church and state, and religious freedom, while the SBC leadership is forsaking Baptist heritage and constructing new creeds. CBF claims (with much substance to back the claim) that it is more Baptist than the current SBC.

As to the future of CBF, mainline conservative-moderate leaders themselves are not certain what will transpire in the next few years. Sherman noted that most moderates are watching the CBF, but he also recently declared that it is too early to tell what will become of the Fellowship, although the next few years are very crucial to the organization.[19]

Whether or not CBF will emerge as a serious challenge to the SBC in terms of members and monetary resources is yet unknown. CBF experienced remarkable growth in its first four years. A total of 391 Southern Baptist churches supported the CBF in its first year, 1991. By the end of 1994, the number of supporting churches had grown to over thirteen hundred. Likewise, contributions to CBF rose from $4.5 million in its inaugural year to over $11 million in its third year, with over $13 million projected in 1995.[20] This growth has taken place despite the mandate of SBC leaders for Southern Baptists to dissassociate themselves from the Fellowship.

CBF is using its money largely to support missionaries and evangelism. As of November 1993, CBF had employed twenty-six global missionaries. By September 1995, the number of missionaries had risen to seventy-seven, with a forecast of continued rapid growth.[21] Former Foreign Mission Board president Keith Parks now heads the missions efforts of CBF. In contrast, the Foreign Mission Board is losing missionaries faster than ever, but has managed to sustain a statistical increase (such as it reported in 1993 and 1994) because of the fairly recent practice of including short-term missionaries (as well as the relaxing of qualifications in regards to the definition of "short-term" missionary) in its personnel count. In a similar manner, the Home Mission Board personnel count now includes Mission Service Corps volunteers as missionaries "appointed" by the board, although, in fact, the board merely "approves" these volunteers, and has virtually no contact with them following a few days of orientation.

The influential Woman's Missionary Union (WMU) voiced its support of CBF in 1993. One of several actions taken by the WMU in support of the CBF was the organization's agreement to manage a "missionary house" program for CBF, in which WMU will help CBF find stateside temporary residences for its furloughing missionaries.[22] In 1995 fundamentalist SBC leaders led SBC messengers to remove WMU from the role of being the primary sponsor of the annual Lottie Moon and Annie Armstrong mission offerings, in light of WMU's support of CBF missions (although under the pretext of the reorganization of the denominational structure). WMU, however, has not been deterred from supporting CBF missions, and has since started developing mission material for CBF, despite the continued ire of the SBC leadership. WMU support of the CBF is expected to grow in the future.

The future of the conservative-moderate vision which is developing primarily through the avenue of CBF is slowly coming into focus. The various conservative-moderate organizations previously mentioned seem to be coalescing around the CBF. The Fellowship, in turn, seems to be gradually moving toward formal status as a new Baptist organization entirely separate from the SBC. The SBC fundamentalist leadership is certainly pushing the CBF in that direction, and has accomplished that task to some degree. The future of CBF may yet be unclear, but the fact that it continues to experience growth, as well as the fact that more and more large state Baptist conventions are including the CBF in their definition of Cooperative Program, bears witness to its continued vitality.

For its part, the Fellowship recently approved a formal mission statement, which in summary declared, "We are a fellowship of Baptist Christians and churches who share a passion for the Great Commission of Jesus Christ and a commitment to Baptist principles of faith and practice. Our mission is to network, empower and mobilize Baptist Christians and churches for effective missions and ministry in the name of Christ."[23]

THE REALITY AT HAND

In the midst of the competing visions and ideologies in Southern Baptist life at the close of the twentieth century, the most basic reality in Southern Baptist life is division and fragmentation. As Baptist historian Walter Shurden noted, the "splintering" is "in process."[24] While mainline conservative and moderate leaders are harboring no illusions that the current SBC leadership will be toppled, the momentum of the "splinter" CBF continues to grow.

Despite the fact that Southern Baptists have always been a diverse people, the impending split would be the first major, formal division which Southern Baptists have experienced. The reality is that the current splintering of the SBC has led to a decline of America's largest Protestant body. The sad fact is that suffering and anguish have characterized Southern Baptist life since 1979. Furthermore, Southern Baptists have come to be looked upon in more and more of a negative light by both the secular world and much of the Christian world. In truth, the fundamentalist invasion of the SBC and the subsequent internal struggle have hindered the work of Southern Baptists and the cause of Christ.

In short, visions aside, the reality at hand for the SBC is not a pretty sight, despite the glorious picture painted by the current national leadership. Any one of a number of scenarios arising from the downward slide of the SBC might come to pass in the next few years. Although speculation concerning the immediate future of Southern Baptist life may have limited value at this point in time, the serious nature of the current reality in the SBC makes it imperative that Southern Baptists carefully examine where they are headed in relation to effectiveness as a body of people who profess to be followers of and witnesses for Jesus Christ.

STATE BAPTIST CONVENTIONS: FORGING A NEW ROLE IN SOUTHERN BAPTIST LIFE?

Thus far, the fundamentalist battle for control of the SBC has been largely waged on the national level. However, as the fundamentalists have solidified their control of national SBC agencies, they have begun focusing more of their attention and efforts on the state level.

Although not much has been written about the role state Baptist conventions will play in the eventual picture that emerges from the throes of the fundamentalist takeover of the SBC, indications are that the various state conventions will be vital players in determining which scenario eventually transpires.

The importance of the state conventions lies primarily in the fact that local Southern Baptist churches send their Cooperative Program allocations to their respective state conventions. The state conventions then divide the contributions, keeping a certain percentage for state work and sending a certain percentage on to the national body. In other words, the SBC receives the bulk of its operating money from the state conventions, rather than directly from local Southern Baptist churches.

The significance of Baptist state conventions, therefore, lies in the fact that they hold the purse strings when it comes to disbursement of Cooperative Program funds to the agencies and programs of the SBC. As in the SBC, business decisions are made in state conventions during annual meetings to which individual churches in the states send messengers, who, in turn, vote on officers and business matters. These messengers have the power to change the distribution process in which Cooperative Program receipts are disbursed, as well as who the recipients of the funds will be.

State Baptist conventions could very well cut off the financial pipeline to the fundamentalist-controlled SBC, a fact of which the fundamentalist leadership is now well aware.

Not surprisingly, state conventions, through years of conditioning, have historically sent a large percentage of their Cooperative Program funds to the SBC. In recent years, however, some state conventions have largely sided (in state officer elections) with the mainline conservative-moderates in the face of the fundamentalist takeover of the SBC.

Fundamentalists have, in recent years, taken their campaign to the state convention level. However, their efforts to capture these conventions have not been as successful as they would have liked. In the fall of 1993, for example, fundamentalists and mainline conservatives and moderates squared off against each other in the election of state officers in nine large state conventions. Mainline conservative-moderates won seven of these nine confrontations (Florida, Kentucky, Louisiana, Missouri, North Carolina, Texas, and Virginia), compared to two wins for the fundamentalists (Arkansas and South Carolina). In 1994 fundamentalist candidates won in only two large state conventions where the two parties squared off (Alabama and Georgia). In both instances, the margin of victory was razor-thin.

If 1993 and 1994 were any indication, the fundamentalists are a long way from controlling Baptist state conventions. In Louisiana, the fundamentalist candidate for the 1993 presidency of the state convention was a national SBC leader who has been a leader in the fundamentalist takeover of the national body. Yet, he lost the presedential election in his home state. In both Louisiana and Texas, mainline conservative-moderate candidates won on platforms which openly denounced the new fundamentalist leadership of the SBC. In effect, they told the current SBC leadership to leave their states alone.[25]

With mainline conservatives and moderates largely in control of many state Baptist conventions, it is not surprising that the conventions are beginning to rethink their commitment to the SBC. Virginia and North Carolina led the way in the effort to divert Cooperative Program funds away from the SBC. In 1990 the Baptist State Convention of North Carolina voted to give churches the option of contributing to the state convention while bypassing some SBC support.[26] Virginia Baptists also gave their churches that option beginning in 1990.[27] North Carolina and Virginia Baptists can officially send a portion of their offerings to mainline conservative and moderate agencies rather than to the fundamentalist-controlled SBC agencies.

In the 1993 annual meeting of the Georgia Baptist Convention, messengers voted to appoint a committee to study what it meant for a church to be in harmony and cooperation with the state convention. At issue was whether Georgia Baptist churches could designate Cooperative Program outlays to the state convention, bypass the SBC, and still be considered "cooperating" churches. The matter was decided in 1994 when the Georgia Baptist Convention voted that participation on the state level should be measured only by what the local church contributes to state convention work, as opposed to the national SBC.[28]

A more recent and far-reaching development regarding state and national SBC relations has emerged in the wake of the firing of Southwestern Seminary President Russell H. Dilday. When fundamentalists viciously and maliciously fired Dilday in March 1994, conservatives and moderates (and some less-militant fundamentalists) from across the nation voiced loud, sustained protest. A number of state conventions soon went on record condemning the firing, and by the summer of 1994, Texas Baptist leaders were proposing that the Baptist General Convention of Texas stop automatically sending any Cooperative Program funds to the SBC Executive Committee. In September, the Cooperative Missions Giving Study Committee, appointed by the Baptist General Convention of Texas, had finalized its proposal, which recommended that money designated for CBF and CBF causes be counted as Cooperative Program giving, along with money designated for the SBC Executive Committee. Texas Baptists overwhelmingly passed the proposal the following month. In the fall of 1995, the Texas executive board went even further by significantly decreasing the percentage of state receipts which are forwarded to SBC causes.[29]

This Texas Baptist proposal is resulting in more money being channeled to state missions and to the CBF and CBF-related organizations. The overall amount of Southern Baptist money affected by Texas's decision is very significant—Texas boasts more Southern Baptists than any other state, and Texas has historically forwarded more Cooperative Program money to the SBC Executive Committee each year than has any other state convention. Also of significance is the speculation that other state Baptist conventions may follow the lead of North Carolina, Virginia, and Texas. The Cooperative Program is well on its way to radical transformation by individual state conventions which have been isolated by SBC fundamentalist leaders.

As the funds flowing into the SBC continue their roller coaster ride, fundamentalist leaders are understandably worried about these developments on the state level. As more and more state conventions begin exploring options to allow their churches to bypass sending Cooperative Program allocations to the SBC, the financial future of the SBC may become bleaker. Although some small state conventions have recently voted to increase the percentage of their receipts allocated to the SBC, more and more larger state conventions (whose purse strings determine the financial fate of the national SBC) are directing money away from the SBC Executive Committee through reducing the SBC percentage and/or allowing constituents to send money to non-SBC entities.

As the situation now stands, more and more state Baptist conventions are aligning themselves with (or at least becoming inclusive of) mainline conservative-moderate organizations which were founded to counter the fundamentalist invasion of the SBC. On the state level, Southern Baptists appear to be in the very early stages of developing a dual-alignment movement, with states affiliating with both the SBC and the CBF. If this is indeed the case, such a movement would represent a radical reworking of denominational polity. Indications are that the time may be right for just such a reworking of our Southern Baptist structures.

In a nutshell, the current movement underfoot in the larger Baptist state conventions spells continued financial trouble for the SBC through lost revenues. On the other hand, the actions of many of the large state conventions are lending increasing support for the mainline conservative and moderate cause. The state Baptist conventions, the larger ones in particular, hold a crucial key to the immediate and long-term future of Southern Baptists.

LOCAL SOUTHERN BAPTIST CHURCHES: SANCTUARIES OF APATHY?

Each Southern Baptist church is free to make its own decisions without having to get approval from a higher earthly authority. Autonomy of the local church has been a cherished Baptist tradition from the beginning, as the early Baptists sought to avoid the hierarchical system of the Roman Catholic Church and the Church of England. Southern Baptists, born on the frontier of eighteenth- and early nineteenth-century America, where individualism was a way of life, have ardently embraced local-church autonomy.

With the advent of the Cooperative Program in the 1920s, local church autonomy began taking on a new nuance. Southern Baptist churches were encouraged to pool together monetary resources for the common goal of supporting missions, evangelism, and theological education on a national scale. Although some Southern Baptist churches were already cooperating with one another on the associational level, as well on the state level in some instances, cooperation on the national level had been scattered and uncoordinated up to this point.

As the Cooperative Program grew and expanded, and local churches were convinced to take part, Southern Baptists began realizing what could be accomplished if they pooled a portion of their resources together. On the state level, state Baptist conventions were funding Baptist educational institutions, missions, and a variety of ministries, such as nursing homes, children's homes, and hospitals. On the national level, Cooperative Program money forwarded to the SBC Executive Committee in Nashville funded a growing number of missionaries and agencies. As expansion occurred and the structure of the SBC became more centralized, even more churches bought into this new national and international vision.

By the 1970s, Southern Baptists had the largest missions organization and the largest number of seminary students enrolled in their seminaries of any other denomination. Thanks partially to the selling of, and subsequent success of, the Cooperative Program, Southern Baptists had become a mighty army in the world of Christendom.

By this time, most Southern Baptist churches and individuals (at least those who were active in their local churches) had bought into the Cooperative Program and were strong supporters of the things the Cooperative Program was about. The most notable exception to this trend was the refusal of fundamentalist Southern Baptist churches, by and large, to support the program, based on their perception that denominational leaders were not conservative enough.

The ardent support which most mainline conservative-moderate Southern Baptists have long given to the Cooperative Program has played a major role in the way in which the current controversy has played out. At least two-thirds of Southern Baptists are opposed to the current fundamentalist agenda in the SBC. However, only a minority of churches and individuals have openly stood against the fundamentalist coup. This incredible disparity between inner convictions and outer actions can partially (if not largely) be explained by the fact that most mainline conservative-moderates have become so acclimated to the Cooperative Program as the Southern Baptist "way of doing things" that major change is viewed as being too dramatic, or perhaps too disruptive. Many Southern Baptists declare that, although they do not agree with the direction the SBC is heading, they cannot abandon their Cooperative Program support through the SBC Executive Committee.

The Cooperative Program has become a sacred cow for many Southern Baptists. To back off from or to alter it is considered heresy. Many Southern Baptists with conscionable objections continue sending their money to Nashville because it is simply what they are supposed to do. The most obvious excuse given for continuing to support that with which they disagree is that to withdraw from the Cooperative Program on the national level would hurt the great missions programs of the SBC. Although this is a valid argument, it skirts the real issue of whether or not God's hand is still upon the SBC and its ministries.

For the local church, the crux of the matter is this: local-church autonomy allows mainline conservative-moderate churches to remain a part of the SBC without openly taking part (other than through Cooperative Program giving to the Executive Committee) in what is going on at the national level under the new fundamentalist leadership. Or so the myth goes.

Baptist historian Walter Shurden identified this attitude as the "Myth of Isolation." "It won't affect our church; it doesn't matter what they do at the Southern Baptist Convention; we'll do what we want at the local church level."[30] For churches, that is an unfortunate perception of reality.

Studies conducted by sociologist Nancy Ammerman revealed that fifty percent of the leaders of Southern Baptist churches believe that the changes that have occurred at the national SBC level have not affected their local churches. Viewing themselves as autonomous bodies, they do not believe they are affected by the fundamentalist coup. They plan to continue supporting the Cooperative Program, while maintaining their distance from the new leadership.

The problem with this stance, however, is that it is either fantasy or ignorance, as opposed to realism. These fifty percent of Southern Baptist churches, having stated their independence from the SBC on a national level, continue to support the Cooperative Program on the national level, just as they have been trained to do for the last seventy years. They are sending a portion of their tithes and offerings to help support an agenda with which they do not agree. They probably are continuing to send their young people to Southern Baptist seminaries which are under fundamentalist control. They continue to use denominational literature in their Sunday School classes—literature which is now fundamentalist-controlled.

Are these local Southern Baptist churches, in fact, exercising their autonomy? Have they insulated themselves from the national SBC and its new leadership? In theory, maybe. In practice, no.

The disparity lies in the fact that although local Southern Baptist churches are autonomous (that is, void of bishops and a structured hierarchy), the connections between the local church and national denominational life are both ever present and pervasive. Prior to the fundamentalist takeover, too many churches, after years of conditioning, had tied themselves so closely to the SBC Cooperative Program and the issuances of the SBC Executive Committee that they blindly allowed the national SBC to be their spokesperson on all matters of faith, practice, and ministry. Despite the takeover, some of these churches are yet blind followers of SBC decrees in many areas. This "connectionalism" (which sometimes leads to the point of unquestioningly following someone or some human entity which is perceived as a higher authority) can tend to make "local church autonomy" more theory than fact within some church congregations.[31]

Many mainline conservative-moderates are, in effect, excusing themselves from the conflict by declaring a hands-off approach. In all likelihood, many churches and individuals are keeping their eyes closed to the fact that a hands-off attitude silently recognizes the legitimacy of the minority faction that now controls the SBC on the national level.

With the twenty-first century now at hand, it may be time for many mainline conservative-moderate Southern Baptists to ask themselves if the centrally structured national SBC, supported through the "traditional" Cooperative Program, has lulled them into a state of complacency and lukewarmness. God works primarily through local-church fellowships, not national or international organizations or denominations. Although denominations and Christian organizations often serve to advance the kingdom of God and are good in many respects, the concept originated with man, not God. When any local church becomes so closely intertwined with a man-made denomination or organization that it chooses to look away even when sin and pride permeate the leadership of that man-made body, it is time to evaluate where that local-church's priorities lie. Departing from the SBC may not be the answer for some non-fundamentalist churches and individuals, but choosing not to address the ungodliness among the Convention leadership should never be the answer.

Up to this point, many mainline conservative-moderates, who represent the clear majority of Southern Baptists, have indeed been straddling the fence. The time is rapidly approaching, however, when sitting on the fence may no longer be possible. That watershed point for some may be the day when the CBF declares itself a new denomination. At that point, there will be two distinct organizations of Baptists in the South competing for the loyalty of Southern Baptists, and hard choices will have to be made. Or, the day of reckoning for many others may be the day that the SBC fundamentalist leadership issues a mandate that all Southern Baptist ministers and congregations must subscribe to strict inerrancy. Furthermore, there may come a day when the SBC Executive Committee leads the SBC to refuse to recognize any local churches which are related to the CBF. In such instances, very hard choices would have to be made.

The future of the now fundamentalist-controlled SBC and the success of the CBF, the champion of historic Southern Baptist principles and beliefs, will hinge to a large degree upon whether or not the fifty percent of Southern Baptist churches which are resting upon their claims of local-church autonomy actually act on that autonomy, or simply follow their connectionalistic traditions. Also, the point to which that fifty percent will go along with the possible future inerrancy mandate could be an important factor in deciding the fate of both the SBC and the CBF.

The feeling on both sides of the controversy is that only a small percentage of Southern Baptist churches will abandon their traditional SBC ties. Ammerman surmised that only ten to twenty percent of churches would, in the long run, actively resist the new fundamentalist leadership. Of those, not all would join the CBF, for many would move in an independent direction.[32]

Will the indifference of many local Southern Baptist churches continue until the last possible moment? At that decisive moment, will the majority mainline conservative-moderates by and large sell out their convictions to remain on the SBC team? It is still just a little too early to tell, but it appears that denominational loyalty is, and will remain, a major hurdle.

Nancy Ammerman placed these questions in a larger context. She observed that denominations in general are undergoing many kinds of changes in organizational methodology as the twenty-first century approaches. She detected a trend away from centralized "headquarters" in denominational life toward a less structured relationship between the local church and the denomination. Ammerman noted that out of this new direction may emerge a new understanding of denominational identity. Within this context, she saw the "denominational monopoly" of the SBC Cooperative Program as already breaking apart.[33]

The future direction of Southern Baptist life lies largely in the hands of those local churches and individual leaders who to this point have been straddling the fence. The choice may ultimately be between personal convictions and connectionalistic traditions bound up in denominational loyalty. Decisions made will have enormous influence.

INTO THE TWENTY-FIRST CENTURY

Although the future of Southern Baptists is murky at this point, a number of recent trends may well be barometers as to what lies ahead for the SBC and the fledgling CBF. The Southern Baptist fabric, long woven together, despite having stripes of different colors, is rapidly coming apart at the seams and appears to be on the verge of complete cleavage. Now is the time for Southern Baptists to evaluate where they stand and where they are going. Following are some scenarios that may likely take place as Southern Baptists move beyond their 150th anniversary celebration and toward a new century.

Fundamentalist Leaders Continue Their Quest for Total Control. To begin with, fundamentalism is very exclusive in nature. Fundamentalism requires strict adherence to a particular set of beliefs and/or actions. Fundamentalist leaders are primarily concerned about making sure that their constituency "toes the line." Protestant Christianity does not have a monopoly on fundamentalism. Fundamentalism exists among Roman Catholics, and fundamentalism within the religious bodies of the Middle East is well documented. Well-known Islamic author Salmon Rushdie remains in hiding because the Islamic leadership has sentenced him to death for his book, *The Satanic Verses*, which criticizes fundamentalist Muslims.

The sixteen-year track record of fundamentalist leaders on the national SBC level has revealed that they are dedicated to erecting stricter and stricter parameters in regards to who can be a "cooperating" Southern Baptist in national SBC life. Whereas SBC agencies have historically honored diversity under the Lordship of Christ within agency and missionary personnel, the new fundamentalist leadership, despite claims of seeking "parity" earlier in the controversy, has systematically sought to weed out from national SBC life all who do not agree with them. Only the "theologically correct" and the "politically correct" now have opportunity to advance in the ranks of national SBC leadership. Even missionaries and agency personnel are being purged when they openly voice disagreement with the fundamentalist leadership.

The main parameter which the fundamentalists have erected is the belief in the Bible as inerrant in the strict sense. Recent SBC presidents, including the sitting president, have loudly decreed that only "inerrantists" will be permitted to hold positions of leadership in national SBC life. Fundamentalist leaders claim to speak for the majority of Southern Baptists as they trumpet their inerrancy agenda. However, the majority of Southern Baptists are not inerrantists in the strict sense, and the very existence of inerrancy as a valid theory of biblical inspiration is questionable on the basis that it is built upon humanistic understanding and misleading terminology, rather than coming from the biblical text itself.

Nevertheless, the fundamentalist leadership is busy ruthlessly forcing inerrancy upon Southern Baptists. One recent example of the extent to which the "enforcers" will go was an incident at Midwestern Baptist Theological Seminary in October 1993. Wilburn Stancil, a well-respected professor who is a strong, committed conservative Christian leader and who has served the seminary well for a number of years, was up for tenure. In the spring of 1993, trustees had voted 17-16 to grant him tenure, but the fundamentalist trustee chair ruled that a two-thirds majority was required to grant tenure. In truth, the bylaws contained no such provision, and the chair's ruling was in violation of the bylaws, which merely mandated a majority vote. The chair's ruling was, in effect, a dishonest and illegal move to buy time for the fundamentalist trustees.

In October the trustees met again and decided that only a majority vote was needed to grant tenure. However, instead of letting their earlier vote stand, they chose to vote again, and this time the fundamentalist majority voted to deny tenure to Stancil. The entire episode was one of duplicity and dishonesty on the part of the fundamentalist trustees who illegally bypassed the established system to make sure that they got their own way.

The issue upon which Stancil was denied tenure was his refusal to use the word "inerrant" to describe his view of the Bible. Midwestern Seminary president Milton Ferguson noted that Stancil had a higher view of the Bible than some inerrantists. Self-avowed inerrantist Marvin Nobles, a Missouri trustee, declared that although Stancil did not use the word "inerrancy," his beliefs were, in effect, the same as Nobles' were. These observations fell largely on deaf ears, however, as Stancil was denied tenure mainly because he refused to use the word "inerrancy" to describe his beliefs about the Bible. The opinion of fundamentalist trustees bent on enforcing theological correctness was that if Stancil would not embrace the term, he did not believe the Bible, and should not be tenured.[34]

The recent 1994 firing of Southwestern Seminary president Russell H. Dilday further reveals just how far some fundamentalist leaders will go to make certain they maintain absolute control in SBC life.

Dilday, president of Southwestern since 1978, had long been known to be a staunch conservative. However, he was also a vocal critic of the fundamentalist takeover of the SBC. As the controversy grew more intense in the late 1980s and early 1990s, Dilday managed to maintain his denominational position because Southwestern had long been considered the most conservative of the six Southern Baptist seminaries. Also, Dilday, although critical of the fundamentalist agenda, did strive to work with the fundamentalists to some degree. This uneasy arrangement, however, was destined not to last. Ultimately, Dilday refused to bow down to the wishes of the fundamentalist trustees of Southwestern, and the trustees, angry that he would not be their puppet, finally decided to forcefully remove him from office.

The manner in which the trustees removed Dilday from office was so extraordinarily unChristian and unBaptist that tens of thousands of Southern Baptists from across the nation immediately raised their voices in protest over his firing. Of the several hundred letters to the editors in state Baptist papers between mid-March and late May, only a dozen or so expressed support for the trustees (and several of those were authored by the same person).

The ruthless bent of the trustees was evident from the beginning. On March 8, the day before the firing took place, Dilday questioned the chair of the trustees about rumors regarding his dismissal. The trustee chair adamantly denied any such intentions. When the firing did occur the next day, the trustee chair acted as if the incident was unplanned. The facts, however, revealed otherwise.

Certain trustees, it turned out (including the trustee chair), had been plotting Dilday's removal for quite some time. Preprinted ballots had been prepared for trustees to vote on his dismissal. Two letters to the Southwestern faculty had previously been printed in regards to his termination—one if Dilday chose to accept the "buyout" package key trustees had decided to offer him, and the other in case he refused the offer and forced a vote. Some faculty actually received the wrong letter. Trustees also had arranged ahead of time to have the locks changed on Dilday's office during the moments following his dismissal—he was not even allowed to return to his office to gather his personal belongings. Furthermore, some trustees had plotted ahead of time to immediately force Dilday out of the presidential house, but they did back down and allowed him to remain in his house for a few more months.

Despite the trustees' denial that a plot was underfoot, the facts that surfaced following the incident clearly revealed that not only was the removal of Dilday planned well ahead of time; the plot was also carefully carried out with cold-blooded, loveless, calculated precision.

Moments prior to the trustee vote on Dilday's status, Dilday asked the chair of the trustees why they wanted to fire him. The trustee chair's reply was, "We don't need a reason; we can do it." When questioned by the press, the trustee chair initially refused to give an explanation. The arrogance on the part of the hostile trustees (not all voted for the firing) was evident.

Later, with the fallout from the firing continuing to grow, the trustee chair scrambled to do some damage control. Dilday's firing was blamed on his not being conservative enough—that is, not being an avowed inerrantist. Most knowledgeable Southern Baptists, however, saw through the thinly veiled guise of painting Dilday as a liberal. Well into the summer, resolutions from Southern Baptist groups across the nation rebuking the trustees' ungodly, political actions continued to be issued. A number of state Baptist conventions went on record as supporting Dilday, and of the many state Baptist paper editors, only one backed the trustees' actions.[35] Since Dilday's firing, many faculty and administrative members have taken early retirement or accepted other positions elsewhere, and the word from some students is that campus morale is low.

Although inerrancy is the main tenet which fundamentalists are forcing upon the SBC, they are also constructing other parameters which are designed to ensure theological and political correctness. Among these agendas are a hard-line opposition to all abortions from the moment of conception (many are against abortion even if the life of the mother is in danger), the universal exclusion of women as pastors or ordained ministers, an attempt to expel Freemasons from SBC life (which has caused division in the fundamentalist camp), a direct aligning with the Republican Party, a campaign to tear down the separation of church and state, the transformation of Southern Baptist seminaries into centers of indoctrination (several are already officially committed to hiring only inerrantists on their faculties), and the upholding of the pastor as a dictator, as opposed to a shepherd.

The events of 1995 at Southern Seminary reveal just how paranoid the fundamentalist leaders are in their quest for minute theological correctness as determined by their personal opinions. The events also paint a picture of a regime which continues to place seemingly no boundaries on the unethical and unChristian means which they are willing to employ in order to enforce their personal will upon the masses. President Albert Mohler, declared Calvinist, has led this modern-day witch-hunt.

Since Mohler's inaguration, the situation at Southern has turned from bad to ugly. Mohler has set out to rule Southern with an iron fist, and his edicts have been coming primarily from his own personal opinions, and not from Scripture. The forced resignation of professor Molly Marshall in 1994 (Mohler decreed that her views were not compatible with his interpretation of the seminary's Abstract of Principles) turned out to be a precursor of things to come.

The following year turned out to be a pivotal year for the seminary as Mohler's iron fist, with the support of fundamentalist trustees, came down hard. In February, professor Timothy Johnson resigned amidst charges of racism and broken promises on the part of Mohler. The following month, Mohler fired Diana Garland, dean of the Carver School of Social Work, resulting in the most serious crisis of his administration to date.

Despite the fact that no policy existed which declared what prospective faculty members must believe regarding women in ministry, Mohler took the matter into his own hands and deemed that he would hire no one who believed in women's ordination. Garland was fired primarily because she publicly aired her disagreements with Mohler over his refusal to hire a solidly conservative professor on the grounds that the prospective professor supported women's ordination. Garland explained that as most evangelical denominations are becoming more open to women in ministry, finding an evangelical scholar who could meet Mohler's personal criteria was virtually impossible. Mohler summarily fired Garland for publicly stating her views.

Reaction to Mohler's move was swift. Students, faculty, pastors, laity, and editors of Southern Baptist papers declared that Mohler had overstepped his bounds by imposing his personal opinions upon the faculty hiring process. Students affirmed their support of the School of Social Work, but Mohler brushed aside both students and the school. He declared that students had no business getting involved in the matter, and that students could not hold him or the administration accountable for any of his actions. Furthermore, Mohler declared that "the culture of social work and the culture of theological education are not congruent." (Never mind that at least half of Jesus' ministry here on earth was involved with spreading the Good News through social work!) He also stated that his only obligation to faculty was to pass on to them word of the administration's policies, and he paid no heed to the objections of Southern Baptists across the nation.

The trustees, however, responded by rewarding Mohler for his actions. They voted to make belief against women's ordination a prerequisite for future faculty, and they voted basically to give Mohler a free hand in filling all future faculty positions. As a result, accreditating agencies are once again turning a doubtful eye toward Southern, over a dozen professors left within a few months (with a little encouragement from Mohler's administration), alumni support dropped to an all-time low, Southern faces a severe financial crisis, enrollment has plummeted, and many Baptist colleges and universities no longer allow Southern to recruit on their campuses.[36] Despite all of this, it does not seem to have occurred to Mohler and the trustees that their unChristlike spirit and actions are the cause of Southern's drastic downturn.

As the tragedy at Southern illustrates, fundamentalist leaders have been and are still in the process of forcefully paring the SBC down to their own personal beliefs. Opposing opinions are considered to be invalid, and the fundamentalist leaders have revealed over and over again that they have no interest in cooperating with those who do not believe as they do. The strict enforcing of their theological/political agenda is all-consuming.

A telling sign of the totalitarian regime which fundamentalist leaders have enacted took place in the spring of 1994. Two self-identified fundamentalists decided to run for the SBC presidency in June 1994. The fundamentalist power brokers threw their weight behind a particular candidate because he was the more hard-line of the two. When asked why they opposed the other candidate, some of the power brokers expressed the fear that he would be too soft when it came to dealing with non-fundamentalists, to the point where he might even "appoint the wrong people" to national positions of leadership. The all-consuming nature of the fundamentalists' power play is self-evident.[37]

At least two-thirds of Southern Baptists do not support the fundamentalist agenda. Furthermore, as Ammerman's surveys have revealed, only eleven percent of Southern Baptists use the term "fundamentalist" to describe themselves. As such, the fundamentalist leadership is seeking to impose an agenda upon an organization whose members are largely hostile to such intentions. The fact that the fundamentalist leaders have succeeded in the face of hostility is, in part, a testimony to their political skill and duplicity.

Fundamentalist leaders continue their passionate pursuit of theological and political correctness. They are willing to do anything, whether it be ethical or not, to see that their agenda is carried out. Their quest for control and conformity apparently knows no boundaries in methodology.

When the Woman's Missionary Union (WMU), an autonomous organization that has historically worked with the SBC in missions awareness and funding, stated its intentions in January 1993 to support the CBF, fundamentalists responded with rage. John Jackson, chairman of the SBC Foreign Mission Board, declared that WMU had become an "adulterer" by agreeing to help the CBF.[38]

At the heart of the fundamentalists' rage was the issue of control—since WMU is an autonomous national organization which voluntarily relates to the SBC, fundamentalists cannot enforce their agenda upon the organization. One fundamentalist leader expressed his displeasure with the situation when he declared that WMU should be "hard-wired" into the Convention, and therefore brought under fundamentalist control. As Daniel Vestal, a conservative Southern Baptist who went from being unaligned in the controversy to becoming a leader within the CBF, discovered during his tenure on the 1987 Peace Committee of the SBC that fundamentalists desired "control, total control, absolute control."[39]

All indications point toward a fundamentalist leadership which has no disposition to ease up on efforts to gain complete control of SBC life through the enforcing of a theological and political agenda. WMU has been a thorn in their side as it gravitates toward lending more and more of its considerable organizational clout to support of the CBF. The WMU-sponsored Lottie Moon and Annie Armstrong mission offerings have historically contributed a huge chunk of the annual budgets of the Foreign and Home Missions Boards. WMU is largely responsible for the success of both mission boards, but the SBC Executive Committee, through the 1995 restructuring proposal, has led the SBC to strip mission fund-raising responsibilities from the WMU, turning such responsibilities over to the mission boards (which are to be renamed the International Mission Board and North American Mission Board). This, along with the prior formation of a new women's organization by the Baptist Sunday School Board,[40] has effectively removed WMU from playing any vital role in SBC life other than missions education. Ironically, the SBC leadership sees no inconsistency in working with non-Baptist evangelical groups while at the same time condemning WMU for teaming up with the CBF.

If WMU has been a thorn in the side of the fundamentalist leadership, the CBF itself has been a migraine headache. Although only five years old, the CBF is growing at a steady rate even as the SBC continues its roller coaster ride. More and more churches are sending their money to the CBF rather than to the SBC Cooperative Program.

In addition, CBF-friendly seminaries are more than successfully competing with fundamentalist-controlled SBC seminaries for Southern Baptist students. Smyth and Helwys Sunday School literature is competing with Sunday School Board literature. Even a CBF missions offering is competing against the Lottie Moon and Annie Armstrong mission offerings. The Christian Life Commission is battling with the Baptist Joint Committee and the Baptist Center for Ethics in regards to social and church-state concerns. In short, the fundamentalist leadership of the SBC is finding itself competing against CBF-friendly organizations and agencies at almost every turn. For their part, these alternate conservative-moderate organizations taken together are beginning to show signs of being the "little engine that could."

The fundamentalist leadership openly dealt with the CBF during the 1994 SBC annual meeting. There have also been recent calls by fundamentalists for those Southern Baptists who do not support the fundamentalist agenda to leave the Convention. It would be fitting if the two-thirds (or more) of Southern Baptists who do not support the new fundamentalist agenda would indeed depart, leaving the fundamentalists holding a mostly empty bag.

There is much anticipation that fundamentalist leaders will lead the SBC into disfellowshiping those churches and individuals who are supporting the CBF. The fundamentalist leadership has already severed the SBC from the CBF from a financial standpoint by requiring SBC agencies to refuse money that is channeled to them through the CBF. The complete disfellowshiping of CBF churches, possibly only a few short years or less down the road, would be consistent with the fundamentalists' desire for total control over those churches affiliated with the SBC.

Although fundamentalist leaders will continue extending their quest for control in all areas of SBC life, as evidenced by the 1995 organizational restructuring which proposed to do away with, among other agencies, both the Education Commission and Historical Commission (two SBC agencies which had never fully cooperated with the fundamentalist leadership), the CBF and the entities which are affiliated with it are beyond the control of fundamentalists. As such, these organizations have assured themselves that they will be viewed as chief antagonists of the SBC fundamentalist leadership. Since control is not an option which the fundamentalists possess in regards to these organizations, the most likely response will be disfellowshiping CBF-friendly churches which support the conservative-moderate structures. To rid the SBC of all churches which do not support the fundamentalist agenda (even if the support is coerced and based on fear) would be the finishing touches of the fundamentalist coup.

Independent Fundamentalist Baptists May Join the SBC. Recent SBC president H. Edwin Young and independent fundamentalist Baptist leader Jerry Falwell have publicly voiced their support for more cooperation between the independent fundamentalist Baptist churches and the SBC. The strong ties between the SBC fundamentalist leadership and Falwell seem to be pointing toward a merger of some type between the Baptist Bible Fellowship, the largest of the independent fundamentalist Baptist denominations and the denomination to which Falwell's church belongs, and the SBC. Such a merger could be only a few short years away.

The merger would be a strategic move on the part of the SBC fundamentalist leadership. The growing success of the CBF is already causing financial and numerical distress on the SBC national level. The gravitation of the CBF towards a new denominational entity will statistically pull the SBC further down. Merging with the Baptist Bible Fellowship would instantly beef up the SBC, statistically speaking.

As a foreshadowing of this very real possibility, black Baptists are accusing the SBC leadership of using the recent SBC resolution on racial repentance as a tool to add new congregations to the SBC roster. SBC leaders have promised numerical growth in terms of the numbers of SBC-affiliated churches, and have resorted to various tactics (such as wooing blacks and independents) to engineer such growth. Also, the definition of "church" has been reworked to allow more "churches" to appear in SBC reports.

How far can the "engineered success" of the SBC leadership carry the SBC? Fundamentalist leaders are hoping that the typical Southern Baptist will be gullible and apathetic enough to allow them to continue the facade for quite some time.

State Conventions Assert Their Independence. By the time the fundamentalists put the finishing touches on their coup of the SBC, a number of individual Baptist state conventions will have openly expressed patterns of independence from the SBC (North Carolina, Virginia, and Texas have already done so). The mainline conservative and moderate leanings of the majority of the major state conventions will continue to facilitate this trend, although some state conventions in newer convention areas which rely on Cooperative Program money for their existence may line up solidly behind (or at least not voice opposition to) the national SBC fundamentalist leadership in order to ensure their own survival.

The trend toward independence is already gaining momentum in the wake of Texas's recent redefining of their Cooperative Program. A president of Texas Baptists, Jerald McBride, is the pastor of a church which supports the CBF. The Baptist General Convention of Texas openly thumbed its nose at the fundamentalist leadership of the SBC during 1993. McBride threw down the gauntlet when he declared that the Texas Baptist Convention was not a "farm team" of the SBC and would not allow the SBC to dictate its whims to Texas Baptists. Texas Baptists have chosen to respect the rights of local churches to contribute to either the SBC or the CBF. In 1994, following the firing of Russell Dilday as president of Southwestern, Texas Baptists overwhelmingly voted to redefine "Cooperative Program" to include the CBF and CBF-related entities. This move by Texas stirred the wrath of SBC fundamentalist leaders, because Texas has historically contributed more annual money to the SBC Executive Committee than any other state Baptist convention. Now, only money which churches specifically direct to the SBC Executive Commitee will be forwarded to the SBC.

State Baptist convention meetings of 1993, 1994, and 1995 also saw other states exploring various ways to distance themselves from the national SBC. If the fundamentalists have their way, there will be a price to pay for those states which continue to support, or decide to support, the CBF openly. The executive committee of the Home Mission Board voted in June 1994 to study how the HMB should relate to state Baptist conventions which are channeling designated funds to the CBF. The author of the motion referred to such states as not being "loyal to Southern Baptists" and voiced a thinly veiled warning, "We need to send a message to these conventions—don't be uncooperative."[41] When HMB personnel did sit down to meet with state directors, the rhetoric was toned down, but the HMB has continued to strongly advocate, to the point of insisting, that state Baptist conventions remain loyal to the national SBC.

Although many other Bible-belt state conventions continue to verbally voice support for the SBC Cooperative Program, fundamentalists have not fared well in the election of state officers furing the past three years, and the firing of Dilday has eroded much support for traditional Cooperative Program giving. The conservative-moderate trend on the state level (which many regard as a truer indication of Southern Baptist thought and will) is paving the way for established state conventions to more strongly assert their independence from the SBC.

The current movement seems to be toward dual alignment (whether explicitly or implicitly) with the SBC and the CBF. If the SBC fundamentalist leadership continues its longstanding policy of harassment and intimidation, the dual-alignment status of some state conventions could eventually give way to primary support for the CBF. With the recent call by some fundamentalists to form alternative state Baptist organizations in certain CBF-friendly states (with the proposed organizations being fundamentalist in nature and relating only to the SBC on the national level), a movement toward primary support of the CBF in those states could possibly come about within a shorter period of time.

The Cooperative Baptist Fellowship Becomes a New Convention. Even now, the CBF and CBF-friendly conservative-moderate agencies and organizations have all the markings of a separate convention: a central organization, a rapidly growing financial base, a rapidly developing missionary force, the increasing support of several key state Baptist conventions, theological institutions, worldwide constituency, state fellowship groups, a national annual convocation, a quality publishing house, an ethics agency, a historical society, and skilled, capable leadership. There is a growing consensus that the CBF will eventually take on the "denominational" label, an issue which was brought up at the 1995 annual CBF meeting. Since that time, CBF leadership has appointed a committee to study the denominational "question." Some supporters of CBF are encouraging a formal split with the SBC, while many others are expressing a more cautious attitude. A formal recommendation about direction could come forth in 1996.

There are basically two ways in which the CBF could arrive at the point of becoming a separate convention. The first would be for those Southern Baptist churches and individuals who are connected to the Fellowship to vote for CBF to become a separate organization independent of the SBC. Should the current CBF denominational study committee recommend temporarily delaying or indefinitely postponing the move towards formal denominational status, a second scenario enters the picture. This second possibility would involve the fundamentalist-led national SBC disfellowshiping those churches which are a part of CBF, which would in effect force the Fellowship into declaring itself a fully independent Baptist entity. A big step was taken in this direction during the 1994 annual SBC meeting in Orlando when messengers voted, at the urging of the SBC Executive Committee, to order SBC agencies and institutions to stop accepting money channeled through the Fellowship office. Although local churches who support the Fellowship were not targeted for disfellowship, the SBC Executive Committee has positioned the SBC towards barring Fellowship-supporting churches from SBC life in the not-too-distant future. Already, members of CBF-related churches are not allowed to hold positions in the national SBC denomination.

Should the CBF take the initiative to formally launch a new convention, many Southern Baptist churches which are in sympathy with the Fellowship might find it difficult to depart from traditional SBC structures and cast lots with the new kid on the block. The exodus of churches would most likely be rather small and insignificant, a fact of which CBF leaders are well aware. Any meaningful growth within the new denomination would come about over a period of time, rather than immediately.

On the other hand, if the fundamentalist-led SBC, in its continual quest for control, votes to disfellowship CBF churches from the Convention, many of the two-thirds or more of Southern Baptist individuals who are not supportive of the fundamentalist agenda in the SBC may take a hard look at the heavy-handed tactics of the fundamentalist leadership. With the SBC being viewed as the wrongful oppressor, a significant number of Southern Baptist churches might seriously entertain the notion of abandoning the SBC in favor of the CBF. Significant growth, accordingly, could very well take place right away.

If the CBF is to emerge as an organization of significant numbers in the near future, it will almost certainly have to do so against the backdrop of an SBC which is clearly perceived to be a heavy-handed oppressor of all who dissent from the party-line. The firing of Russell H. Dilday from Southwestern and the forced removal of Molly Marshall from the Southern Seminary staff (both in 1994), as well as the firing of Diana Garland in 1995, are three recent incidents which have served to reinforce this ever-growing perception of the SBC leadership.

Up to this point, only a minority of mainline conservative-moderates have fully opened their eyes to the hate-filled tactics of the fundamentalist leadership. More and more conservative-moderate churches and individuals are lining up behind the CBF, and although the numerical growth of the CBF continues upward, the Fellowship is merely five years old and has a long way to go before it numerically rivals the SBC—if it ever does.

Another potential turning point for the CBF relates to the fallout of the removal of the WMU from coordinating the missions offerings for the SBC mission boards. There is some speculation that the WMU, having been trodden underneath the feet of the crusading fundamentalists, will soon turn much of its fund-raising clout and expertise towards the CBF.

Yet another critical point for the conservative-moderate cause could be the possible merger between the fundamentalist Baptist Bible Fellowship and the SBC. An effort by the fundamentalist SBC leadership to bring Jerry Falwell and his organization into the SBC would certainly arouse a lot of ire among heretofore silent mainline conservative-moderates, and would likely result in many undecideds fleeing to the CBF.

The more the fundamentalist leaders of the SBC flex their muscles, the more the CBF will see its ranks swell, such as through the Dilday and Garland firings. The more persecution SBC leaders heap upon conservative-moderate Southern Baptists, the more solid will become the likelihood that the CBF will become a viable organization for the long term. The continued forced removal of the WMU from any meaningful role in SBC life, the acceptance of independent fundamentalist Baptist churches into the SBC, and the formal disfellowshiping of CBF churches from the SBC could well be the best things that happen to the CBF.

Baptists were born out of persecution at the hands of an official state church. Southern Baptists were born out of what they perceived as a slighting by their northern brothers. The CBF as a separate convention is also being birthed out of the pangs of persecution—this time at the hands of some of their own Southern Baptist brethren. The timing of the final delivery, and the circumstances surrounding its coming into the world, will be very, very crucial.

THE NEW SOUTHERN BAPTIST WITNESS

By the time the twenty-first century arrives, indications are that Sosouthern Baptists will likely be presenting two contrasting witnesses to the world. One will be that of the SBC, by then fully fundamentalist and possibly smaller as a result of the split (how long the leadership can continue to manipulate the statistics remains to be seen, and Falwell remains the wild card). The witness presented by the SBC will be a strict, legalistic mind-set pitted squarely and militantly against the perceived evils (whether real or not) of this modern world—this, after all, is what fundamentalism is all about.

By this time, the fundamentalist leadership of the SBC will likely be engaged in major internal strife, which will contribute further to the decline of the SBC. Already, there are signs of internal conflict within the fundamentalist leadership. The SBC presidential race of June 1994 witnessed two fundamentalists pitted against one another. One of the two candidates was endorsed by the fundamentalist presidents who had served during the previous fifteen years, while the other, Jim Henry of Florida, viewed by some as a less militant fundamentalist, was endorsed by Russell H. Dilday, recently fired president of Southwestern Seminary. Dilday had been fired at the hand of a trustee board comprised largely of extremist fundamentalists. In part because of the Dilday firing, Henry won the presidency, becoming the first man since 1978 to win the SBC president without the endorsement of the SBC "inner circle" fundamentalist leadership.

The ramifications of this new fundamentalist infighting within the SBC have yet to surface. Although Jim Henry did win the presidential election without the backing of past fundamentalist presidents, he has been supportive of the fundamentalist takeover, and is "dear friends" with members of the fundamentalist "inner circle." The main difference between past fundamentalist SBC presidents and Henry is the fact that Henry's church has long been a stalwart supporter of the Cooperative Program, while the previous presidents' churches have given the Cooperative Program only token support.

Although not handpicked by the "inner circle," Henry is fully supportive of the fundamentalist agenda and has stated his intentions to continue that agenda. A few non-fundamentalists have expressed very cautious optimism regarding Henry's term, but Henry has plainly stated his intention to maintain the fundamentalist policy of allowing only avowed inerrantists to hold positions of leadership within the SBC.

Henry's election seems to have changed nothing in regards to the fundamentalist takeover. His tenure as president, however, may mark the beginning of a struggle within the fundamentalist movement to further define itself and its image. At this point, it is doubtful that his election will reverse the downward spiral of the SBC. Indeed, during the 1994 annual SBC, there was no toning down of the continuing fundamentalist quest for total and complete control of the SBC, as fundamentalists led messengers to severe financial ties with the CBF and give approval to the trustees who had removed Russell H. Dilday from the presidency of Southwestern in an unChristian and mean-spirited manner.[42] The 1995 annual meeting followed in the same tone, as the fundamentalist leadership led messengers to dismantle the Historical Commission, among other agencies, and cut WMU out of any meaningful role in SBC life.[43] Signs of inner turmoil in fundamentalist circles continued, however, as SBC Executive Director Morris Chapman and Home Mission Board President Larry Lewis traded sharp words in a disagreement over the details of the proposed restructuring proposal.

If current trends continue, the SBC's witness at the turn of the century will reflect more of an independent, fundamentalist Baptist flavor than a Southern Baptist texture. SBC leaders' claims to hold the monopoly on all truth will make it more and more difficult for the SBC to speak to an increasingly pluralistic, technological, biomedical, and scientific world. Easy answers may temporarily satisfy those who are searching for higher meaning, but we no longer live in a world where easy answers will suffice in the long run. Added to this picture will be a Convention whose image will have been damaged in the eyes of the secular world and the larger Christian church by a ruthless, unethical leadership.

In short, the SBC, as it turns the corner of a new century, will, if current trends and indications hold out, be a body of Christians whose witness for

Christ has been badly damaged by internal strife, strict adherence to old extra-biblical traditions, and hypocritical, unethical, and mean-spirited leadership.

The other witness which Southern Baptists will be presenting to the world will be through the CBF. Although the Fellowship will not bear the Southern Baptist label in name, this organization will be more Southern Baptist in practice than will the SBC. The CBF will continue to uphold the historic Southern Baptist principles of biblical authority, the priesthood of all believers, religious liberty, and the separation of church and state. The CBF will maintain the Southern Baptist distinctives and identity that mainline conservative-moderates have long championed. The Fellowship will also reflect the inclusive nature of the pre-fundamentalist SBC.

If its current mission statement is an indication, the CBF will likely be a vibrant, growing organization centered around missions and evangelism, and dedicated to sharing the gospel of Christ with integrity to a dying world. The Christian witness of CBF will be more evident and effective in a twenty-first-century world. Furthermore, if the timing and circumstances of the impending split are right, the CBF could be an organization of considerable size by the turn of the century. The CBF will have problems and difficulties as it grows and further defines itself and wrestles with various issues, but it will most likely bear a more faithful Baptist and Christian witness in the early twenty-first century than will the SBC.

Thus, indications are that the Southern Baptist witness will be disjointed as the new century begins. The SBC will have finished rewriting the mission of the SBC to reflect the fundamentalist bent of the organization. The CBF will be carrying the torch of non-creedalism and unity amidst diversity under the Lordship of Christ that Baptists of old carried, distinctives that the fundamentalist-controlled SBC has already abandoned. The national SBC leadership will continue to present a strict, legalistic God to the world, while the CBF will be bearing witness of a God who has love for and compassion upon the human beings he created as he calls them back to him. Despair and hope will coexist together in Southern Baptist life.

The result of the current failure to be able to work together despite diversity will have caused much pain and suffering and will have damaged the Southern Baptist witness for Christ. Southern Baptists are just now beginning to face the future which the controversy has put in motion. The finalization of the impending divorce will not be pleasant. There will be much soul searching as those churches and individuals who have sought to ignore the controversy are forced to choose sides. Hopefully, Christian conscience will not become a victim of fear and intimidation.

What good can come out of this destruction of the SBC as it was known only two decades ago? God ultimately is in control, and is more than capable of bringing good out of the direst of circumstances. The Israelites of old had a habit of forsaking God for their own schemes, until the disasters which followed brought them back to God on bended knee, opening the way for God to be glorified through his people again.

The current leadership of the SBC seems to have led the SBC far astray from God's agenda for Southern Baptists in the midst of embracing and enforcing their own personal agendas. Nevertheless, this chapter in Southern Baptist life is far from being the last. God may or may not have removed his hand from the SBC at this juncture, but he is not finished with the people of his kingdom who are known as Southern Baptists:

> "Just as I watched over them to uproot and tear down, and to overthrow, destroy and bring disaster, so I will watch over them to build and to plant," declares the Lord. . . . "The time is coming," declares the Lord, "when I will make a new covenant . . ." (Jer. 31:28, 31a, NIV).

Notes

Chapter One
 1. *New England Baptist*, October 1993, 6.
 2. Leo Rosten, *Religions of America* (New York: Simon and Schuster, 1975), 339.
 3. For more information, see Rosten, or National Geographic Society's *Great Religions of the World* (National Geographic Society, 1978).
 4. H. Leon McBeth, *The Baptist Heritage: Four Centuries of Baptist Witness* (Nashville: Broadman, 1987), 21-152.
 5. Ibid., 153-608.

Chapter Two
 1. Williston Walker, *Christian History* (New York: Charles Scribner's Sons, 1985), 35.
 2. Ibid., 36-40.
 3. Ibid., 74-77.
 4. Ibid., 129-51.
 5. Ibid., 153-279.
 6. Ibid., 283-385.
 7. Ibid., 344-47.
 8. Ibid., 419-20.
 9. Ibid., 421-41.
 10. Ibid., 441-47.
 11. Ibid., 448-62.
 12. Ibid., 471-80.
 13. Ibid., 481-562.
 14. H. Leon McBeth, *The Baptist Heritage: Four Centuries of Baptist Witness* (Nashville: Broadman, 1987), 19-31, 52-56.
 15. Ibid., 32-44.
 16. Ibid., 44-48, 66-91.
 17. Ibid., 123-47.
 18. Robert G. Gardner, *Baptists of Early America: A Statistical History,*

1639-1790 (Atlanta: Georgia Baptist Historical Society, 1983), 63.
   19. McBeth, 200.
   20. Winthrop Hudson, *History of American Christianity* (New York: Charles Scribner's Sons, 1965), 115.
   21. McBeth, 200.
   22. Ibid., 202-06.
   23. Ibid., 206-27.
   24. Ibid., 227-35.
   25. Ibid., 235-51.
   26. Ibid., 252-83.
   27. Ibid., 152, 343-60.
   28. Ibid., 360-70.
   29. Ibid., 371-76.
   30. Walter B. Shurden, *Not a Silent People: Controversies That Have Shaped Southern Baptists* (Macon, Ga.: Smyth & Helwys, 1995), 22-27.
   31. McBeth, 371-76.
   32. Ibid., 376-77.
   33. Ibid., 377-80.

Chapter Three
   1. H. Leon McBeth, *The Baptist Heritage: Four Centuries of Baptist Witness* (Nashville: Broadman, 1987), 381-392.
   2. Ibid., 413-24.
   3. Ibid., 424-32.
   4. Ibid., 432-46.
   5. Ibid., 461-63.
   6. Walter B. Shurden, *Not a Silent People: Controversies That Have Shaped Southern Baptists* (Macon, Ga.: Smyth & Helwys, 1995), 41.
   7. McBeth, 447-57.
   8. William E. Ellis, *A Man of Books and a Man of the People* (Macon, Ga: Mercer University Press, 1985), 33.
   9. McBeth, 457.
   10. Ellis, 32-36.
   11. McBeth, 609-23.
   12. Ibid., 650-72.
   13. Ibid., 679.
   14. Ellis, 53-60.
   15. Ibid., 74.
   16. Ibid., 78.
   17. Ibid., 75.
   18. Ibid., 112-13.
   19. Morris Ashcraft, "The History of Fundamentalism," *Review and Expositor* 79 (Winter 1982): 36-37.

20. Ellis, 66, 135-36.
21. McBeth, 671.
22. Ibid., 620-21.
23. Ibid., 671.
24. Ibid., 679-80.
25. Ellis, 151.
26. Ibid., 151-61.
27. Ibid., 163-68.
28. Ibid., 189-99.
29. McBeth, 678.
30. Ibid., 679-80.
31. Robert A. Baker, *A Baptist Source Book* (Nashville: Broadman, 1966), 200.
32. Ibid., 201-05.
33. McBeth, 678-79.
34. Ibid., 677-78.
35. Ellis, 207-08.
36. McBeth, 626-27.
37. Ibid., 626-28.
38. Ibid., 628-30.
39. Ibid., 630-32.
40. Ibid., 673-74.
41. Ibid., 673.
42. Ralph H. Elliott, *The Genesis Controversy* (Macon, Ga.: Mercer University Press, 1992), xi.
43. McBeth, 674.
44. Elliott, xi, 10.
45. McBeth, 674.
46. Ibid., 674, 680.
47. Leon McBeth, "Fundamentalism in the SBC in Recent Years," *Review and Expositor* 79 (Winter 1982): 88-89.
48. Ibid., 81.
49. Elliott, 33-34.
50. Ibid., 22.
51. Ibid., 25.
52. McBeth, "Fundamentalism," 90.
53. Ibid., 87.
54. Shurden, 74.
55. McBeth, "Fundamentalism," 90.
56. Shurden, 75.
57. Joe Edward Barnhart, *The Southern Baptist Holy War* (Austin, Tex.: Texas Monthly Press, 1986), 26.
58. Shurden, 75-79.

59. McBeth, "Fundamentalism," 91-92.

60. Nancy Tatom Ammerman, *Baptist Battles* (New Brunswick: Rutgers University Press, 1990), 70.

61. McBeth, *Heritage*, 681.

62. McBeth, "Fundamentalism," 92-95.

63. Ibid., 95-97.

64. Ammerman, 70.

65. McBeth, "Fundamentalism," 96.

66. Ammerman, 174.

67. Barnhart, 26.

68. Ibid., 26.

69. Ammerman, 71, 173.

70. McBeth, *Heritage*, 681.

71. Ibid.

72. McBeth, "Fundamentalism," 98-101.

73. Ammerman, 168-76.

74. McBeth, *Heritage*, 681.

75. Barnhart, 2-3.

76. McBeth, *Heritage*, 682.

77. Ammerman, 177-78.

78. Ibid., 181.

79. Ibid., 178.

80. Ibid., 182-86.

81. Ibid., 10, 190.

82. Ibid., 121.

83. Ibid., 112-13.

84. Ibid., 8-9, 120-21, 195, 200. Also, Daniel Vestal, "The History of the Cooperative Baptist Fellowship," *The Struggle for the Soul of the SBC*, edited by Walter B. Shurden (Macon, Ga.: Mercer University Press, 1993), 253.

85. Ammerman, 195-97, 220.

86. Cecil E. Sherman, "In the Beginning: How the Cooperative Baptist Fellowship Came to Be," paper released in late spring, 1992, 3-4.

87. Ammerman, 223-29.

88. Jack U. Harwell, "Update and Overview of Post-Takeover Southern Baptist Convention Agencies," *Baptists Today* 10 (December 15, 1992): 6.

89. Ammerman, 230-32.

90. R. Albert Mohler, Jr., "Rushlikon Defunding Stands; Baptists Debate Future of Missions," *The Christian Index* (December 19, 1991): 1, 3, 8. Also, Grady C. Cothen, *What Happened to the Southern Baptist Convention?* (Macon, Ga.: Smyth & Helwys, 1993), 340.

91. Harwell, "Update," 6.

92. Ibid., 6-7.

93. Mark Wingfield, "Two Deans Stepping Down at Southern

Seminary," *Baptists Today* 11 (April 29, 1993): 2. *Biblical Recorder* 160 (April 2, 1994): 1-3, 8-10, 13.

94. Baptist Press, September 20, 1995.
95. Harwell, "Update," 6.
96. Robert Dilday, "Rogers Says SBC Should Control WMU," *Western Recorder* 167 (March 9, 1993): 2.
97. Baptist Press, June 20, 1995.
98. Sherman, 4.
99. "Baptist Cooperative Missions Program Inc." (Report by BCMP to the Fellowship Convocation of May 1991 in Atlanta, Ga.)
100. Walter B. Shurden, "An Address to the Public from the Interim Steering Committee" (Message presented to the Fellowship Convocation of May 1991 in Atlanta, Ga.)
101. Harwell, "Update," 7.
102. Ibid.
103. Cothen, 260, 304-05, 332-33, 338, 359, 369. Also, Sarah Zimmerman, "Decline in SBC Baptisms Concerns Evangelism Leaders," *The Religious Herald* 166 (December 23, 1993): 3.
104. "Cooperative Baptist Fellowship Appoints 16 New Missionaries," *Baptists Today* 13 (August 1995): 3.
105. Greg Warner and Jack U. Harwell, "Keith Parks Will Lead CBF Missions Program," *Baptists Today* 10 (December 15, 1992): 1.
106. "Newest Mission Staffer Off to Quick Start," *Fellowship News* 3 (September/October 1993): 2.
107. Ammerman, 78-79, 181.
108. Ibid., 252-257.

Chapter Four

1. Leland D. Baldwin, *The American Quest for the City of God* (Macon, Ga.: Mercer University Press, 1981), 161.
2. Ibid.
3. Walter B. Shurden, *Not a Silent People: Controversies That Have Shaped Southern Baptists* (Macon, Ga.: Smyth & Helwys, 1995), 29-32.
4. H. Leon McBeth, *A Sourcebook for Baptist Heritage* (Nashville: Broadman, 1990), 252-55.
5. Shurden, 35.
6. McBeth, 285-86.
7. Ibid., 286-87.
8. Ibid., 287.
9. H. Leon McBeth, *The Baptist Heritage: Four Centuries of Baptist Witness* (Nashville: Broadman, 1987), 782-86.
10. Robert A. Baker, *A Baptist Source Book* (Nashville: Broadman, 1966), 154-56.

11. Ibid., 186.
12. Shurden, 37.
13. Ibid.
14. Ibid., 36.
15. Ibid., 36-38.
16. Paul F. Parsons, *Inside America's Christian Schools* (Macon, Ga.: Mercer University Press, 1987), 113-26.
17. Cecil E. Sherman, "An Overview of the Moderate Movement," and Robert Parham, "The History of the Baptist Center for Ethics," *The Struggle for the Soul of the SBC*, edited by Walter B. Shurden (Macon, Ga.: Mercer University Press, 1993), 36, 210-11.
18. *The Tennessean*, September 5, 1995, p. 7A.
19. Winthrop S. Hudson, *Religion in America* (New York: Charles Scribner's Sons, 1965), 131-39.
20. Nancy Tatom Ammerman, *Baptist Battles* (New Brunswick: Rutgers University Press, 1990), 27-28.
21. Hudson, 141.
22. Ammerman, 29-31.
23. Baldwin, 156-60.
24. Ibid., 160-63.
25. Ammerman, 35.
26. Baldwin, 186.
27. Ammerman, 36.
28. Baldwin, 139.
29. Hudson, 198.
30. Baldwin, 189.
31. Hudson, 218.
32. Ammerman, 36; *Encyclopedia of Religion in the South* (Macon, Ga.: Mercer University Press, 1984), 722.
33. Ammerman, 65.
34. Ibid., 65-66.
35. Ibid., 66-67.
36. Ibid., 67-69.
37. Ibid., 68, 99, 236-39.

Chapter Five
1. Leo Rosten, *Religions of America* (New York: Simon & Schuster, 1975), 40-41.
2. Ibid., 33-34.
3. *Encyclopedia of Religion in the South* (Macon, Ga.: Mercer University Press, 1984), 533.
4. H. Leon McBeth, *A Sourcebook for Baptist Heritage* (Nashville: Broadman, 1990), 316.

5. H. Leon McBeth, *The Baptist Heritage: Four Centuries of Baptist Witness* (Nashville: Broadman, 1987), 448-54.
6. McBeth, *A Sourcebook*, 317.
7. McBeth, *The Baptist Heritage*, 449-54.
8. McBeth, *A Sourcebook*, 318-20.
9. McBeth, *The Baptist Heritage*, 456-57.
10. Walter B. Shurden, *Not A Silent People: Controversies That Have Shaped Southern Baptists* (Macon, Ga.: Smyth & Helwys, 1995), 41-44.
11. McBeth, *A Sourcebook*, 317, 320-25.
12. Shurden, 46-47.
13. McBeth, *The Baptist Heritage*, 458-59.
14. William E. Ellis, *A Man of Books and a Man of the People* (Macon, Ga.: Mercer University Press, 1985), 32-36.
15. Shurden, 15.
16. Jesse C. Fletcher, *The Southern Baptist Convention: A Sesquicentennial History* (Nashville: Broadman & Holman, 1994), 28.
17. James C. Hefley, *The Truth in Crisis* (Dallas: Criterion Publications, 1986), 3.
18. Shurden, 48-49.
19. Ibid., 16.
20. William E. Hull, "Pluralism in the Southern Baptist Convention," *Review and Expositor* 79 (Winter 1982): 125.
21. Shurden, 77-78.
22. Martin E. Marty, "Fundamentalism As a Social Phenomenon," *Review and Expositor* 79 (Winter 1982): 21.
23. McBeth, *The Baptist Heritage*, 700.
24. Nancy Tatom Ammerman, *Baptist Battles* (New Brunswick: Rutgers University Press, 1990), 220.
25. *Biblical Recorder* 160 (May 21, 1994): 2.
26. Ellis, 61-81.
27. Ammerman, 57, 214.
28. Hull, 136-39.
29. Ibid., 127-32.
30. Ammerman, 227.
31. Stan Hastey, "The Southern Baptist Convention, 1979-1993: What Happened and Why?" *Baptist History and Heritage* 28 (October 1993): 19.

Chapter Six
1. *Encylopedia Americana*, Volume 12 (New York: Americana Corporation, 1977), 240-44.
2. Joe Edward Barnhart, *The Southern Baptist Holy War* (Austin, Tex.: Texas Monthly Press, 1986), 126.
3. Ibid., 125.

4. Bobby D. Compton, "J. Frank Norris and Southern Baptists," *Review and Expositor* 79 (Winter 1982): 72-77.
5. William E. Ellis, *A Man of Books and a Man of the People* (Macon, Ga.: Mercer University Press, 1985), 160-203.
6. Ralph H. Elliott, *The Genesis Controversy* (Macon, Ga.: Mercer University Press, 1992), x.
7. H. Leon McBeth, *The Baptist Heritage: Four Centuries of Baptist Witness* (Nashville: Broadman, 1987), 680.
8. Paul F. Parsons, *Inside America's Christian Schools* (Macon, Ga.: Mercer University Press, 1987), 79-91.
9. Barnhart, 76, 122-23.
10. Nancy Tatom Ammerman, *Baptist Battles* (New Brunswick: Rutgers University Press, 1990), 74-75.
11. *Mercer Dictionary of the Bible* (Macon, Ga.: Mercer University Press, 1992), 408-10.
12. Barnhart, 88-91.
13. Ibid., 202-04.
14. Elliott, 32-35.
15. Ammerman, 136.
16. Ibid., 137.
17. Barnhart, 199.
18. Ammerman, 80-82.
19. Ibid., 115.

Chapter Seven
1. H. Leon McBeth, *The Baptist Heritage: Four Centuries of Baptist Witness* (Nashville: Broadman, 1987), 61, 71.
2. Morris Ashcraft, "The Theology of Fundamentalism," *Review and Expositor* 79 (Winter 1982): 33-36.
3. H. Leon McBeth, *A Sourcebook for Baptist Heritage* (Nashville: Broadman, 1990), 505.
4. Ashcraft, 33-36.
5. Robison B. James, "Authority, Criticism, and the Word of God," *The Unfettered Word: Southern Baptists Confront the Authority-Inerrancy Question*, edited by Robison B. James (Waco: Word Books, 1987), 84.
6. Ibid., 76.
7. Grady C. Cothen, *What Happened to the Southern Baptist Convention?* (Macon, Ga.: Smyth & Helwys, 1993), 79.
8. James, 72.
9. Robison B. James, "Is Inerrancy the Issue? The Lessons of Ridgecrest," *The Unfettered Word*, 84.
10. Nancy Tatom Ammerman, *Baptist Battles* (New Brunswick: Rutgers University Press, 1990), 80.
11. Ibid., 82.

12. Ibid., 83.
13. Ibid., 83-84.
14. Joe Edward Barnhart, *The Southern Baptist Holy War* (Austin, Tex.: Texas Monthly Press, 1986), 9.
15. Ibid., 39.
16. James, "Is Inerrancy the Issue?" *The Unfettered Word*, 177-84.
17. Ammerman, 74-75.
18. Barnhart, 91.
19. Fisher Humphreys, "Biblical Inerrancy: A Guide for the Perplexed," *The Unfettered Word*, 50.
20. Ibid.
21. James, "Is Inerrancy the Issue?" *The Unfettered Word*, 184.
22. As cited in Stan Hastey, "The Southern Baptist Convention, 1979-1993: What Happened and Why?" *Baptist History and Heritage* 28 (October 1993): 20.
23. Jack U. Harwell, "Update and Overview of Post-Takeover Southern Baptist Convention Agencies," *Baptists Today* 10 (December 15, 1992): 6-7.
24. Hastey, 26.
25. Charles H. Talbert, "The Bible's Truth Is Relational," *The Unfettered Word*, 41.
26. James, "Authority, Criticism, and the Word of God," *The Unfettered Word*, 79.
27. Talbert, *The Unfettered Word*, 50-52. Also, Cothen, *What Happened*? 128-29.
28. James, "Is Inerrancy the Issue?" *The Unfettered Word*, 184.
29. Ammerman, 195-96, 222-23.
30. McBeth, *A Sourcebook*, 531.
31. Ammerman, 74-75.
32. James, 182-83.
33. Talbert, 52.
34. James, 184.
35. James, 183-84.
36. Barnhart, 176-77.
37. David S. Dockery, *The Doctrine of the Bible* (Nashville: Convention Press, 1991), 86-87.
38. Ibid., 88-89.
39. James Emery White, *What Is Truth?* (Nashville: Broadman and Holman, 1994), 190.
40. Ibid., 80.
41. William R. Estep, Jr., "Biblical Authority in Baptist Confessions of Faith," *The Unfettered Word*, 155-72.
42. H. Leon McBeth, "Fundamentalism in the SBC in Recent Years," *Review and Expositor* 79 (Winter 1982): 96.
43. Dockery, 88.

44. James, 184.
45. Clark H. Pinnock, "Afterword," *The Unfettered Word*, 185.
46. Talbert, 60.
47. *The Christian Index* (October 28, 1993): 3.

Chapter Eight
1. Grady C. Cothen, *What Happened to the Southern Baptist Convention?* (Macon, Ga.: Smyth and Helwys, 1993), 152-55.
2. Ibid., 1-2.
3. Ibid., 96.
4. Ibid., 96, 97.
5. Ibid., 264.
6. Ibid., 12-16, 74-75.
7. Ibid., 172-73.
8. Ibid., 187-88, 193-204.
9. Nancy Tatom Ammerman, *Baptist Battles* (New Brunswick: Rutgers University Press, 1990)), 10-11.
10. Cothen, 229-31.
11. "A Chronology," *The Struggle for the Soul of the SBC*, edited by Walter B. Shurden (Macon, Ga.: Mercer University Press, 1993), xiv.
12. Cothen, 90-91.
13. Clark H. Pinnock, "Afterword," *The Unfettered Word: Southern Baptists Confront the Authority-Inerrancy Question*, edited by Robison B. James (Waco: Word Books, 1987), 185.
14. Joe Edward Barnhart, *The Southern Baptist Holy War* (Austin, Tex.: Texas Monthly Press, 1986), 4, 17-18, 73, 235.
15. Ibid., 4.
16. Ibid., 70.
17. Cothen, 40.
18. Ibid., 195.
19. Ammerman, 105, 153, 361.
20. Barnhart, 235.
21. Ammerman, 105-06.
22. Ibid., 106.
23. *Baptist Beacon* (October 28, 1993): 7; *Baptists Today* 12 (June 16, 1994): 7, 19.
24. Ammerman, 99.
25. Cothen, 64.
26. Ibid., 355.
27. Ibid., 145-46, 152-56, 167-68.
28. Erling Jorstad, *Being Religious in America* (Minneapolis: Augsburg, 1986), 87-88.
29. Ammerman, 5, 184. Also, Shurden, *Struggle*, 213.

30. Cothen, 5, 167-68.
31. Ibid., 353-54.
32. Ibid., 351. Also, Robert Parham, "The History of the Baptist Center for Ethics," *The Struggle for the Soul of the SBC*, 206-07.
33. Frederick Clarkson, "The Christian Coalition: On the Road to Victory?" *Church and State* (January 1992): 4-7.
34. Frederick Clarkson, "Inside the Covert Coalition," *Church and State* (November 1992): 7.
35. Cecil E. Sherman, "An Overview of the Moderate Movement," *The Struggle for the Soul of the SBC*, 35.
36. Cothen, 21-23.
37. "Christian Reconstructionists Hope to Stack Library Stacks, Duo Argues," *Church and State* (January 1993): 14.
38. Cothen, 7.
39. Ammerman, 185.
40. Barnhart, 4.
41. Joseph L. Conn, "Courtroom Contender," *Church and State* (June 1992): 5.
42. Rob Boston, "Sects, Lies and Videotape," *Church and State* (April 1993): 9.

Chapter Nine
1. *Mercer Dictionary of the Bible* (Macon, Ga.: Mercer University Press, 1992), 680-84.
2. "Agencies Asked to Consider Ties to CBF, Some Businesses," *The Christian Index* (June 24, 1993): 10. Also, "CBF Ties Lead to Removal," *Baptist Standard* 106 (January 5, 1994).
3. Grady C. Cothen, *What Happened to the Southern Baptist Convention?* (Macon, Ga.: Smyth and Helwys, 1993), 91.
4. Ibid., 157-58.
5. H. Leon McBeth, *A Sourcebook for Baptist Heritage* (Nashville: Broadman, 1990), 531.
6. Nancy Tatom Ammerman, *Baptist Battles* (New Brunswick: Rutgers University Press, 1990), 11.
7. Ibid., 225.
8. Cothen, 339-41.
9. Cecil Sherman, "An Overview of the Moderate Movement," *The Struggle for the Soul of the SBC*, edited by Walter B. Shurden (Macon, Ga.: Mercer University Press, 1993), 33.
10. Cothen, 91.
11. John H. Hewett, "A History of the Forum," *The Struggle for the Soul of the SBC*, 74, 90.
12. Cothen, 91.

13. Ibid., 205.
14. Ibid., 90, 91.
15. Ibid., 105.
16. Ammerman, 115.
17. Joe Edward Barnhart, *The Southern Baptist Holy War* (Austin, Tex.: Texas Monthly Press, 1986), 71, 123.
18. Sherman, 33.
19. Barnhart, 80.
20. Ibid., 168.
21. Ibid., 4.
22. Ibid., 98.
23. Ibid., 240.
24. James C. Hefley, *The Truth in Crisis* (Dallas: Criterion, 1986), 143-44.
25. Ibid., 144.
26. Slayden A. Yarbrough, "Biblical Authority in Southern Baptist History, 1845-1895," *Baptist History and Heritage* 27 (January, 1992): 4-8.
27. Barnhart, 167.
28. James H. Slatton, "The History of the Political Network of the Moderate Movement," *The Struggle for the Soul of the SBC*, 67; Hewett, 74, 84-86.
29. H. Leon McBeth, *The Baptist Heritage: Four Centuries of Baptist Witness* (Nashville: Broadman, 1987), 620.
30. See *The Genesis Controversy* by Ralph H. Elliott (Macon, Ga.: Mercer University Press, 1992).
31. Cothen, 90, 91.
32. Hewett, 81.
33. Joel Gregory, *Too Great a Temptation: The Seductive Power of America's Megachurch* (Arlington, Tex.: Summit, 1994).
34. Ammerman, 71, 119-20, 157-58.
35. Cothen, 89
36. Ibid., 186, 188, 194, 198, 201-02, 204, 210-11, 215, 218, 241, 243-45, 256, 285-86, 299, 301-02, 309, 313, 324-30, 333, 339-40, 344, 350-51, 371. Also, Sherman, 31; Slatton, 64, 69.

Chapter Ten
1. Bill J. Leonard, *God's Last and Only Hope* (Grand Rapids: Eerdmans, 1990), 1-24.
2. H. Leon McBeth, *The Baptist Heritage: Four Centuries of Baptist Witness* (Nashville: Broadman, 1987), 609, 622.
3. Cecil E. Sherman, "An Overview of the Moderate Movement," *The Struggle for the Soul of the SBC*, edited by Walter B. Shurden (Macon, Ga.: Mercer University Press, 1993), 17-29.
4. Ibid., 37-44.

5. Ibid., 40-43; James H. Slatton, "A History of the Political Network of the Moderate Movement," *The Struggle for the Soul of the SBC*, 58-62.
6. Sherman, 44.
7. Nancy Tatom Ammerman, *Baptist Battles* (New Brunswick: Rutgers University Press, 1990), 175-78.
8. Ibid., 259.
9. Stan Hastey, "The Southern Baptist Convention, 1979-1993: What Happened and Why?" *Baptist History and Heritage* 28 (October 1993): 26.
10. Alan Neely, "The History of the Alliance of Baptists," *The Struggle for the Soul of the SBC*, 125.

Chapter Eleven
1. Joe Edward Barnhart, *The Southern Baptist Holy War* (Austin, Tex.: Texas Monthly Press, 1986), 166, 172.
2. Nancy Tatom Ammerman, *Baptist Battles* (New Brunswick: Rutgers University Press, 1990), 82.
3. James C. Hefley, *The Truth in Crisis* (Dallas: Criterion, 1986), 216-17.
4. Grady C. Cothen, *What Happened to the Southern Baptist Convention?* (Macon, Ga.: Smyth & Helwys, 1993), 369. Also, *The Christian Index* (October 14, 1993): 6.
5. *The Christian Index* (May 11, 1995): 2.
6. Baptist Press, December 8, 1993.
7. Ammerman, 250.
8. Cothen, 294.
9. *Illinois Baptist* (November 10, 1993): 19.
10. Ammerman, 250.
11. *The Christian Index* (December 21, 1989): 5.
12. Baptist Press, December 8, 1993.
13. James Dotson, "Mohler Nominated to Presidency of Southern Seminary," *The Christian Index* (March 4, 1993): 1, 3-4.
14. *Illinois Baptist* (November 10, 1993): 19.
15. Paige Patterson, "My Vision of the Twenty-First Century SBC," *Review and Expositor* 88 (Winter 1991): 37-52.
16. Ammerman, 78-79, 181.
17. Cecil E. Sherman, "An Overview of the Moderate Movement," *The Struggle for the Soul of the SBC*, edited by Walter B. Shurden, (Macon, Ga.: Mercer University Press, 1993), 17-46.
18. Ibid., 45-46.
19. Ibid., 46.
20. Cecil E. Sherman, "An Update on CBF," *Fellowship News* 3 (November/December 1993): 2; *Baptists Today* 13 (August 1995): 3.
21. *Baptists Today* 13 (August 1995): 1.
22. *Fellowship News* 4 (September/October 1994): 1.

23. "Mission Statement Approved," *Fellowship News* 5 (July/August 1995): 10.

24. Walter B. Shurden, "The Struggle for the Soul of the SBC: Reflections and Interpretations," *The Struggle for the Soul of the SBC*, 290.

25. "Moderates Prevail in Key State Conventions," *Baptists Today* (December 16, 1993): 1; also *Baptists Today* 12 (November 30, 1994): 1-5.

26. Ibid., 2.

27. *Indiana Baptist* (December 7, 1993): 12.

28. *Baptists Today* 12 (November 30, 1994): 5.

29. *Baptists Today* 12 (November 10, 1994): 1; *Indiana Baptist* 37 (August 29, 1995): 5.

30. Shurden, 285.

31. Nancy Tatom Ammerman, "The SBC: Retrospect and Prospect," *Review and Expositor* 88 (Winter 1991): 18.

32. Ibid., 18-20.

33. Ibid., 20.

34. "Trustees Deny Professor Tenure at Midwestern," *The Christian Index* (October 28, 1993): 3

35. *Biblical Recorder* 160 (March 19, 1994): 1, 6-10; (April 2, 1994): 1, 3, 8-10, 13; (April 30, 1994): 11-12; *The Christian Index* 173 (March 31, 1994): 1-2; *SBC Life* (June/July, 1994): 4.

36. *Word & Way* (March 30, 1995): 2, 6; *The Christian Index* (March 30, 1995): 1, 2; (April 13, 1995): 3; (April 27, 1995): 2, 6; *Baptists Today* 13 (May 18, 1995): 3; (July 17, 1995): 12.

37. *Word & Way* 131 (May 5, 1994): 10.

38. Jack U. Harwell, "Diverse Reactions to WMU Actions Reported," *Baptists Today* (February 4, 1993): 1-2.

39. Daniel Vestal, "The History of the Cooperative Baptist Fellowship," *The Struggle for the Soul of the SBC*, 290.

40. "Concerns Expressed About New Women's Ministry," *The Christian Index* (November 18, 1993): 1, 3.

41. Baptist Press, June 14, 1994.

42. *The Alabama Baptist* 159-22 (June 2, 1994): 1, 11; *Indiana Baptist* 35 (June 7, 1994): 8-9; Baptist Press, June 15-16, 1994.

43. Baptist Press, June 20, 1995.